Praise for *Invitation to Poetry*

"Lisa Steinman has taken all the insights of a lively seminar, guided by an expert, and offered the rest of us a chance to eavesdrop. Her book is more than an introduction to poetry; it is also a demonstration of impassioned reading, an immersion in the languages of the lyric. To the casual reader, Steinman explains how poems work; to the critical reader, why they keep working. Ranging over several centuries, styles, genres, and modes of English verse, *Invitation to Poetry* provides both the tools needed to 'play with poems' and a manual in their use."

C. D. Blanton, University of California, Berkeley

"Lisa Steinman's *Invitation to Poetry*, with its effortless scholarship and engaging manner, offers a wonderful introduction to the study of poetry. Her book reminds one of what the best of university teaching can be like: readers are guided through a variety of linked questions arising from examples selected from English and American poetic traditions. She is attentive to the social context of poetry, to tradition and genre, to the practice and ambition of individual poets; and above all to language itself as a medium for the music and meaning of a poem, with its changing history and resonances. This is a beautifully written book which offers many pleasures, and for those who read attentively, a tremendous depth of reference underpinning its argument."

Tim Armstrong, Royal Holloway, University of London

This book is dedicated to my students.

Invitation to Poetry

The Pleasures of Studying Poetry and Poetics

Lisa M. Steinman

Blackwell
Publishing

© 2008 by Lisa M. Steinman

BLACKWELL PUBLISHING
350 Main Street, Malden, MA 02148–5020, USA
9600 Garsington Road, Oxford OX4 2DQ, UK
550 Swanston Street, Carlton, Victoria 3053, Australia

First published 2008 by Blackwell Publishing Ltd

1   2008

Library of Congress Cataloging-in-Publication Data

Steinman, Lisa Malinowski, 1950–
    Invitation to poetry : the pleasures of studying poetry and poetics / Lisa M. Steinman.
        p.   cm.
    Includes bibliographical references and index.
    ISBN 978-1-4051-3163-6 (hardcover : alk. paper)—ISBN 978-1-4051-3164-3 (pbk. : alk. paper)   1. English poetry—Study and teaching—Methodology.   2. American poetry—Study and teaching—Methodology.   3. Poetry—Study and teaching—Methodology.   4. Poetics—Study and teaching–Methodology.   I. Title.

    PR504.5.S74 2008
    811'.0071—dc22

                                        2007019832

A catalogue record for this title is available from the British Library.

Set in 10.5 on 12.5 pt Minion
by SNP Best-set Typesetter Ltd., Hong Kong
Printed and bound in Singapore
by Markono Print Media Pte Ltd

For further information on
Blackwell Publishing, visit our website at
www.blackwellpublishing.com

To The Reader
Pray thee, take care, that tak'st my book in hand,
To read it well: that is, to understand.
                                    Ben Jonson (1616)

Contents

Preface

This book is based on a class called "An Introduction to Poetry and Poetics," which I have taught in different forms over the past decade or so at Reed College. The book, like the class, develops, with later discussions drawing on earlier vocabularies, technical terms, and readings of lyric poems. In this sense, I suspect this volume will be most fruitful for those who read it from the first to the last chapter, in the same way that my students participate in class discussions over several months. Throughout what follows I have likened learning to think and talk about poetry to learning a language; in the same way as a chapter in a grammar book on the use of past participles or the use of the subjunctive in a new language will be less useful to someone who has not yet practiced forming simple sentences using the present tense or who has not yet internalized a basic vocabulary of common nouns, verbs, and pronouns, so here the later chapters may seem less transparent to new readers of poetry who have skipped ahead.

That said, I include a list of terms at the end of each chapter (and highlight these within the chapter where they are first introduced) so that someone reading a single chapter out of sequence might be able to look back to these for help should they encounter a previously unknown technical term. I would hope, too, that individual chapters – chapters 3 and 4 on sonnets, chapters 4 and 5 on the sound of poems (rhythmic and tonal), chapters 6 and 7 on modal terms (odes and pastorals), or chapters 2 and 8 on intertextual conversations – could be read on their own, especially by those with some previous experience of reading poems. Finally, I have listed and provided dates for the poems discussed in each chapter title so that those puzzled by a particular poem or set of poems will be able to read selectively to further their thinking about what might be said about an individual text or texts from a particular period.

Since this is both an invitation and an introduction to poetry, I have concentrated on lyrics, which are more easily read at one sitting (or in one class session), as well as on poems in modern English that are easily found – or accompanied by poems found – in standard anthologies. As I say throughout, the poems included here by no means represent all the kinds of poetry that have been, are being, and presumably will be written.

Acknowledgments

The author and publisher gratefully acknowledge the permission granted to reproduce the copyright material in this book:

Wallace Stevens, "The Idea of Order at Key West," *The Collected Poems of Wallace Stevens* (New York: Random House, 1978), pp. 128–30. © 1936 by Wallace Stevens and renewed 1964 by Holly Stevens. Used by permission of Alfred A. Knopf, a division of Random House, Inc., and Faber and Faber Ltd.

Robert Frost, "Design," *The Poetry of Robert Frost*, edited by Edward Connery Lathem (New York: Holt, Rinehart & Winston, 1967), p. 302. Copyright © 1947, 1969 by Henry Holt and Company. Copyright © 1975 by Lesley Frost Ballantine. Reprinted by permission of Henry Holt and Company, LLC, and The Random House Group Ltd.

William Carlos Williams, "To Greet a Letter-Carrier," *The Collected Poems of William Carlos Williams*, vol. 1, *1909–1939*, edited by A. Walton Litz and Christopher MacGowan (London: Carcarnet Press, 2000), p. 458. © 1938 by New Directions Publishing Corp. Reprinted by permission of New Directions Publishing Corp. and Carcanet Press Ltd.

Josephine Miles, "Purchase of a Blue, Green, or Orange Ode," Josephine Miles, *Collected Poems, 1930–83* (Urbana and Chicago: University of Illinois Press, 1983), p. 38. © 1983 by Josephine Miles. Used with permission of the Estate of Josephine Miles and the University of Illinois Press.

John Ashbery, "Le Livre Est Sur La Table," *Some Trees* (New York: Ecco Press, 1978), pp. 74–5. © 1956 by John Ashbery. Reprinted by permission of Carcanet Press Ltd and Georges Borchardt, Inc., on behalf of the author.

Frank O'Hara, "The Day Lady Died," *The Selected Poems of Frank O'Hara*, edited by Donald Allen (New York: Alfred A. Knopf, 1974), p. 146. ©

1964 by Frank O'Hara. Reprinted with permission from City Lights Books.

James Wright, "A Blessing," James Wright, *Collected Poems* (Middletown, Conn.: Wesleyan University Press, 1971), p. 15. © 1971 by James Wright. Reprinted with permission from Wesleyan University Press.

Denise Levertov, "O Taste and See," Denise Levertov, *Poems 1960–67* (New York: New Directions, 1983), p. 125. © 1964 by Denise Levertov. Reproduced by permission of New Directions Publishing Corp. and Pollinger Ltd and the proprietor.

Elizabeth Bishop, "Filling Station," *The Complete Poems 1927–79* (New York: Farrar, Straus and Giroux, 1984), pp. 127–8. © 1979, 1983 by Alice Helen Methfessel. Reprinted with permission from Farrar, Straus and Giroux, LLC.

Howard Nemerov, "Quaerendo Invenietis," Section "1" (The Spiral Way). Part II, four-line extract, *The Collected Poems of Howard Nemerov* (Chicago and London: University of Chicago Press, 1977), p. 413. © 1977 by Howard Nemerov. Reprinted with permission from the author's estate.

C. G. Giscombe "(the future)" and "(1962 at the end of town)," C. S. Giscombe, *Here* (Normal, Ill.: Dalkey Archive Press, 1994), pp. 14 and 22. © 1994 by C. S. Giscombe. Reprinted with permission from Dalkey Archive Press.

Every effort has been made to trace copyright holders and to obtain their permission for the use of copyright material. The publisher apologizes for any errors or omissions in the above list and would be grateful to be notified of any corrections that should be incorporated in future reprints or editions of this book.

The author would also like to thank the readers, editors, and copy-editor for Blackwell, as well as her colleagues at Reed College – especially Walter Englert, Robert Knapp, Nick Moschovakis, Katie Pelletier, Jim Shugrue, and Ellen Stauder – for their useful suggestions, willingness to give of their time, and above all for their attentive readings of portions and early versions of this text.

Chapter 1

Conceptual Syntax: An Introduction to the Way Poems Invite Different Approaches and Position Readers

in Howard Nemerov's "Quaerendo Invenietis" ("The Spiral Way") (1973) and William Carlos Williams's "To Greet a Letter-Carrier" (1938)

The purpose of this book is most simply to talk about how to read and understand poetry. More specifically, it is to introduce readers to the pleasures of poetry as well as to familiarize them with the technical language often used to describe the features of poetic language and with theories about poetry. While no introductory book can be exhaustive, this book does try to examine a range of poems, poetic styles, and theories. It tends to emphasize shorter lyrics and earlier British (and to a lesser degree American) poetry in English, focusing on poems that are less likely to be encountered outside of classrooms. It deals exclusively with written work in modern English.

Given the many ways in which poetry has been conceptualized and written, it would simply not be possible to discuss all poetic traditions, although in some chapters I have tried to suggest how individual poets can draw on more than one type of poetry. As I hope to illustrate, most poems draw on at least one poetic tradition, even if to resist or change it. How else, after all, does someone know that what he or she is writing is a poem, if not from having read and been moved by poems and having entered into conversation with what he or she has read? Here, I most often concentrate on poems or series of poems that show how such relationships can work. My hope is that readers will be able to use the ideas and skills offered to read longer poems, more contemporary poems, and poems in genres or modes or styles (such as satire or elegy or contemporary experimental poetry) slighted here for reasons of time and space. In short, I would open with a plea that readers do not take what is included as defining all poetry, even as I trust that the book will serve as both invitation to and preparation for reading all manner of poems.

If this book does not claim to define all poetry, how *would* one define poetry in general? That is, what makes a piece of writing count as a poem? While I pose the question, it is one to which I have no easy, certainly no tidy, answer. At the most basic level, as a reader I am prone to assume I have a poem in front of me simply when something visually "looks like a poem": that is, when lines are justified with the left-hand margin of a page but do not go all the way to the right-hand margin. However, not only does such an assumption exclude a fair amount of poetry not written in English; even in English there are prose poems and what are called "shaped poems" (one might look at George Herbert's "The Altar," published in 1633), pieces of writing that are widely counted as poems, but of which the definition above would not be true, just as there is much advertising copy of which it would be true. (Of course, in the early twentieth century, the critic Kenneth Burke called advertising "applied poetry," but one might want a less inclusive definition.) I would offer as a working hypothesis that poems are generally pieces of language that position readers in certain ways, that indeed count on readers to expect and pay attention to often condensed, carefully deployed, usually moving, language in which features we usually overlook – such as sound, line breaks, formal repetitions, con-notations, even puns, and echoes of other people's utterances in speech or writing – are meaningfully part of the effect of the language. As I have already implied, poems are often responses to or in conversation with other poems; perhaps because poets "speak poetry," their feelings and thoughts are often, though by no means exclusively, couched in and prompted by reading the language of other poets.

Indeed, reading poems is both simpler and more difficult than the title of this book suggests. That is, on the one hand, there is no rule book you can consult that will easily make you a speaker of poetry, certainly not of all poetry. On the other hand, reading poems is no more esoteric or special-ized than speaking any other language; in one sense, poetry (in English) is simply a dialect of English. While speaking poetry was once related to knowing a classical tradition of Greek and Latin poetry and more specifically tended to be tied to upper-class culture, reflecting access to education, these days it is those who write poetry who tend to read it and to internalize the ways that poems make meaning; poets are, if you will, native speakers of poetry. For most people, however, poetry is not a language heard every day in the way discursive prose or narratives and stories are heard – although, as I noted, it may be that advertising is a dialect related to poetry, as is the language of song lyrics. In any case, no one without any experience with poems should expect to wake up one morning speaking poetry-in-English any more than one would expect to wake up one morning speaking Spanish or French or some other language. However, I do believe that practice, as is the case when learning any language, will give you the ability to "speak poetry."

Those who teach language say that the best way to learn another language is to move to a country where it is spoken. This brings up an oddity of writing a book on how to read poems. I have been using words like "speaking" and "conversation," and "learning a language," which are metaphors, since reading is only "like" speaking with someone else face-to-face. Still, I've chosen these metaphors because I hope they suggest active participation in an exchange. And most poems are, indeed, not for passive consumption: they invite and require engagement. So to write a book about how to engage in conversation with poems is difficult. Certainly insofar as this book is taken as the last word it will be a failure. Insofar as my readers test what I have to say against their responses to the poems I discuss, and enter into exchanges with one another and with me about my suggestions, I will be content.

I have noted that there are technical terms used to describe features of poetic language. For help with these you can go to various reference books, such as *The New Princeton Encyclopedia of Poetry and Poetics*; *The Princeton Handbook of Poetic Terms*; Jack Myers and Michael Simms's *Dictionary of Poetic Terms*; or Lewis Turco's *The Book of Forms*. Such books are necessary if not sufficient resources. That is, although it is probably the case that an **iamb** is always an iamb (the metrical foot whereby a stressed syllable follows an unstressed syllable, as in the word "behold"), there are numerous theories about how easily English accommodates metrical feet, about the origins and significance of meter, and about the relationship between meter and meaning. So why we might care about iambs is not a question to which a reference book can give a definitive answer. When it comes to fixed **forms** like sonnets, or to rhetorical terms or to tropes as basic to poetry as metaphor, things can become even muddier. Throughout, I offer basic definitions, usually with caveats about the theories that have yielded those definitions or about the range of definitions available.

A good example would be use of the word **verse**. The word comes from the Latin for "turn" and most basically refers to language arranged in lines, or more simply to rows of written lines. We can also point to a **stanza** or section of a poem wherein groups of lines share the same meter and call that "a verse." After what is often called "free verse" – that is, poems that do not use regular meter or rhyme – became standard practice, "verse" became for some a negative term, referring to poetry that was formally regular but superficial or uninteresting, with the implication that the language was chosen only to fill out meter and rhyme: "mere verse."

How one uses such terms is, always, a matter of context, including historical context. There are also, always, assumptions – theories – underlying the ways in which one talks about the meaning and features of poems, which is why reference books (and the footnotes in anthologies) and books like this one are useful resources, but, again, should not be read as if they offer the last word. It is true that some terms or definitions will not radically shift in the hands of different critics or editors. However – while there are meanings that are simply implausible – there are often multiple "proper" or fruitful or interesting ways of using terms . . . and of reading the same lines or images in poems. For instance, when reading Spenser's line about how someone raised her "plastic arm," it will almost certainly not prove fruitful for a reader to think of polymer solutions and describe the adjective "plastic" as referring to a certain artificiality. In Spenser's day, "plastic" meant "malleable" or "changeable." It's often useful to consult the *Oxford English Dictionary* or, from the mid-nineteenth century, Noah Webster's *An American Dictionary of the English Language*, which can alert you to when certain meanings of words first come into use or to what are now archaic uses in Great Britain and the United States respectively.

Checking a dictionary will not always resolve one's questions, however. Let me offer another example. If you read in Anne Finch's "Nocturnal Reverie" the phrase "In such a night, let me abroad remain," and think that she is talking about a trip overseas or across the Channel, you probably will end up in a cul-de-sac. "Abroad" in Finch's day could mean "at large" or "moving freely" or "out of one's home" or (a fourth meaning) "out of one's home country." In context, as I will suggest in the second chapter here, the first three meanings are far more likely to be those that inform Finch's poem; the last meaning, although perhaps a more common usage these days – as when we talk of spending the junior year of college "abroad" – makes less sense, given that Finch's poem throughout sets up a series of contrasts between being confined and being free to move about, and between being inside a house and outside in the natural world (without any particular reference to being in or not in a nation-state *per se*).

It is in this way that making decisions about meaning in poems involves looking to what seems in context most fruitful or interesting. True, these days some critics read against the grain (as we now say). That is, one can deliberately offer anachronistic readings or readings that either could not have been or were presumably not culturally or authorially intended. Moreover, someone looking at the origins of nationalism, for instance, might want to see in Anne Finch's use of "abroad" something more than a claim to being outside social or domestic constraints, perhaps drawing on the fact that she and her husband were in fact exiled from the center of national power, that is, from court, after James II was deposed (James having fled to France in 1688).

My assumption in this book is that one can read poems in multiple ways, but that one should be clear about whether and to what extent one is reading with or against the grain. My own predilection is to begin by attempting as clear a thematic and historically embedded reading as possible, and only then to challenge or build on such a basic reading. My ambition, however, is not to rest with basic readings. An introductory text does need to be clear and to define terms and justify arguments, but it need not be unsophisticated. I presume readers new to reading poems are nonetheless intelligent readers, open to challenges.

Another of my assumptions is that poems often set their readers in certain positions, which is to say that the language and features of poems raise expectations and guide readers. This, in fact, offers poets a variety of tools that we may not think about when reading or responding to other literary **genres**, or kinds of literature, to which readers bring slightly different sets of expectations – or, for that matter, when reading non-literary writing. That is, when reading guidelines for tax forms or following instructions on how to assemble a piece of machinery, we do not look for tacit or implicit meanings. However, if a poem has fourteen lines, especially if they are arranged in an opening group of eight lines followed by a separate section of six lines, we, as readers, can expect – indeed, we might convincingly say the poem has led us to expect – that we have a Petrarchan **sonnet** (a form on which I will say more in chapter 3), with an **octave** (eight lines) followed by a **sestet** (six lines). The expectations we have from reading other poems in this form, then, might lead us to expect other features of a Petrarchan sonnet: a certain rhyme scheme, a turn in the argument or images of the poem between the octave and the sestet, perhaps even a certain theme, namely love. If, then, the poem refuses these expectations, being unrhymed, or turning in a different place (or looking as if it will turn in line 9, with "But" or "Yet" or "Still" marking an apparent turn in the poem's argument that then is not followed though), such refusals make meaning: they are significant because they are expectations raised and refused. They perform work in the reader who is familiar with what we might call the conceptual syntax of Petrarchan sonnets. This is why speaking poetry is a skill one learns with practice. At least as early as Shakespeare's well-known Sonnet 130, which opens with the line "My mistress' eyes are nothing like the sun," we have a poem that gains impact or meaning because it is refusing an expectation set by Petrarch (and numerous followers of Petrarch) in which the poet praises his love using a series of complimentary metaphors or **similes** (a simile – the word comes from the Latin for "like" – is a rhetorical figure usually using "like" or "as" to compare attributes of two things, for example, saying one's lover's eyes are "as bright as the sun").

I want to spend the rest of this chapter considering other ways in which poems position their readers by looking at two poems as test cases of sorts. The first is actually an excerpt from a longer poem, but an excerpt that has been reprinted on its own elsewhere with the author's permission. The following – sometimes entitled "The Spiral Way" – is from Howard Nemerov's longer "Quaerendo Invenietis":

> It is a spiral way that trues my arc
> Toward central silence and my unreached mark.
> Singing and saying till his time be done,
> The traveler does nothing. But the road goes on.

While I will talk about Nemerov's poem in detail in a moment, let me first give you another poem, of roughly the same length, also by a twentieth-century American poet: William Carlos Williams's "To Greet a Letter-Carrier."

> Why'n't you bring me
> a good letter? One with
> lots of money in it.
> I could make use of that.
> Atta boy! Atta boy!

I think it is useful to have both poems in one's ears at once because even on a first reading they sound so very different. One uses formal diction ("trues my arc" is almost archaic, certainly highly formal, and "till" is a "poetic" contraction, sounding, in context, like a somewhat stilted literary gesture). The diction in Williams's poem makes it sound more like a transcription of speech, and in particular of colloquial American speech as used by a not especially well-educated speaker. "Why'n't," for example, is not a word or a contraction one will find in a dictionary; "lots" is not a noun one would encounter in most written documents. I did not open this book saying I would offer you "lots of poems," for instance, because the statement is too casual, too vague a gesture, even if strictly speaking true. Williams's poem also has lines that do not rhyme and that end in unexpected places, using what we call **enjambment** as at the end of the second line " . . . one with / lots of money . . . ," where the syntactical unit, the prepositional phrase "with lots of money," is disrupted by the line break at the end of line 2. Finally, "To Greet a Letter-Carrier," despite the relative formality of the language in the title, is not only colloquial in tone but uses **free verse**. That is, although all the lines have five to six syllables (and so two to three stresses), there's little sense that the poem is organized metrically. In fact, at the time the poem was written (in 1938), the lack of clear meter or rhyme would have been relatively surprising. As late as the 1960s, at least some readers wondered if what Williams wrote *was* poetry (given the lack of formal features, the highly colloquial – even "improper" – use of English, and the rather mundane subject matter, in this case waiting for the postal service to deliver the mail). Moreover, given expectations about poetry when the poem was written, its refusal to act like a poem is a feature of the poem. This is, one might then say, a rebellious poem.

Nemerov's poem, on the other hand, uses far more traditional features of poetry. I have already mentioned the formality, even the literary nature, of the diction. It also uses **heroic couplets**. That is, each pair of lines, or **couplet**, rhymes – lines 1 and 2 use **perfect rhyme** ("arc" and "mark") and the next couplet uses **slant rhyme** (also called **off rhyme** or **near rhyme**, repeated sounds often depending on the same final consonant, as with "done" and "on") – and each line within each couplet has roughly five iambs (a pattern called **iambic pentameter**). Moreover, each of Nemerov's couplets forms an independent syntactical unit: a **closed couplet**. And what of the title of the Nemerov poem? If one does not have Latin, one has to look up the very meaning of "Quaerendo Invenietis." So, to start, the poem is assuming a well-educated reader, although even a well-educated reader must from the start make certain decisions – or begin with certain working hypotheses – about the meaning of the title, or at least about its connotations. "Quaerendo Invenietis" does have a literal meaning, namely "You will discover by inquiry." But the phrase also has a history; the language has lived in different places historically. First, it has a biblical history, as a few alternative translations suggest: "Let he who has ears hear" or "Seek and ye shall find." At the same time, an educated reader (and we have already found that the poem seems to position us as such) might think of

Bach's 1746 fugue entitled "Quaerendo Invenietis," and notice that the musical form Bach uses involves counterpoint; in particular, it involves two voices, with the second imitating the rhythm and internal content of the first. Finally, if you are a twenty-first-century reader who has used an internet search engine to position yourself as the well-educated reader Nemerov seems to require, you will find numerous websites called "Quaerendo Invenietis," encyclopedic sites that offer to answer questions (often about how to buy consumer goods, sometimes offering general knowledge).

Here, and now focusing on what the Nemerov poem might mean, it helps to know when the poem was written (since, as I noted above, the meanings of words can change over time). "Quaerendo Invenietis" appeared in Nemerov's 1973 book entitled *Gnomes & Occasions*. This tells us that Nemerov cannot be alluding to internet searches (there was no World Wide Web in 1973), although it does not tell us whether the echo of religious language or of musical form or – for that matter – of some pre-internet version of a site of knowledge is what we are asked to bring to mind. At this point, it seems wise to keep all three meanings somewhere in mind; after all, poems can work in multiple registers and have rich reso-nances (that is to say, echoes or **allusions**, a word derived from the Latin for "to touch lightly on a subject"). I use the word "resonance," although it is not a common technical term, to mean the ways in which images or word choices in poems seem to be thematically full or to have what we might call undertones – meanings that we are intended to call to mind (or that work to enrich the poem when we do so) but that are not quite part of the literal meaning of the poem. One might call resonance a lighter version of allusion. That "Quaerendo Invenietis" has a title calling to mind biblical injunctions or classical music lends at the very least a sense of seriousness to the poem that follows, but a paraphrase or even a summary of the theme of the poem would not necessarily need to mention Bach or the Bible (while full-blown allusions more typically do call on readers to consider more explicitly that to which the poem alludes).

The salient formal features of Nemerov's poem, its brevity and formal-ity, also tend to make one think one is dealing with a "serious" and perhaps a traditional subject: if not religion, then some statement on how to live one's life, perhaps. And reading the first couplet, which discusses a path or "way" and refers to getting something right ("trues my arc" suggests being on the right path), furthers our sense that the poem is working **allegori-cally**. In other words, it seems as if the "spiral way" and the "arc" – not to mention the "central silence" and "unreached mark," which suggest some ultimate goal – stand for something other than themselves, for some larger abstraction. It is, in this sense, not difficult to see that if the poem has moved us in some way, it is perhaps because we are thinking of a life's journey toward death (a "silence" reached when one's "time be done"), with some further goal or "mark" (whether a worldly ambition or the reward of some afterlife).

However, if you have begun to read the poem's first couplet allegorically, the second couplet seems a bit more confusing. For one thing, the speaker seems to have changed. We have a first-person speaker ("*my* arc," "*my* unreached mark") in the first couplet. In the second couplet we have a "traveler," who would seem to be the "I" from the first couplet – who said he was on a "spiral way," journeying, in an arc, toward a goal – now referred to in the third person. Bearing in mind the musical form of Bach's fugue, one could propose that the second couplet is a second voice, repeating the content (as it patently repeats the rhythm) of the first couplet.

If we are analytic readers or simply practiced readers of poetry – with what Wallace Stevens called a "rage for order" – we may even try to align the first couplet's "spiral way" (spirals do, in fact, contain or consist of arcs) with what the second couplet identifies as an active road (going on) and a passive traveler (doing nothing). One is tempted, then, to propose that this is a poem of spiritual advice, one advocating "going with the flow" or accepting what life offers – or at least, one might propose that the poem represents such an acceptance on the part of one who travels through life doing "nothing" as one way of following a non-linear (spiral-like) path that will ensure one arrives where one is supposed to be. Here, I might point out, that in aligning "central silence" and an "unreached mark" with "where one is suppose to be," I am relying on the definition of "true" used as a verb, which means "to bring or restore something to a desired precision." At the same time, the poem ensures we will maintain somewhere in mind – as a resonance or undertone – the definitions of the adjective "true," meaning accurate or loyal or even conformable to a pattern, all of which again bolsters the sense that we are reading a poem about the pattern of a life lived well. This interpretation seems also to be supported by the tidy, closed heroic couplets, with their clear rhyme and regular iambic pentameter, perhaps, in context, even by the lack of enjambment and the regularity of the syntax. There is, further, a pause between sentences in the last line, called a **caesura**, which in this case makes the final sentence – "But the road goes on" – read almost like a punch line or final piece of wisdom, which we reach only after pausing to take a breath at the caesura.

If offering this wisdom were the sole purpose of the poem, I have to say I would find it a formally well-crafted but not otherwise particularly interesting poem, although others might be more disposed to find what it says attractive. In writing about how to read poems, I do not imagine that everyone will thrill to every poem I offer here. One wants, after all, to be able to listen to and understand even what one is *not* already predisposed to like. Yet whatever one's response to what seem to be the poem's central concerns on first reading, the above interpretation – while plausible – leaves some unanswered questions. Why does the poem specify a "spiral" instead of just a "wandering" way? Why bother with the form (except perhaps to suggest a universal pattern)? And is not the message – don't bother working for your "mark," since you will get where you are going by doing "nothing" – a bit vague, without exemplification or complication?

If one were prone to agree that such passivity is the way to live, one might just nod amiably. If one found the "message" unwelcome, this poem would hardly change one's heart or mind or make one think again. Moreover, why does the poem describe the "mark" as "unreached"? Or align that goal not only with a center but with "central silence" and one's time being "done"? If we are being counseled to accept Nemerov's "spiral way," it seems he has chosen less than attractive descriptions of where we will end up. For some readers at least, describing the end of one's life's journey as "central silence" (especially contrasted with the description of the traveler as anything but silent in line 3) would not be especially appealing. For those inclined to embrace the joys of living, I imagine that "singing and saying" and *not* reaching one's fated "mark" any sooner than absolutely necessary would be a far more attractive "way." This is not what the poem says, of course. But the question remains, what *does* the poem want from us or want to convey to us? Does it say its piece effectively?

At this point, I will simply spring on you a piece of knowledge I have withheld. This is a **riddle poem**, and, at least on some accounts, a poem first written on commission to sell a product. That is, there is at stake a far more material, concrete reference – pointing outside of the poem to an object or type of object – than we thought at first. If I had offered you the full, three-stanza, version of "Quaerendo Invenietis," the poem's status as a puzzle would have been slightly (but only slightly) clearer because each of the three numbered, four-line sections of the poem poses a riddle (each with a different answer). And the title, in that context, seems to pose a rather more secular challenge than might first appear, asking if we can find the answer to a puzzle we're being set.

Before returning to "Quaerendo Invenietis" with this new piece of information in mind (information that positions us differently as readers and raises different expectations), let me directly address one obvious question. How can one know that one has a riddle here (rather than a parable or allegory or piece of vaguely spiritual advice)? I pose the question starkly, but I have no real answer. I first encountered Nemerov's poem in a 1970s poetry anthology, where it was grouped with other riddle poems. In short, while a little research in books about Nemerov's poetry and his life might have provided me with this suggestion, I know what I know because someone fed me the answer. Moreover, even research might not have provided a definitive answer, since many of Nemerov's poems and essays use the image of spirals metaphorically, which is to say that the subject of "The Spiral Way" appears to have appealed to the writer because spirals apparently stood for something – operated allegorically, if you will – in Nemerov's mind. Certainly there is nothing obvious on the face of the poem that reveals or requires the information that it is a riddle poem. However, I *do* know that riddle poems are a traditional kind of poem, especially in Old English, and considering "Quaerendo Invenietis" as a riddle poem *does* make it suddenly a far more interesting, and a far more precise, poem. If you will, *my* "arc" as a reader coming to an understanding of the poem seems to be "trued" by knowing the poem is a riddle, that is, by knowing its genre.

I suggested, above, that interpreting poems involves looking to what seems in context most fruitful or interesting. If I now explore what happens when I take "Quaerendo Invenietis" as a riddle and consider both how it has positioned me as a cultured or educated reader and the title's possible invocation of musical form, something interesting happens. With this new context, I can take the images offered literally, or at least in material rather than in metaphysical terms. I often sketch what poems describe – here, a spiral with a vocal ("Singing and saying") speaker arcing toward a center, a point that is both unreached and that involves silence. Moreover, the "I" is not actively traveling the arc, or road, but nonetheless seems to move toward a central point. Ironically, perhaps, the riddle is harder now than when this poem was written, technologies for producing or reproducing sound having shifted a good deal since the 1970s; in 1973 the image Nemerov offers would have been quite familiar, even if – because we have a poem with apparent high seriousness and metaphysical implications – still not immediately obvious. On a second, recontextualized reading, however, we can see that what we have is a quite literal description of a now old-fashioned record player. The stylus or phonograph needle and the arm that holds it do indeed head (or arc) directly toward the center of the phonograph record, the spiral way being the grooves on the phono-graph (metaphorically the "road" that "goes on" – indeed, moves – while the stylus that is moved does "nothing"). And when a phonograph record has been played, the stylus does not move to the very center of the record, but does reach the end of recorded sound: that is, there is "central silence" and an "unreached mark." Unlike the more metaphysically suggestive reading of the poem that first comes to mind, this interpretation (and it is an interpretation, even if it feels more like a set solution to a set problem) leaves very few questions about the choice of images (spirals and central silence reached by "singing and saying," the truing of arcs, the passive traveler and the active road).

However, now one has two possible readings of Nemerov's poem. On the one hand, it is a vague, high-minded (if not perhaps philosophically very original) poem about living; and on the other hand, it is a quite precise description of – perhaps, given the implication that readers will be cultured people, even a savvy advertisement for – a phonograph player. In either case, whether read as high-minded allegory or as riddle, the poem seems to yield most when each trope (the spiral, the road, the doing nothing, and so on) is read carefully, and, indeed, read as if it can be translated on some other (whether higher or more literal) level. At the same time, the poem yields two rather different interpretations. Moreover, unlike some poems, the literal and the allegorical poem do not seem intimately related. That is, I am not convinced (although I have an open mind and suppose I could be convinced some day) that the poem is suggesting that living one's life well is like being a stylus. On the contrary, the poem may be humorous. It actively invites us to use our familiarity with the high seriousness of formally staid poetry and apparently high diction (not to mention the suggestion of ultimate things that the biblical echoes bring to mind) to read the poem as a piece of philosophical wisdom. And then, with a kind of surprise turn – perhaps even an "unfair" turn, given the more down-to-earth reference to the language of riddles and consumer culture – it deflates our expectations. It's "just about" a record player.

There are two more things I would like to point out here. First, as a riddle the poem may indeed be unfair or at least spring a surprise on its readers, since, as I mentioned above, there's little in the words on the page or the form of the poem telling us to read it as a riddle with a literal answer. On the other hand, this surprising turn of the poem, for those who find poems esoteric or (as I sometimes hear it said) elitist, is doubly surprising because it is surprising in its plainness. That is, knowledge of widely used consumer items like record players, especially in 1973, cannot easily be called elite or esoteric knowledge. In fact, I'd suggest that the poem may playfully be challenging any assumptions I brought to it about the elite nature of poetic material. Had the poem seemed to be about a record player but turned out to be about religious beliefs or even Bach (with such meaning available only to those with the appropriate education), then it could, I imagine, be said to appeal to an elite. However, "Quaerendo Invenietis" works the other way around: the poem first appears to be abstractly high-minded, but then works far more precisely when it is read as a description of an everyday, modern material object (even if one that calls to mind a recording of a Bach fugue). That record players now are less common than they were when the poem was written over thirty years ago, and that the poem might one day need a footnote to explain what phonographs were, suggests not elitism but the perhaps ironic fact that the more contemporary, temporally relevant, references a poet uses (and this would assuredly pertain to political events or fashion as well as to consumer goods), the more likely such references are to become dated.

Second, as what I have already said implies, I think I would find Nemerov's poem no more stunning as "just" an advertisement for or riddle about a record player than I did as a message about the path of human life. Ultimately, whatever or whoever originally inspired the poem, even if Nemerov was first hired to write a clever and sophisticated advertisement, the poet also reprinted "Quaerendo Invenietis" in a volume of poetry where he clearly intended it to be taken seriously as a poem. Indeed, what I enjoy about "Quaerendo Invenietis" is that in the long run I "seek and find" two discordant ways of reading it, both of which challenge me to read the language and references of the poem carefully, so that to "true [one's] arc" comes also to implicate me, my process of thinking through or thinking with the poem, as well as challenging the assumptions I bring to the reading of poems. If there is a "higher" message, it would seem to me to be this: that we often go looking for (or resent being asked to go look for) obscure references to answer questions, specifically to unpack the meaning of poems that seem puzzling, but we might more usefully just look at the material world around us, using our common knowledge.

Whether or not this final implication was, indeed, part of Nemerov's purpose in writing the poem, it is a feature of the poem – not a failure of our readings of the poem – that it invites two, not easily reconciled, interpretations. And, while it is most rewarding to read poems with precision (that traditionally being one of the distinguishing features of poetry's language, that it carries a good deal of meaning in a small space by virtue of the precise linguistic choices it embodies), I would suggest that it is also one of the pleasures of reading poems that one does not need to shoehorn them into tidy or preconceived schemata. That is, if a poem, like Nemerov's, read with careful attention to the details, appears to say two things at once (even contradictorily), one might pause to ask what might be at stake, or what might be interesting, about that fact – rather than insisting that *one* meaning must be the proper and only meaning.

Finally, one might notice that after dwelling on Nemerov's poem for several pages here, I have come to propose that it is, despite one's initial impression, something of a rebellious poem in the way that it both draws on expectations of higher meanings in poetry and then almost jokingly calls them into question. I have also suggested that Nemerov's poem would not be as interesting if I had not gone through the process of trying, first, to read it as an allegory, pointing to second-order religious or philosophical abstractions lying outside the text. Part of the gentle humor of the poem comes from the fact that, whether I am reading an allegory or a riddle, the process of figuring out what I am invited to seek is much the same. In short, riddles have things in common with allegories: both use coded language, although riddles tend to have concrete references rather than the abstractions to which allegories point. So perhaps Nemerov's riddle is not that unfair; the poem does invite me to bring to it my expectation that I will be solving a kind of puzzle. It is simply that the precise kind of puzzle is not what I'd first expected.

I have just suggested that Nemerov's poem might be called "rebellious" – a term I used earlier of the poem by William Carlos Williams which I juxtaposed with Nemerov's at the beginning of this chapter. Yet "To Greet a Letter-Carrier" clearly positions its readers differently. That is, the language of Williams's poem does not invite us to draw on specialized knowledge or to see ourselves being set a puzzle. We are in the workaday world from the start, with nothing – neither language nor images nor references – to make us try to read the poem as allegory *or* riddle. The first sentence (as I also already noted) is slightly indecorous for a poem, certainly for a poem written in 1938 in the United States. "Why'n't you bring me / a good letter?" does not sound like a serious poetic statement, both because of the diction and because of the enjambment. And one would feel a bit silly asking what "a good letter" stands for, as if it were a kind of code with "letter" metaphorically standing for something else. What we have by the end of the third line of this five-line poem seems to be a kind of **dramatic monologue**: that is, we are overhearing a speaker whose speech characterizes him (or, less likely in 1938, her). Some critics would call the poem a **dramatic lyric** or even a **mask lyric** or a poem using a **persona**, depending on whether they see the speaker ironically revealing more of himself than he means to show (the dramatic monologue) or whether the poet's relationship to the speaker is less distanced (using a persona), even difficult to distinguish from the poet (the mask lyric).

How one thinks William Carlos Williams positions himself in relation with his speaker in "To Greet a Letter-Carrier" will be a matter of interpretation, depending on other considerations that can be detailed and debated. To start, it seems obvious that Williams's speaker and the scene his poem dramatizes are quite different from Nemerov's. I have never seen anyone read "Quaerendo Invenietis" as if it were an expression of the poet's biographical experience (although it may of course nonetheless express things in which Nemerov, biographically, believed). Certainly, despite the first-person pronouns in "my arc" and "my unreached mark," the poem does not suggest at all that it is a transcription of spoken English (the diction, rhyme, and meter are simply too formal), and the disappearance of any first person in the final couplet further dissuades most of us from any reading of "Quaerendo Invenietis" as a lyrical outcry from Howard Nemerov's heart. Williams's poem, however, does seem to capture and characterize a speaker. That Williams was an educated man (and a medical doctor, although doctors in 1938 did not have quite the prestige they might now) suggests to me that the speaker is not Williams but a character. That said, however, I do not think we are invited to make much of this distinction: we hear an apparently heartfelt utterance (not only is the diction colloquial, but "One with / lots of money in it" is not even a full sentence). Only the fact that there are line breaks (if decidedly non-standard line breaks) tells us this is a poem, in fact, rather than – say – an ethnographer's transcription of speech by an ordinary person from around 1938. Williams, I would suggest, is counting on the fact that what he wrote "looks like" (and was published as) a poem to make readers pay careful attention to the apparently unpoetic language he uses.

Reading the poem as ethnography that nonetheless takes ordinary language to be worthy of the kind of attention we give to the language of poems, I would probably say it uses a persona, that is, the poet is imaginatively identifying with (not ironically exposing) the fictional speaker, even if that speaker differs from what we know of the author. In making this judgment about how the poem shapes my attitude toward the speaker whose words I overhear, however, I am also drawing on some extra-literary knowledge. Earlier I mentioned that the most temporally relevant references in poems are, perhaps ironically, just those most likely to seem obscure after some time has passed. This may be true of Williams's poem in two ways. First, "Atta boy!" now sounds to many Americans as if it could only be said to a dog, or as a form of condescension. However, in 1938 – and according to dictionaries of American English even now – the phrase indicates approval or encouragement and comes from the chatter of baseball players in the field. It is a piece of American slang that entered the language in the first decades of the twentieth century (so it was relatively "up-to-date" slang when Williams wrote his poem), a shortened version of "That's the boy!" Comparable interjections we might now use would be

"Way to go" or "You're the man." In other words, in 1938 "Atta boy!" was a commonplace, even working-class, male expression of solidarity, as if one were on the same (baseball) team as one's mail carrier.

The other contemporary reference in the poem is not precisely a reference, but rather an extra-literary context that may affect how the poem was originally heard and originally intended to be heard. "To Greet a Letter-Carrier" was written during what is called the Great Depression – lasting from 1929 to 1941 – in the United States. The poem's tacit definition of a "good" letter as one containing money might be read in this context. That is, this is not an expression of, say, corporate greed; it is the voice of a working-class person who is living through hard times, expressing a hope, namely that a windfall will arrive. Even more than Nemerov's poem, Williams's poem resists from the very start any expectation that the poem will transport its readers to some metaphysical or more abstract realm. Indeed, it seems almost incantatory, suggesting the speaker is using language – the language of an ordinary speaker of American slang – as if it might cast a spell on the mail delivery man and make something "good," a letter with "lots of money in it," appear. This is in some ways similar to the way words of encouragement might indeed encourage a baseball player to play well, although of course letters tend not to respond to words of encouragement. One could say it is ironic that an apparently pragmatic, down-to-earth speaker (he wants what he can "make use of" in a material sense) is using language as if it could cast a spell on the mail. Yet rather than irony at the expense of the speaker, we seem to have here a portrait – even a generous, or at least affectionate, portrait – of an ordinary person's relationship both to the world and to language.

In saying this, I am drawing on yet another kind of extra-literary knowledge, or at least on what I know of William Carlos Williams's aims as a poet. What a poet says she or he wants to do cannot always be used as a guide for reading the poet's poems. Poets' aims, like anyone else's, can change over time; poets can say they believe one thing in theory but can surprise themselves or find themselves ambivalent or unconsciously at odds with themselves in actual poems. However, it does not hurt to test a poem against a poet's stated poetic goal. And it does add something to one's reading of "To Greet a Letter-Carrier" to know that Williams said he wanted to write in and celebrate the American language (which he saw not as the Queen's English but as more populist and as more inflected by immigrant languages). Williams's interest in promoting ordinary spoken language as appropriate for use in poetry informs my suggestion, then, that his poem is not only a sketch of an ordinary person but also an exploration of what one might call the poetic quality of ordinary language – language used as if it had almost magical qualities. In this light, too, the title of Williams's poem takes on rich undertones: "To Greet a Letter-Carrier" sounds like the title of a section of an etiquette book, or perhaps a recipe, the latter underlining the incantatory, near-magical belief in the efficacy of using language ("This is what you must say to receive money in the mail"), the former underlining how what is "proper" (the etiquette for using language in poems) is for Williams something other than the high, non-spoken language or diction and tone people in 1938 (and still in 1973, to judge by Nemerov's poem) expected from serious poetry.

While Williams's rebellion against what one might call traditional expectations for poetry is far more overt than Nemerov's, in ways it is similar. One can read "To Greet a Letter-Carrier" without knowing how unpoetry-like it would have seemed in its day because, unlike Nemerov's poem, Williams's does not entirely depend for its effect on his readers having such expectations. Still, the discrepancy between more genteel poetry and "To Greet a Letter-Carrier" did once add a certain bad-boy quality to Williams's work that may now be lost to us without some act of historical imagination (and research). Indeed, given Williams's stated aims, one suspects that he unwittingly did depend on exactly what he was trying to overturn, namely expectations of a certain decorousness in the language and subject matter for poems, knowing his poem would gain a certain shock value by resisting expectations.

These days, however, many of us have had our ears for poetry formed by Williams and those who followed his lead. Ironically, his very success means that his poem no longer sounds so rebellious. Even so, the poem's presentation of the power of ordinary speech does not require one to "speak poetry" in the way Nemerov's poem does; the poem is clearly concerned with how ordinary language – anyone's language – attended to with care can be seen to reveal something about human desires. What is lost in reading "To Greet a Letter-Carrier" out of context is simply the edgy, rebellious tone. It would be more difficult to read "Quaerendo Invenietis" had one never read any other poetry; without hearing or feeling the appeal to and surprising redefinition of allegories and riddles, "Quaerendo Invenietis" is less likely to affect us.

Despite some similarities, the two poems position us differently as readers and yield most to different acts of interpretation. Of course they don't come with instruction manuals telling us we are entering one sort of poem or another. Yet familiarity with other poems, with how they make meaning, as well as using one's historical imagination to put one's self in another era, does provide a way of figuring out what kind of reading will prove most humanly and linguistically resonant, and of hearing the conceptual syntax – the manner in which ideas or feelings work together and move from one position to another – in each poem.

The ways in which poems work with, or against, or in conversation with other poems is sometimes called **intertextuality**. In this chapter, I have focused on how Nemerov's and Williams's poems, in different ways and to different degrees, depend on readers' expectations. Their conversations or arguments with poetic tradition involve their knowledge of how readers approach poems, including what kinds of diction or subject matter seem appropriate. In the following chapter, I want to think about intertextuality on a more thematic level. That is, I want to turn to poems that suggest the later writers read and were more specifically and more self-consciously responding to the earlier writers' poems.

Terms used

allegory	intertextuality
allusion	mask lyric
caesura	near rhyme
closed couplets	octave
couplet	off rhyme
dramatic lyric	perfect rhyme
dramatic monologue	persona
enjambment	riddle poem
form	sestet
free verse	simile
genre	slant rhyme
heroic couplets	sonnet
iamb	stanza
iambic pentameter	verse

Other poems that might be read

Old English riddles (*The Norton Anthology of Poetry*, for one, includes translations of several tenth-century riddles) and Robert Browning, "My Last Duchess" (1842)

John Donne, "A Valediction Forbidding Mourning" (1633) and Anna Laetitia Barbauld, "The Rights of Women" (1795)

A. E. Housman, "Loveliest of Trees, The Cherry Now" (1896) and Langston Hughes, "Weary Blues" (1926)

Marianne Moore, "Roses Only" (1917) and Edmund Waller, "Song" ("Go, lovely rose," 1645)

W. S. Merwin, "Odysseus" (1960) and James Wright, "A Note Left in Jimmy Leonard's Shack" (1959)

Useful further reading

M. H. Abrams, *A Glossary of Literary Terms* (Boston: Thomson/Wadsworth, 2005).

T. V. F. Brogan and Alex Preminger, eds., *The New Princeton Encyclopedia of Poetry and Poetics* (Princeton, NJ: Princeton University Press, 1993).

Jack Myers and Michael Simms, *The Longman Dictionary of Poetic Terms* (New York and London: Longman, 1989).

Alex Preminger, ed., *The Princeton Handbook of Poetic Terms* (Princeton, NJ: Princeton University Press, 1986).

Adina Rosmarin, *The Power of Genre* (Minneapolis: University of Minnesota Press, 1985).

John Simpson and Edmund Weiner, eds., *Oxford English Dictionary* (Oxford: Clarendon Press; New York: Oxford University Press, 1993).

Lewis Turco, *The Book of Forms: A Handbook of Poetics* (New York: E. P. Dutton, 1968).

Noah Webster, *An American Dictionary of the English Language* (Springfield, Mass.: G. and C. Merriam, 1851).

Chapter 2

Speaking Poetry: Night Pieces and Intertextual Conversations

in John Milton's "Il Penseroso" (1631); Anne Finch, Countess of Winchilsea's "A Nocturnal Reverie" (1713); William Wordsworth's "A Night Piece" (1798); and James Wright's "A Blessing" (1963), with reference to Act V, scene i, lines 1–24 of Shakespeare's *The Merchant of Venice*

In chapter 1, I mentioned that poets often draw on – and are seen to draw on – others' poems in various ways. One of these ways is the use of familiar **motifs**, a motif being a theme, device, event, or character that is repeated and developed not only within an individual poem but over time, often going back to classical (Greek or Roman) literature. Here, I want to look at one particular motif – night – to consider how poetic nights might be seen in relationship to one another. Night-settings are not new to literature in English and can be traced back to well before the piece with which I will open. Indeed, the lines with which I want to begin are not even from a poem *per se*, but from a play: they are part of a scene from William Shakespeare's *The Merchant of Venice*. The scene is in what is called **blank verse**, which is to say it is in lines of iambic pentameter that do not rhyme, although it takes a minute to notice the metrical regularity because the lines are shared by two characters in the scene.

The following is from Act V, scene i, of Shakespeare's play, which we are told is set in Belmont. It is an exchange between two lovers – Lorenzo and Jessica – who are eloping.

Lorenzo: The moon shines bright: in such a night as this,
    When the sweet wind did gently kiss the trees
    And they did make no noise, in such a night
    Troilus methinks mounted the Troyan walls,
    And sigh'd his soul toward the Grecian tents,   5
    Where Cressid lay that night.
Jessica: In such a night
    Did Thisbe fearfully o'erstrip the dew,
    And saw the lion's shadow ere himself,
    And ran dismay'd away.
Lorenzo: In such a night
    Stood Dido with a willow in her hand   10
    Upon the wild sea-banks, and waft her love
    To come again to Carthage.
Jessica: In such a night
    Medea gather'd the enchanted herbs
    That did renew old Jason.
Lorenzo: In such a night
    Did Jessica steal from the wealthy Jew,   15
    And with an unthrift love did run from Venice,
    as far as Belmont.
Jessica: In such a night
    Did young Lorenzo swear he lov'd her well,
    Stealing her soul with many vows of faith,
    And ne'er a true one.
Lorenzo: In such a night   20
    Did pretty Jessica, like a little shrew,
    Slander her love, and he forgave it her.
Jessica: I would out-night you, did nobody come;
    But, hark! I hear the footing of a man.   24

Even without knowing much about the context of the whole play (which I am not going to discuss here), it is fairly clear that the dialogue forms a kind of affectionate sparring between lovers; the whole exchange is part of a subgenre representing the battle between the sexes that would have been as familiar to Shakespeare's audience as it is to us. Line 6 also shows how Shakespeare has kept the iambic pentameter going across the two characters' voices: "Where Cressid lay that night. In such a night." The line has alternating stressed and unstressed syllables for a total of five stresses in what, if this were a poem, would be called a **stepped line**. You can also hear a repeated **refrain** ("in such a night") that interests me because the battle between Lorenzo and Jessica is a tussle over which of them will get the final say on just what kind of night is conjured in their (and our) imaginations. Moreover, virtually all the nights described are literary, by which I mean that Lorenzo and Jessica are characterized as imagining themselves in settings they (and we) know through stories, poems, myths, and other plays.

While you do not have to know much about or have thought deeply about *The Merchant of Venice* in order to enjoy the excerpted scene, the edgy humor of the exchange is clearer if you know something of the stories to which the characters allude. For example, although Lorenzo's first speech begins with a simple description of nature (the wind is kissing the trees, a seductive image for a lover to use), it also appears that Lorenzo is imagining himself and Jessica as heroic lovers: their night is like that experienced by Troilus and Cressida – characters used both by Chaucer and by Shakespeare himself in another play. Not surprisingly, perhaps, Lorenzo imagines the scene from the hero's point of view, as Troilus "sighs" over Cressida. More importantly, however, he has chosen a story in which the female lead, Cressida, represents betrayal and lack of fidelity. Jessica's retort shows her refusal to be cast in such a role; she re-imagines their night as that of Pyramus and Thisbe, lovers from a classical story reminiscent of Romeo and Juliet's, in which both lovers are true (and in which both die for love). Lorenzo then ups the ante, re-reimagining the night as Dido's. Although in Dido's story – again from the classics – it is Aeneas, the male lover, who is untrue, he is also an epic hero who leaves Dido for what Virgil's *Aeneid* clearly figures as a more important mission, namely the founding of Rome. The man is again the hero (for Lorenzo). Jessica, at this point, trumps Lorenzo's classical pair with yet another pair of lovers: Jason and Medea. In that myth, while Jason is also, like Aeneas, heroic (not to mention untrue), Medea is primarily known for getting revenge on her faithless lover. Rather than die a tragic death (of the sort the *Aeneid* provides for Dido), Medea uses her knowledge of herbs, at least in the most common variant of the myth, to poison Jason and, indeed, then to kill their children.

One can think of the verbal sparring in the scene as a kind of one-upmanship (or one-upwomanship). Although the dialogue remains affectionate, Lorenzo keeps imagining the elopement as a story in which he plays a hero-lover, with Jessica as his untrue or unworthy beloved; for her part, Jessica gives as good as she gets, consistently countering with reimagined models in which the woman is true and decidedly not passive. Not only does she literally get the last word (even as she says she has been cut off by the arrival of someone else), what she says contains an interesting image – a telling picture or **emblem** of their whole conversation: "I would out-night you, did nobody come." In short, the two have been trying to "out-night" each other, which is to say each offers in turn a culturally familiar night scene, in which either the male hero or the female lead is more prominent, or more steadfast, depending on whether it is Lorenzo's or Jessica's imagination of night.

In light of the gendered nature of the stories and of later uses of similar gestures (which I will discuss in a moment), Jessica's final words in the scene are even more interesting. She says, "But, hark! I hear the footing of a man." Admittedly, in Shakespeare's play a man does appear. Literally, in context, Jessica is simply saying their conversation has been halted because she hears someone approaching. But, of course, for us as readers (even more than for playgoers listening to the dialogue) the whole exchange has also involved *metrical* feet, since the twenty-four lines in question are in blank verse, five iambic feet per line. Moreover, although a male character does arrive on stage, and although "man" can and typically would be used to mean "person" or "human being," in the context of the pointedly self-conscious exchange about male and female imaginations of heroism, it is difficult not to read the connotations or subtext of Jessica's statement as implying that she has been cut off by specifically male speech. Finally, in a larger context, Jessica's storytelling is curtailed not just by another character arriving on the scene, but by the metrical feet of male authors, of just those classical writers – Virgil, Ovid, Chaucer, Shakespeare himself – who have told the stories of Troilus and Cressida, Pyramus and Thisbe, Aeneas and Dido, Jason and Medea, and (not least) Lorenzo and Jessica.

Whether or not Shakespeare in this dialogue tacitly insists on his own authorial presence is not something one can prove one way or another (although he might well be seen as out-nighting all the earlier authors on whom he has his characters draw). Still, Shakespeare is (and was) known for punning, so the idea that "footing" refers to metrical feet is not far-fetched. Nor is the idea that Jessica's use of the word "man" is meant to be gender-specific; certainly it is difficult after the back-and-forth between Lorenzo and Jessica not to hear "man" as distinct from "woman." The final step – the idea that Shakespeare's own "out-nighting" is at stake – is more problematic, but, again, such self-consciousness is not anachronistic. In any event, it seems later writers were inclined to think of something very like Shakespeare's scene between Lorenzo and Jessica when writing their own night scenes, in a way I want to trace beginning with a seventeenth-century poem by John Milton.

Milton – whatever his ambitions – could not have known when he wrote "Il Penseroso" in 1631, early in his authorial career, that he would become a monumental writer, one of those who seems to us as Shakespeare or Chaucer seemed to him, a great figure referred to by a single name. "Il Penseroso" was written as an exercise when John Milton was still a student at Cambridge (if one with high hopes); his awareness of classical and earlier English precedents is both overt and probably connected with the writing of the poem as a form of apprenticeship. If you were to look in most anthologies that contain poems by Milton, you would notice that "Il Penseroso" – the name is Italian for "the pensive man" – is paired with another exercise poem entitled "L'Allegro," which makes a case for the good life as a life of daylight and engagement in the world rather than as the one of nocturnal contemplation found in "Il Penseroso." The opposition between active and contemplative lives was not new in 1631; nor can one say without question that, of the two, "Il Penseroso" is the poem in which Milton spoke from his heart or declared his personal commitments. "Il Penseroso" and "L'Allegro" mirror one another (in form and structure) even as they praise different ways of living, as if Milton were on a collegiate debate team, arbitrarily assigned to one side of a preset debate – even showing off a bit by taking both sides, one at a time, with equal dexterity.

"Il Penseroso" is a poem that may be difficult for us to read with great enthusiasm these days, and not only because it seems to be an "exercise" poem, participating in a debate we no longer find pressing. It is also laced with allusions and uses of words that are now uncommon (most anthology reprintings are thick with footnotes). Moreover, as I'll show in a moment, the poem draws on rhetorical models that are no longer familiar to us, while its diction and syntax can sound to modern readers so lofty as to be off-putting to many. On the other hand, "Il Penseroso" became a set piece for a large number of later readers and writers. This may have to do with an increased interest in interiority and in the workings of the individual psyche, or with the increasing later association of poetry with the solitary, sensitive individual. It is primarily because of its influence on later literature – and for the way in which Milton's poem itself draws on and reimagines (or out-nights) earlier night pieces – that I want to give you "Il Penseroso" in full, even if it is quite long.

Indeed, given the length of Milton's night piece, I am not going to (although one certainly could) offer here a line-by-line close reading. I do, however, want to consider how the poem unfolds – its conceptual syntax – and to dwell on a few images and gestures, especially some that may be opaque to modern readers. I have drawn lines to mark breaks between the sections of the poem's argument that I want to highlight, although it did not originally contain such lines. Nor is "Il Penseroso" arranged in stanzas;

rather than arranging lines in such formally defined units, Milton characteristically uses units of thought or **verse paragraphs** that arrange lines in
units of thought rather than in formally defined units. You might notice
as you read that the syntax draws our attention to turns in the argument
with words like "Hence," "But," and "Thus," conjunctions that usually
signal logical relations in the rhetoric of logical expositions.

> Hence vain deluding joys,
> The brood of folly without father bred,
> How little you bestead,
> Or fill the fixed mind with all your toys;
> Dwell in some idle brain,   5
> And fancies fond with gaudy shapes possess,
> As thick and numberless
> As the gay motes that people the sunbeams,
> Or likest hovering dreams,
> The fickle Pensioners of Morpheus' train.   10
> But, hail thou Goddess, sage and holy,
> Hail, divinest Melancholy,
> Whose saintly visage is too bright
> To hit the sense of human sight;
> And therefore to our weaker view,   15
> O'erlaid with black, staid Wisdom's hue.
> Black, but such as in esteem,
> Prince Memnon's sister might beseem,
> Or that starred Ethiope Queen that strove
> To set her beauty's praise above   20
> The sea nymphs, and their powers offended.
> Yet thou art higher far descended;
> Thee bright-haired Vesta long of yore,
> To solitary Saturn bore;
> His daughter she (in Saturn's reign,   25
> Such mixture was not held a stain).
> Oft in glimmering bowers and glades
> He met her, and in secret shades
> Of woody Ida's inmost grove,
> While yet there was no fear of Jove.   30
> Come pensive Nun, devout and pure,
> Sober, steadfast, and demure,
> All in a robe of darkest grain,
> Flowing with majestic train,
> And sable stole of cypress lawn   35
> Over thy decent shoulders drawn.
> Come, but keep thy wonted state,

With even step and musing gait,
And looks commercing with the skies,
Thy rapt soul sitting in thine eyes: 40
There held in holy passion still,
Forget thyself to Marble, till
With a sad leaden downward cast,
Thou fix them on the earth as fast.
And join with thee calm Peace and Quiet,   45
Spare Fast, that oft with gods doth diet,
And hears the Muses in a ring
Aye round about Jove's altar sing.
And add to these retired leisure,
That in trim gardens takes his pleasure;   50
But first, and chiefest, with thee bring,
Him that yon soars on golden wing,
Guiding the fiery-wheeled throne,
The cherub Contemplation;
And the mute Silence hist along,   55
'Less Philomel will deign a Song,
In her sweetest, saddest plight,
Smoothing the rugged brow of night,
While Cynthia checks her dragon yoke,
Gently o'er th' accustomed oak;   60
Sweet bird that shunn'st the noise of folly,
Most musical, most melancholy!
Thee chantress oft the Woods among,
I woo to hear thy evensong;
And missing thee, I walk unseen   65
On the dry smooth-shaven green,
To behold the wandering moon,
Riding near her highest noon,
Like one that had been led astray
Through the Heaven's wide pathless way;   70
And oft, as if her head she bowed,
Stooping through a fleecy cloud.
Oft on a plat of rising ground,
I hear the far-off curfew sound,
Over some wide-watered shore,   75
Swinging slow with sullen roar;
Or if the air will not permit,
Some still removed place will fit,
Where glowing embers through the room
Teach light to counterfeit a gloom   80
Far from all resort of mirth,

Save the cricket on the hearth,
Or the bellman's drowsy charm,
To bless the doors from nightly harm;
Or let my lamp at midnight hour,   85
Be seen in some high lonely tower,
Where I may oft out-watch the Bear,
With thrice great Hermes, or unsphere
The spirit of Plato to unfold
What worlds, or what vast regions hold   90
The immortal mind that hath forsook
Her mansion in this fleshly nook;
And of those dæmons that are found
In fire, air, flood, or underground,
Whose power hath a true consent   95
With planet, or with element.
Some time let gorgeous Tragedy
In sceptered pall come sweeping by,
Presenting Thebes, or Pelops' line,
Or the tale of Troy divine.   100
Or what (though rare) of later age,
Ennobled hath the buskined stage.
But, O sad virgin, that thy power
Might raise Musæus from his bower,
Or bid the soul of Orpheus sing   105
Such notes as, warbled to the string,
Drew iron tears down Pluto's cheek,
And made Hell grant what Love did seek.
Or call up him that left half told
The story of Cambuscan bold,   110
Of Camball, and of Algarsife,
And who had Canacee to wife,
That owned the virtuous ring and glass,
And of the wondrous horse of brass,
On which the Tartar king did ride;   115
And if aught else, great bards beside
In sage and solemn tunes have sung,
Of tourneys and of trophies hung;
Of forests and enchantments drear,
Where more is meant than meets the ear.   120
Thus, Night, oft see me in thy pale career,
Till civil-suited morn appear,
Not tricked and frounced as she was wont,
With the Attic boy to hunt,
But kerchiefed in a comely cloud,   125

While rocking winds are piping loud,
Or ushered with a shower still,
When the gust hath blown his fill,
Ending on the rustling leaves,
With minute drops from off the eaves.   130
And when the sun begins to fling
His flaring beams, me, Goddess, bring
To arched walks of twilight groves,
And shadows brown that Sylvan loves
Of pine or monumental oak,   135
Where the rude ax with heaved stroke,
Was never heard the nymphs to daunt,
Or fright them from their hallowed haunt.
There in close covert by some brook,
Where no profaner eye may look,   140
Hide me from day's garish eye,
While the bee with honeyed thigh,
That at her flowery work doth sing,
And the waters murmuring
With such consort as they keep,   145
Entice the dewy-feathered sleep;
And let some strange mysterious dream,
Wave at his wings in airy stream,
Of lively portraiture displayed,
Softly on my eye-lids laid.   150
And as I wake, sweet music breathe
Above, about, or underneath,
Sent by some spirit to mortals good,
Or th' unseen genius of the wood.
But let my due feet never fail,   155
To walk the studious cloister's pale,
And love the high embowed roof,
With antic pillars massy proof,
And storied windows richly dight,
Casting a dim religious light.   160
There let the pealing organ blow,
To the full-voiced choir below,
In service high, and anthems clear,
As may with sweetness, through mine ear,
Dissolve me into ecstasies,   165
And bring all heaven before mine eyes.
And may at last my weary age
Find out the peaceful hermitage,
The hairy gown and mossy cell,

Where I may sit and rightly spell,   170
Of every star that heaven doth show,
And every herb that sips the dew;
Till old experience do attain
<u>To something like prophetic strain.</u>
These pleasures, Melancholy, give,   175
And I with thee will choose to live.

Thought, form, and syntax often signal how poems are structured, almost subliminally urging us as readers to switch gears where form, sentences, or images mark turns in the poem's unfolding. Although someone else might want to mark slightly different – or more – sections, I've marked eight, which will let me talk about the overall movement of the poem and in particular about the way it might have been read when it was written in 1631.

In "Il Penseroso," you can see how the first ten lines form a unit conceptually, in terms of the formal arrangements of the lines, and syntactically. Lines 3–10 form one sentence; lines 1–4 and 5–10 form two rhyming units (rhyming *abba* and then *cddeec*, as if lines 5–10 have had a stray couplet – *ee*, where "sunbeams" and "dreams" rhyme – inserted into the near-**quatrain**, or unit of four lines, one is led to expect by the rhyme scheme in the first four lines [*abba*] and even by the next three lines, which for a moment seem to launch a second quatrain). Most obviously, lines 1–10 form what is called a **valediction**; they dismiss (in this case) joys, which are commanded to go ("hence") and characterized as superficial delusions. One can then feel the poem switching gears in line 11 as a new sentence begins and the form shifts to rhymed couplets at the same time that the speaking voice turns from the valediction to welcome the figure that serves as muse of this poem, namely Melancholy.

You might at first wonder why Milton specifies joy's fancies as "fond" (line 6), given that today the word usually means "affectionate"; but if you look the word up in the *Oxford English Dictionary* you will find that in Milton's day it meant "silly" or "foolish." This is one of those moments when, as a modern reader of a seventeenth-century poem encountering a word that seems to interrupt the expected meaning of the poem, you need to check the dictionary. It is not, I would add, that unexpected turns or assumptions do not appear in poems; they do, and often such turns or surprises are where poems become interesting. But you would want first to know if a poet and his original readers could have heard the same surprising turn you think you are hearing.

In line with this suggestion that it is useful to know what is or is not anachronistic, I want also to say a few words about the presiding muse of

"Il Penseroso," Melancholy, to whom Milton turns in the second section of the poem. This second section is technically an **apostrophe** or address to an absent quality, thing, or person as if it were present. Lines 11–30 in effect conjure Melancholy, hailing her, describing her, and even giving her genealogy in lines 22–6. What I have marked as a third section invokes or calls for melancholy. Lines 31–44, formed of two sentences that both begin "Come," are an **invocation**, a form of apostrophe that underlines the absence of what is called for (since if Melancholy were actually present the speaker would not need repeatedly to call for her to come). The repeated words at the beginning of lines ("Come" or "And") deploy a rhetorical device called **anaphora**.

The question at hand is why a poet would want to invoke Melancholy. These days we might turn to psychology and suggest the depressive speaker should be given Prozac or undergo psychoanalysis, especially given that Melancholy is said to look "black," her eyes are called "sad," and indeed she is said to be the product of an incestuous union of Vesta and Saturn (a pseudo-classical myth, one Milton invented). But our sense of pathology – like our definitions for words like "fond" (or "sad," for that matter, which in 1631 could mean "serious") – may not be Milton's. To say this, though, is a bit misleading. "Fond" unequivocally meant "foolish" in 1631; however, the concept of melancholy was less straightforward. Even at that date the term could be used to describe despondency, which may have modern remedies but is not an exclusively modern ailment. Yet in Milton's day there were other forms of melancholy, associated with the "humor" (the Renaissance took from Greek medicine the physiological theory according to which a person's state of health, mind, and character depended on a balance between four bodily fluids or humors) that inspired poetry and spirituality.

Thus it is not so easy to know which form of melancholy Milton is invoking. My sense of Milton's muse relies in part on a history of critical commentary about "Il Penseroso." The very fact that scholars have felt called upon to trace from where and with what associations Milton derives his idea of melancholy already tells you that the concept is open to debate. Yet, even without being a specialist in the period, you can see ways in which the text itself suggests what kind of melancholy – and by line 121, what kind of night, associated with Melancholy – the poem invokes. One of my reasons for saying this has to do with the formal qualities of "Il Penseroso," although here one does have to have (or acquire) a passing familiarity with classical rhetoric. I have mentioned that the opening sections of the poem use what would have been familiar rhetorical gestures – a valediction, an apostrophe, and an invocation. Given the tradition of public speaking in which Milton's paired poems ("L'Allegro" and "Il Penseroso") participate, the poem as a whole is clearly a public gesture. In fact, an audience familiar with the classical tradition of orations praising things or people (such a piece was called an **encomium** or **panegyric**) would expect to hear an orderly introduction, followed by a genealogy, a list of the companions of the one being praised, a list of the powers and virtues of the same, through to an epilogue. And "Il Penseroso" seems to have just this form: the valediction in lines 1–10 serves as an introduction; a genealogy (especially in lines 22–6) follows; the companions are listed in the paratactic fourth section (**parataxis** is juxtaposition without logical transition, for instance using the conjunction "and," as Milton does).

I am not using Milton's poem to give you a series of rhetorical definitions, because this book is an introduction to reading poetry. I am suggesting that the poem is, by design, a display of meaningful rhetorical flourishes. Moreover, paired as it was with "L'Allegro," it participates in a longstanding debate over the virtues of the contemplative over the active life; so the formality of the poem not only displays Milton showing off his mastery of classical rhetoric but also marks the poem as a familiar and lofty (because classically rooted) piece of public speaking. Admittedly, it takes an act of historical imagination and generosity, or perhaps hubris, to try to cast one's self in the role of a seventeenth-century reader, but doing so has its rewards: it allows one to hear "Il Penseroso" as a celebration of Melancholy, the muse of the contemplative life, traditionally a life of withdrawal from worldly affairs, but far from a pathological condition.

Along the same lines, if you turn to note the traits and companions Milton associates with Melancholy, the contemplative nature of this muse is underlined even without extra-literary knowledge: her color, black, is a sign of "wisdom" (line 16), not depression; she is nun-like, "devout and pure" (lines 31–2), and has a "rapt soul" (line 40) involving "holy passion" (line 41); and her companions, in lines 45–62, include personified versions of peace, quiet, retired leisure, silence, and, not least, "Contemplation" itself (in line 54). (**Personification** involves the humanization of abstract qualities, what might be seen as a brief excursion into allegory.) The very title of the poem – "Il Penseroso," the pensive or thinking man, not "Melancolico" or "Afflitto," which would have been more negatively charged – suggests we should put aside the negative associations melancholy might have for us.

This said, there remain at least two oddities – surprising moments that even with knowledge of the period do not fit tidily into the interpretative framework I am building (and testing against the poem) here. Such moments are often telling, or at least interesting, because they can serve to test your working hypotheses about what a poem means and allow you to understand something that is not necessarily fulfilling your modern (let alone personal) expectations. Often it is moments that don't seem to fit a gathering understanding of a poem that help you have conversations with poems, that let you hear something new or unexpected. So what are the two oddities, as I've called them? (A more theoretical book might use a word I take from an essay on poetic language by Michael Riffaterre, namely "ungrammaticality.") The first passage I have in mind is the unique genealogy that Milton gives his muse, Melancholy. On Milton's account she is the daughter of Vesta (goddess of purity) and Vesta's father, the "solitary Saturn" (line 24). The poem goes on to say that such "mixture was not held a stain" – as we might put it, incest was culturally acceptable. Still, whatever Milton says, in 1631 lines 23–5 would have seemed a bit racy, describing something unequivocally taboo, especially since the disclaimer about incest having been acceptable is given to us only after we are told that Melancholy is the product of such a union. (We do read sequentially, after all, and poems use first impressions, even ones that are then countered, to invoke certain readerly responses).

The second oddity – the image of Philomel introduced in lines 56–62 – might not seem so odd without the first. Philomel in the myth as recorded by Ovid was raped by her brother-in-law, who cut out her tongue to prevent her from accusing him; eventually she was turned by the gods into a nightingale, whose sweet, nocturnal song compensated for her loss of speech. Without the earlier mention of incest, Philomel might just be a piece of furniture, as it were, which is to say that poets could and did mention Philomel as a classical name for the nightingale (and real, as opposed to mythical, nightingales do sing at evening in Great Britain as well as in parts of the United States). The more disturbing associations – rape, violence, loss of speech – need not be intended or may not add much to the poem. However, "Il Penseroso" explicitly reminds its readers that Philomel's song stems from her "saddest plight," and, reading this just after having been told about Melancholy's untraditional genealogy, we seem to have a pattern of transgressive images. Indeed, I suspect this is why an anachronistic reading might turn to psychoanalyze Milton as melancholic, with coded references to incest and rape.

The references are clearly there. And I, at least, feel uncomfortable simply dismissing such associations once a pattern begins to emerge (and two such references in close proximity in a poem do form a pattern). On the other hand, the incest is "explained" and the story of Philomel forms a light transition to the nocturnal setting of the fifth section of the poem, in which the speaker – even if "Like one that had been led astray" (line 69), another potential image of sin and transgression – is introduced as celebrating night. As is probably clear, I am inclined to think that in context (the formal rhetoric, the place of "Il Penseroso" as a virtuoso piece of debate set against "L'Allegro," the careful characterization of Melancholy as related to contemplation) the poem makes more sense if one does not take the transgressive undertones or connotations to overturn the more explicit meaning and trajectory of the poem. Yet this still leaves me with the question of why the charged images (incest, Philomel) and language ("astray") appear. The best I can do is to suggest that the very lightness of the references allows Milton to add a kind of frisson (or emotional charge) to his poem and his muse, while also – with the constructed genealogy – suggesting that his muse is turned in on herself or contemplative, although that may be an unusual way to think of incest.

I am not arguing that every reader of "Il Penseroso" needs to pause to ask what Vesta and Saturn, Philomel, or the one led astray under a wandering moon are doing in the poem. I have paused to raise such questions because I want to make three related points. The first is that, as with the more modern poems discussed in chapter 1, all poems are most interesting when read with careful attention to the work being done by the details (even when the details seem at first to be something like classical window-dressing or decoration, what I called "furniture"). Second, I am suggesting that when a poem presents puzzling passages – places where your working understanding is challenged – it is almost always useful to stop and ask if the passage requires you to adjust your understanding (or to investigate references, word definitions, and cultural assumptions). Third, by implication, I am suggesting that it almost never fosters understanding to ignore the existence of passages or patterns or images that challenge your first response to or working interpretation of a poem, even if raising questions does not always lead to wholly satisfactory answers. Indeed, I remain open to other arguments about why Milton invented Melancholy's unusual genealogy, without which the other so-called oddities might not seem to form a pattern. For the moment, though, I conclude that these passages do not undermine (although they may add nuance to) my reading of the poem as centrally about the contemplative life and about Melancholy as a positive – if perhaps slightly dangerous – muse of contemplation.

It is not simply the rhetorical formality and semantic content of "Il Penseroso" that lead me to this conclusion. More broadly, too, the poem enacts – as well as talks about – higher contemplation, which is another reason why I marked sections to show the poem's unfolding narrative. Of course, poems most often do not tell stories in the same way that novels or movies do. Yet "Il Penseroso" does move us as readers from one place to another: it unfolds. Look, for instance, at the fifth and sixth sections of the poem, beginning at line 63, which include the first sentence in which a first-person pronoun ("I") appears. We are told the speaker is wooing Philomel, the nightingale, under the "wandering moon" (line 67), and at first it seems we have a story about a physical night-time walk: the speaker uses physical senses; he walks, beholds, and hears (in lines 65, 67, and 64). But then lines 77, 83, 85, 100, 101, 105, 109, 127, 138, and 154 begin with "or" (another use of anaphora). It almost sounds as if the speaker is stricken with indecision – Is he outside walking? Listening to crickets or night watchmen? Reading at night inside? Reading Greek tragedies or epics or earlier English literature? Every time the speaker describes himself as if in a concrete physical setting (for instance, "I walk unseen / On the dry smooth-shaven green" in lines 65–6), the poem shifts us to an alternative setting (as if to say, "or another place will do"). There are twelve uses of the word "or" in the fifty-eight lines I am considering as the fifth section of the poem, with almost as many **internal rhymes**, rhymes that are not at the end of lines, which keep the word in our ears ("sh*or*e," "res*or*t," "d*or*s," "imm*or*tal," "f*or*sook," "g*or*geous," "*Or*pheus," "st*or*y," "h*or*se," "f*or*ests," and "m*or*e") and a series of five more uses of "or" in the thirty-four lines I have marked as the sixth section of the poem. Either Milton is a sloppy writer overusing the word and the sound . . . or there is a purpose to this repetition.

Certainly, the repeated "or" has an effect, namely to show the speaker's mind at work, which also underlines the fact that by line 77 we are not after all reading about settings that are physically present to the speaker. We are eavesdropping on an interior monologue. In Latin – a language Milton knew well, evidenced by the Latinate vocabulary and syntax of his work – "or" can be used not simply to exclude possibilities (in an "either/ or" proposition); there is also what is called the "non-exclusive 'or'" (in Latin, "vel"), whereby the word multiplies possibilities. In "Il Penseroso," it seems we are overhearing an act of rich imaginative contemplation, in which – since the landscapes come to seem interior or imagined – physical and fictional landscapes have equal status (although the ambitious crafts-manship on view and the mention of the classics as well as of major earlier writers in English – Chaucer's and Spenser's tales are referred to in lines 109–20 – all might suggest that Milton is also "out-nighting" earlier poets). It seems, in any case, that it is the pleasures of such rich imaginings or pensiveness that motivate the speaker's dedication of himself to "night" beginning on line 121: "Thus, Night, oft see me in thy pale career." Night is here associated with the pleasures of interior rather than physical sight. It seems that banishing joy and daylight ("Hence"), and calling on

Melancholy ("Hail," "Come") has worked for the speaker. In other words, by the fifth section of the poem, what we have is not a description of contemplation but the performance or process of an act of contemplation, marked by the use of the non-exclusive "or."

Even more interesting, however, is that by line 155, beginning what I have marked as the seventh or penultimate section of the poem, "or" disappears from the poem, although the verbs do tie what I have dubbed sections six and seven together in that the speaker issues first a hope ("Thus . . . see me") and finally what seems more a prayer: "let some strange mysterious dream" (line 147); "let my . . . feet . . . walk" (lines 155–6); "let the pealing organ blow" (line 161), "And may . . . my weary age" (line 167). (The feet of line 155, I'd add, seem, like Jessica's, metrical as much as physical by this point in the poem.) Milton's use of the optative (where the verb expresses a wish or prayer) is finally a bit sneaky. True, following the poem's invocation we are shown thought-in-action. Most of the poem has proposed hypothetical landscapes and scenes (imagined places are, by definition, hypothetical), focusing us on the act of hypothesizing. Still, it is in places difficult to tell whether "let" (like the also repeated "may") operates as an imperative – a command – as in "let there be light" or "let the music begin" (which is one way of paraphrasing line 161) or expresses a wish ("if only this would happen"). So there is a near sleight of hand (or sleight of language) at work when we read: "As may with sweetness, through mine ear, / Dissolve me into ecstasies, / And bring all heaven before mine eyes" (lines 164–6). Reading line 165 by itself, "Dissolve me into ecstasies" suggests either an authoritative command or, at least, the present tense (the speaker dissolves before *our* eyes in a kind of beatific transport or moment of **epiphany**, that is, a sudden and fully present understanding). The lines, in effect, lay claim to the achievement of a high, spiritual state.

Yet if you look back at the grammar of the sentence (which begins four lines earlier), you can see that the speaker seems more literally to be hoping for music of the sort that only "*may*" dissolve him. Similarly, the speaker hopes that he will grow old and knowledgeable (with "old experience," line 173), but the length of the sentence and the line breaks mask for a moment the fact that the speaker is only **proleptically** imagining himself old, meaning he anticipates as if present a future in which his experiences might grant him "something like prophetic" song ("strain" here means "song"). Milton has loaded the dice in other ways, as well. The imagined future scene seems present by lines 173–4. And while the stars and herbs the speaker imagines himself knowing could indicate knowledge of the world (the rise of science in Milton's day did include advances in both astronomy and botany), there were in 1631 still astrologers promising to tell the future by the stars, and herbalists (like Medea) were as often associated with magic (black and white) as with botanical classification. By association, the pensive man speaking in "Il Penseroso" claims a kind of magic foresight – including what is finally indeed "something like" a prophecy – not so much in as of his own old age. The tacit claim of this verbal performance is that the process of contemplation leads to moments of divine ecstasy or spiritual vision – performed, again, in the language of the poem as the speaker's prayer can be seen not simply to anticipate or hope for but imaginatively to rise to a kind of epiphanic vision.

The final couplet of "Il Penseroso" backs away from the above claims in some ways. The language echoes the language of pastoral love poems, specifically Christopher Marlowe's "The Passionate Shepherd to His Love," which will be discussed in more detail in chapter 7. The hypothetical nature of Melancholy's gifts is re-emphasized, as the speaker implies he'll choose Melancholy only *if* she can give the pleasures of contemplation described and exemplified in the body of the poem. Still, when Milton writes of "these" pleasures, in line 175, we are at least invited to see the **deictic** – from the Greek, *deiktos*, "able to show directly" – or indexical "these" as pointing to the pleasures of the vision in the previous lines, suggesting that such pleasures were present, even if (as would make sense for something like ecstasy or prophecy) only fleetingly.

Although the echo of Marlowe's love poem at the very end of "Il Penseroso" might bring to mind the way in which Shakespeare's characters variously identify night with love, there is no obvious sign that Milton had Shakespeare's nights in mind when composing "Il Penseroso." Love, *per se*, does not seem to be one of the thematic concerns of the poem. Milton draws more on classical and some Christian associations of night with a time when one withdraws from affairs of the world (to think or read or pray, and ultimately to leave worldly places entirely – the Greek root of the word "ecstasy" means being "out of place"). Still, whether he meant to or not, he "out-nights" Shakespeare insofar as "Il Penseroso" became for later writers and readers what we call a **locus classicus**, the originating text for certain kinds of night visions.

Indeed, by the eighteenth century, most poems of nocturnal contemplation seem to be in conversation with "Il Penseroso." The poem I want next to consider interests me because the writer, Anne Finch, Countess of Winchilsea, not only invites other ways of thinking about intertextuality, but also because she was explicitly aware of her status as a woman writing poetry in the early eighteenth century (many of her poems address the problems facing women writers), an awareness which I think informs her clear echo of Shakespeare's staged battle between the sexes over the characterization of night. In particular, the anaphoric "In such a night" in Finch's poem borrows from – and calls to mind – the exchange between Lorenzo and Jessica with which I began the chapter. I might add that we have far more poems by women from the early eighteenth century than from previous eras, for various reasons (including the rise of print culture and of literacy, as well as a change – although certainly not a revolutionary change – in the status of women). Finch herself was a court lady, by 1683 maid of honor to the future wife of James II, at whose court she met her husband. When James was deposed in 1688, Finch's husband was arrested for attempting to follow James to France; upon his release, the couple retired in political exile to their country estate in Kent. In 1713, Finch wrote "A Nocturnal Reverie":

In such a night, when every louder wind	
Is to its distant cavern safe confined;	
And only gentle Zephyr fans his wings	
And lonely Philomel, still waking, sings;	
Or from some tree, famed for the owl's delight,	5
She, hollowing clear, directs the wanderer right:	
In such a night, when passing clouds give place,	
Or thinly veil the heavens' mysterious face;	
When in some river, overhung with green,	
The waving moon and trembling leaves are seen;	10
When freshened grass now bears itself upright,	
And makes cool banks to pleasing rest invite,	
Whence springs the woodbind, and the bramble-rose,	
And where the sleepy cowslip sheltered grows;	
Whilst now a paler hue the foxglove takes,	15
Yet checkers still with red the dusky brakes	
When scattered glow-worms, but in twilight fine,	
Show trivial beauties watch their hour to shine;	
Whilst Salisbury stands the test of every light,	
In perfect charms, and perfect virtue bright:	20
When odors, which declined repelling day,	
Through temperate air uninterrupted stray;	
When darkened groves their softest shadows wear,	
And falling waters we distinctly hear;	
When through the gloom more venerable shows	25
Some ancient fabric, awful in repose,	
While sunburnt hills their swarthy looks conceal,	
And swelling haycocks thicken up the vale:	
When the loosed horse now, as his pasture leads,	
Comes slowly grazing through the adjoining meads,	30

Whose stealing pace, and lengthened shade we fear,
Till torn-up forage in his teeth we hear:
When nibbling sheep at large pursue their food,
And unmolested kine rechew the cud;
When curlews cry beneath the village walls,   35
And to her straggling brood the partridge calls;
Their short-lived jubilee the creatures keep,
Which but endures, whilst tyrant man does sleep;
When a sedate content the spirit feels,
And no fierce light disturbs, whilst it reveals;   40
But silent musings urge the mind to seek
Something, too high for syllables to speak;
Till the free soul to a composedness charmed
Finding the elements of rage disarmed,
O'er all below a solemn quiet grown,   45
Joys in the inferior world, and thinks it like her own:
In such a night let me abroad remain,
Till morning breaks, and all's confused again;
Our cares, our toils, our clamors are renewed,
Our pleasures, seldom reached, again pursued.   50

While the staid rhymed couplets in iambic pentameter and the use of anaphora (not only "in such a night," but also "and," "or," "when" or "while") make "A Nocturnal Reverie" easy to follow, one might note that the poem contains only one long sentence: it is (if we bear in mind both the title and the assumptions we might bring to this poem from "Il Penseroso") one long reverie, although we are told how something in the described setting – an owl, traditionally associated with wisdom, or more probably (although the syntax is somewhat confusing) Philomel in an owl's tree – "directs the wanderer right" (line 6). I want to return to this image, but first it seems wise to get a more general sense of the poem's subject and movement. To start, most of us will need to look up some unfamiliar or archaic uses of words ("brakes" are tall ferns; a "fabric" is a structure, here a building; "awful" could mean awe-inspiring as well as causing fear; "kine" are cattle; a curlew is a kind of bird). At the same time, I suspect most of us recognize at first reading that this seems to be a poem about a walk in the English countryside (a reasonably domesticated landscape with cattle and horses) at night.

To say this is already to bring to the fore what might seem a puzzling feature of the poem. I have already suggested it seems like one long reverie (a kind of waking dreaminess, a mental not a physical landscape). This suggestion, moreover, came from my sense that the movement of the poem is like that of "Il Penseroso"; one could almost choreograph the kind of poem I mean as a dreamy, mental "walk," a form of contemplation or thought-in-process, leading to an epiphanic moment (at least a sense of "ah-hah!" if not a traditional spiritual revelation). Not knowing Milton's poem, you might simply dismiss or perhaps admire "A Nocturnal Reverie" as a decorative snapshot of country living. However, like me, and like Finch's original readers, you already know "Il Penseroso" and what kinds of night-time (explicitly as opposed to day-time) pleasures might be at stake. You may even have noticed at first reading that Philomel, wandering, the moon, and a Miltonic use of "or" reappear as verbal echoes of Milton within the "Il Penseroso"-like movement of Finch's poem. There is in Finch's poem a prelude, something like Milton's valediction, in which we are told that "louder winds" are not present, but "safely confined," allowing the delicate perceptions traced in the body of the poem. There are logical shifts in the poem (marked by the syntax), most prominently at line 41. The literal, logical, and emotional grammar of the poem gives us a move-ment, which might be sketched as follows: "In such a night, when or while the mind wanders, it [the mind] comes to seek something higher until the soul has an experience of some sort of transcendence."

You will notice that in distilling what we are told in the poem's sentence, I am underlining a trajectory very like that of "Il Penseroso" (although more briefly put), viewing "A Nocturnal Reverie" through the lens of Milton's poem: an act of interpretation, although one to which Finch's poem easily lends itself. "Il Penseroso" also began with a valediction, then moved through an invocation to Philomel to what seemed a night-time walk but in retrospect seemed more a night-tinged meditation leading to a moment of epiphany (and a concluding couplet). As one "walks" through Finch's poem with the narrator – and "A Nocturnal Reverie," like most poems, does unfold, taking us from one place to another – one can find a conceptual syntax similar to that in Milton's poem.

In one sense, Finch's poem provides more to (and makes more claims on) readers who bring to it certain expectations, specifically to and on readers who can hear resonances with or echoes of Milton's poem. Another way of putting this would be to say that if (as I claim) this is a poem in conversation with "Il Penseroso," then it will be a richer poem for readers who can hear both sides – Milton's as well as Finch's – of the conversation. Yet to say this is not to ignore the fact that – far more than Milton's poem – Finch's night has a physical sensuousness. Indeed, the poem touches on sight (for instance in line 10), touch (line 12), smell (line 21), hearing (line 32), and even potentially taste (if one counts the munching animals in lines 32 through 34), almost as if the senses are systematically catalogued. We get also individuated, rather than generic, plants (woodbind, bramble-rose, cowslip and foxglove), again offering a landscape that seems to be described as physically present (even though we are told that the scene is muted, when lines 9 and 10 mention that the moon and leaves – "waving" and "trembling" – are seen only as reflected in "some river"). In other words, Finch's night piece seems far more linked to a physical (and natural) world than Milton's, even as it is like Milton's, so that the status of what is represented is at first uncertain: Is this a real walk in a real world? Or are we overhearing a reverie, an internalized landscape? The anaphoric refrain, "In such a night," maintains the uncertainty since it suggests a generalized or idealized setting ("oh, yes, that *kind* of night") even as the use of the singular ("in such *a* night," not "in such nights") leads one to think that the night being described is one specific, physically sensed night.

Like Nemerov's poem, discussed in chapter 1, Finch's poem is not well served by ignoring what seem contradictory gestures. "A Nocturnal Reverie" seems to be *both* a contemplative Miltonic reverie – underscored by the title and mimicked in the long, sinuous sentence that makes up the poem – *and* a poem concerned with the world of the senses. Unlike Nemerov's poem, though, "A Nocturnal Reverie" may invite us to reconcile the sensuous details and mental processes, both of which it seems to emphasize. If you look at what we might call the climax of the poem (the epiphanic moment toward which the first forty lines build), you can see that Finch not only has the mind seeking something "too high for syllables to speak" (reminiscent of Milton's "something like prophetic strain"), but also describes how, just after the mind does this, the "free soul" apparently looks *down* on the world ("O'er all below a solemn quiet grown") and "Joys in the inferior world, and thinks it like her own" (line 46). This is an interesting image, as if of someone having an "out of body" experience. When conditions are right ("In such a night"), we have been told, one is calmed, and "musings" – like "reveries" – lead the mind to seek something higher, presumably higher than the natural world. At this point (and the word "Till" that opens line 43 suggests the culmination of a temporal sequence of events), we are told that the soul is free, and that this soul looks *down* on the world it "thinks [is] like her own" (line 46). In other words, the "inferior" world is literally (if also perhaps spiritually) inferior, below a soul that is floating above this world, at the same time that the physical world seems to the soul spiritualized (perhaps the world is even spiritualized by being internalized or brought into the realm of thought as the soul "*thinks* [the world into being] like her own").

You might notice that I am trying to paraphrase the poem in a way that takes into account the details or stages of the epiphany described for us. This is, in part, my attempt to hear what the poem actually says (rather than, for example, hearing only how it sounds like a modern nature poem or like a simple recasting of "Il Penseroso"). The image Finch offers also suggests why her poem might include what seem to be details of a physical (if "inferior") landscape that, in the course of the poem, can be seen as also spiritualized or "like" the world of the "soul." In "A Nocturnal Reverie" – and the whole poem may on second reading be seen to give us the soul's view "from above" – physical detail and contemplation, at least contemplation from the right angle, seem wedded and, moreover, informed by tacit theological assumptions about how the earthly might resemble the spiritual; in fact, the early image of the moon seen reflected in a river – the heavens imaged on earth – suggests as much; it is an emblem of the entire poem's perspective. This interpretation may also illuminate lines 19–20, one of the more puzzling couplets in the poem, especially for modern readers. At least at first reading, the mention of "Salisbury" standing "the test of every light / In perfect charms, and perfect virtue bright" seems an oddity (or an ungrammaticality, given what seemed first to be the conceptual syntax of the poem as a description of a walk at night). Even if you have a footnote telling you that Anne Tufton, the Countess of Salisbury, was friends with Anne Finch, you would still, I think, ask what Salisbury is doing in the middle of a sentence otherwise cataloguing details of a landscape at night.

Yet if one sees the poem as a spiritualized view of the world – so that glow-worms, whose "scattered" lights can only be seen at dusk, might well bring to mind another, more enduring, kind of earthly light (the inner light of virtue) – the appearance of Salisbury is less disconcerting. To understand Salisbury's position does require a second reading; one needs to revisit the poem's "walk" in light of the final image of the soul thinking "the inferior world like its own." On a second reading, however, it seems no accident that the word "charmed" (used of the soul in line 43) reminds us of the earlier use of the word "charm" in the description of Salisbury, with the repeated word linking the thought of Salisbury with the turn to higher and more internalized perspectives at the poem's conclusion . . . not counting the final couplet on how the disclaimed, confused, and decidedly not composed or contented daytime world will return as long as that free soul is still associated with a body and a physical world.

There are other oddities in Finch's poem. Some seem explicable, again at least on a second reading, with the working interpretation I've been constructing. For example, Finch (perhaps having internalized Milton's use of slightly racy images and their power) describes her calm night without letting us forget how fragile (perhaps threatened) it is. If, without giving him or her Finch's poem, you were to tell a friend you were reading a poem that contained the following words – "louder wind," "confined," "Philomel," "wanderer," "stray," "gloom," "stealing," "fear," "unmolested," "straggling," "short-lived," "tyrant," "fierce," and "disturbs" – he or she would presumably be surprised to find the poem was about a feeling of "sedate content." Admittedly, I've taken the words out of context: for instance, "unmolested" is actually the opposite of "molested." Still, why raise the specter of molestation by saying the cattle are "*un*molested"? Here, it seems, the poem is designed to emphasize the fragile nature of "such" moments, not only for the domestic animals but for the poet and reader who in night-time retirement are beyond the cares of daily life, so that the soul is briefly harmonized and sees itself for a precious if precarious moment reflected in calm, rural nature (or in this poem about such a setting). In sum, the apparent oddity of the diction adds to but does not necessarily overturn our sense of "A Nocturnal Reverie" as a celebration and exemplification of spiritual retreat and epiphany.

That said, there are other repetitions and word choices that are less easily explained. It almost seems that, beginning with the refrain taken from *The Merchant of Venice* ("In such a night"), Finch's poem contains also a counter-argument to her praise of retreat and higher vision as opposed to the desires and tyrannies of the socio-political world. As someone herself in political exile, Finch would, one assumes, have given serious thought to the difference between the world of human affairs (from which she and her husband were banished) and her rural retreat in Kent where higher matters could be contemplated. However, the dialogue from Shakespeare alluded to is more precisely a battle of wits that focuses on the question of gender and of the spheres appropriate to men and women. "In such a night," then, locates Finch's readers not only in an English countryside viewed after sunset, and not only in such a landscape viewed through the lens of contemplative night pieces like "Il Penseroso" that traditionally reject the daylight world of active engagement, but also in a night full of the issues from Shakespeare's play. The echo thus raises the question of Finch's role as a woman writing poetry, and of whether, like Jessica in Shakespeare's play, Finch can define the setting in which she finds herself on her own terms. When Philomel is then mentioned by the fourth line of the poem, we seem to be invited to think of the nightingale as an actual bird; as the bird that standardly sings at such times in such poems; and as the mythical Philomel. In the myth, you recall, Philomel sings sweetly as recompense for being rendered speechless, for being unable to speak out. After such an opening, it is difficult to read the end of the poem without asking whether "tyrant man" is not gender-specific and without asking as well what it means to have "the elements of rage disarmed" (when one might want to be better armed); are we perhaps being told that the soul is tricked, as it were, into enjoying an "inferior world" that the soul only "*thinks*" is like her world? In other words, a pattern that does not quite fit with celebrations of the contemplative life of retreat seems to emerge in Finch's poem. The subtext almost seems to be that, banned from saying what she really means, the speaker (as a woman) has to settle for sweet night music, but as a consolation prize of sorts.

It is difficult to pinpoint how far Finch meant her counter-argument to be taken. In the poem as I began reading it (and reading it, I would add, in a context an eighteenth-century reader – one of Finch's contemporaries – would have found familiar) "the inferior world" of nature is set against the world of the soul, not obviously against the world of political or male power. The end of the poem (from line 39) also seems a genuine celebration of retreat. Yet Shakespeare's Jessica ends the dialogue to which Finch alludes, "I would out-night you, did nobody come; / But, hark! I hear the footing of a man." Also, as I mentioned, Finch wrote about the plight of woman writers. So it is not entirely out of the question – not wholly anachronistic – that her celebration of retreat is guarded in the sense that it depicts the rewards and epiphanies of night as a recompense for not being able to speak out more straightforwardly.

Can we then say that Finch's poem is both an interestingly sensuous variation on "Il Penseroso" (in that it finds a higher strain imaged in rather than beyond the world) *and* a poem that at least tacitly suggests Miltonic retreat yields a kind of second-best form of speech, like Philomel's song? This is a question on which you or I might take a position, but not one to which a definitive answer is available. For example, I could argue that, yes, as a woman subject to several kinds of exile, Finch could have understood her turn to nature and higher matters as what we might now call sublimation. Or, I could argue that Finch wrote a poem suggesting that higher spiritual revelations were what she was left with, or consigned to, given that she was banished from claims to more worldly political or poetic power (as both a woman and a political exile), but that her counter-argument was not consciously crafted: it just made subliminal sense, at which point I would be psychoanalyzing Finch. Or, I could argue that simply by raising questions about gender in "A Nocturnal Reverie" I am reading against the grain: I took a poem of certain kind (a night piece, an "Il Penseroso"-like poem of contemplation and epiphany) and raised questions that in 1713 night pieces would not have been expected to raise (even if the answers prove interesting to us).

In the final analysis, my hunch is that Finch meant to celebrate retreat, not to mark night pieces as, like Philomel's music, poor substitutes for lost speech – a hunch informed by my sense of how people would have read the poem in its own day. Yet, given the way in which Shakespeare's refrain is used and given Finch's other poems on women as writers, I would say that Finch knew her poem would raise issues about women's positions. Ultimately, I suspect she thought she was laying *claim* to (not dismissing) a kind of poetic power previously reserved for male poetic voices. In other words, the echo of Shakespeare seems to me too prominent to ignore; the battle of the sexes is simply there, having an effect on us as readers that it presumably would also have had on Finch's contemporaries. The way in which I tried to interpret Philomel as an image of *lesser* singing, or singing that masks a loss of power, however, is probably reading against the grain: a form of interpretation one may undertake (as I have done), but the anachronistic status of which one would need to make clear.

I have been calling the kind or type of poem I am examining a "night piece." If you look in a form book or dictionary of poetic terms, you will not find "night piece" listed. At the same time, I suspect anyone well read in poetry will know just what you mean if you mention "night pieces," and will think of "Il Penseroso" and of a later poem, Wordsworth's "A Night Piece," among others (but perhaps not of Finch's poem, which was not as well known through the eighteenth, nineteenth, and most of the twentieth centuries). Nonetheless, Wordsworth's poem, to which I now turn, interests me because it seems self-consciously in conversation with Finch's poem: the intertext for "A Night Piece" is not just the *kind* of poem Finch wrote, but specifically "A Nocturnal Reverie." (Some critics, I'd add, would thus say Finch influenced Wordsworth, reserving the word "intertextuality" for less self-conscious conversations. If you are interested in this critical debate, you might look at the chapter in the book by Jonathan Culler listed at the end of this chapter.) One could do research – people know quite a lot about what Wordsworth read and admired – and find that Wordsworth singled out Finch as one of the few earlier English poets to write poems depicting the natural world in a way Wordsworth admired; we even know that Wordsworth's sister Dorothy read "A Nocturnal Reverie" out loud to him around the time he wrote "A Night Piece." But even without such scholarly knowledge, I think one can hear Wordsworth's conversation with Finch (some eighty years after she wrote her poem):

> —The sky is overcast
> With a continuous cloud of texture close,
> Heavy and wan, all whitened by the Moon,
> Which through that veil is indistinctly seen,
> A dull, contracted circle, yielding light   5

So feebly spread, that not a shadow falls,
Checquering the ground—from rock, plant, tree, or tower.
At length a pleasant instantaneous gleam
Startles the pensive traveller while he treads
His lonesome path, with unobserving eye,   10
Bent earthwards; he looks up—the clouds are split
Asunder,—and above his head he sees
The clear Moon, and the glory of the heavens.
There, in a black-blue vault she sails along,
Followed by multitudes of stars, that, small   15
And sharp, and bright, along the dark abyss
Drive as she drives: how fast they wheel away,
Yet vanish not!—the wind is in the tree,
But they are silent; —still they roll along
Immeasurably distant; and the vault,   20
Built round by those white clouds, enormous clouds,
Still deepens its unfathomable depth.
At length the Vision closes; and the mind,
Not undisturbed by the delight it feels,
Which slowly settles into peaceful calm,   25
Is left to muse upon the solemn scene.

As I have done with all the poems discussed, I want first to consider how this poem unfolds, to offer a first reading. After all, even if one "speaks poetry" like a native, poems become richer on rereading, when one sees in retrospect how (as in Finch's poem, for example) the end of a poem may qualify or inform earlier passages. Yet rereading always requires a first reading, one that takes note of how we, as readers, are first led (and even sometimes deliberately misled) through a poem. Let me note to start that, although it is unstanzaic, "A Night Piece" unfolds in three or four sections. The syntax gives us four sentences: lines 1–7; lines 8–13; lines 14–22; and lines 23–6. At the same time, the use of anaphora – the repeated "At length" – in lines 8 and 23 makes the poem feel as if it has an introduction and then two subsequent gestures (begun in lines 8 and 23, with "At length" telling us that a period of time has passed in each case). Further, somewhere around line 11, in the middle of the second section, the diction of the poem seems to change, with the dashes, the multiple caesurae, and the ways in which commas and semi-colons give us the effect of a shortness of breath in lines 11 and 12: "Bent earthwards; he looks up—the clouds are split / Asunder,—and above his head he sees." Notice how the enjambment works almost like a visual pun: the lines and the verb phrase are themselves "split / Asunder."

To rehearse what is happening – how we are being led thematically through the poem – though, we should dwell a bit longer in the introductory section, lines 1–7. The nightscape seems to be seen through the eyes of someone who is sunk into himself: the sky is not only "overcast," but "close" (as in "restricted") and "Heavy and wan"; the moon is "dull" and "contracted" (seen through a "veil" of clouds); its light is "feebly spread." The half-line that starts the poem (called a **hemistich**) may here, in context, add to the sense of restriction. Although the first section of "A Night Piece" gives us simply a description of the natural world at night, the description seems to be emotionally charged – negatively so, unlike Finch's or Milton's descriptions – as if the world is seen from a particular (and not particularly cheerful) perspective. When a traveler is introduced in lines 9–11 as "pensive," "tread[ing] / A *lonesome* path," "unobserving," and "Bent earthwards," as if he is troubled, or perhaps late for an appointment, with "bent" (and the verb "treads" as well) suggesting he is heavy-hearted, we are encouraged to think the first scene is given to us from his perspective. Of course we are told that he is unobserving of details, but then the world through which he travels is not described in great detail (unlike Finch's): the poem says there are no checkering shadows (lines 6–7) cast by the rather generic landscape features listed, namely "rock, plant, tree, or tower" (line 7).

What occurs in the next section (or sections, depending on whether one traces the sentences or the narrative) is most basically that the traveler is pulled out of himself by a "gleam" of moonlight, after which he has a vision of the moon. The narrative and the syntax are disorderly, however. We as readers are told that "a pleasant instantaneous gleam / Startles" even before we are told who is startled or what he is startled out of (namely himself) or by (namely the moon). Reading sequentially, we are probably not sure until line 13 what to make of "the gleam" (encountered in line 8) that pierces the dim, cloudy scene; for five lines the poem defers knowledge of what exactly is being described. When *we* encounter the "clear Moon," then, it comes as a surprise to us. And lines 13–22, the third sentence of the poem, are even more of a surprise because of the heightened diction introduced. On the one hand, we have a fairly literal story: a moonbeam startles a traveler who looks up to see the clouds have parted. But the excited language (which begins with the clouds "split / Asunder") continues as the moon is described as "the glory of the heavens," in a "vault" (something like Milton's cathedral at the end of "Il Penseroso"), with "multitudes" of stars, an "abyss," stars that "wheel away," "Immeasurably distant," and finally – in a near paradox – placed in an "unfathomable depth" that deepens further. While the classical allusions of Finch's (and, more, Milton's) poems are conspicuously absent, Wordsworth's language still sounds more biblical or visionary than mere natural description usually does, even while it is not entirely clear whether the heightened diction comes from an observer's excitement or as a sign that what is observed is not just a natural landscape (here, a skyscape). One can say that the poem shifts images, perspective, and diction in ways that are not at all tidily aligned with the sentence structure or the storyline (such as it is), a misalignment that may be designed to surprise (perhaps to "delight" and "disturb") readers in much the way the traveler is described as surprised, delighted, and "not undisturbed."

Certainly, well before we are told in line 23 that what is described is a "Vision," the status of Wordsworth's moon is called into question by the poem. Is this a visionary moon? A symbol of "something too high for syllables to speak"? Or just an image of a breathtaking glimpse of the moon at night? I want to try to address these questions in several ways, starting with how "A Night Piece" depends on its conversations with and its readers' familiarity with the conceptual syntax of earlier night pieces. I suspect I do not need to rehearse how "A Night Piece" uses the conceptual syntax familiar from both Finch's and Milton's poems: we find a "traveller" at night, who comes to have a "Vision" (an epiphany), and the poem focuses on a contemplative or mental process (as the last four lines about "the mind" make clear). Yet the poem is not in couplets, but in blank verse, and it doesn't move through a described landscape gradually revealed to be an internalized scene in the same way its predecessors do; in "A Night Piece," in fact, it seems the moon taps the traveler on the shoulder, moving him *out* of thought, not into reverie. Unlike Finch's narrator, who looks down at the moon reflected in the river (an emblem of a spiritualized view of the natural world), Wordsworth's narrator explic- itly looks up to see the moon face-to-face. In fact, there are a number of salient differences between "A Night Piece," "A Nocturnal Reverie," and "Il Penseroso."

Now, this could simply mean that "A Night Piece" is a different kind of poem, not related to Finch's and Milton's poems, which I – perhaps misleadingly – called night pieces in my attempt to identify a poetic subgenre of night-time, contemplative, epiphanic poems. At the same time, along with the setting and the rough similarity of the poems' trajectories, there seem to be too many pointed echoes of both Finch's and Milton's poems in "A Night Piece" to ignore. To start, the main human presence in the poem (if not the speaker, the one whose point of view the poem seems to adopt) is called "the pensive traveller," almost a direct translation of Milton's title, "Il Penseroso." Moreover, there are an impressive number of words, images, or phrases that come directly from "A Nocturnal Reverie." It could be coincidence (or "natural" when one is describing a night walk) that we find repeated **imagery** – pictures, figures of speech, or descriptions – of clouds, moon, and clouds veiling the moon, images that appear in both poems. (You might look back at Finch's "clouds" [line 7]; "moon" [line 10], and "veil" [line 8].) However, something more pointed seems to be at stake when you reread lines 15 and 16 of Finch's poem ("a paler hue the foxglove takes, / Yet checkers still with red the dusky brakes") next to lines 6 and 7 of "A Night Piece": "not a shadow falls, / Checquering the ground." The word "checker" is not the first that comes to mind in describing twilight unless one has read "A Nocturnal Reverie." And why would we need to be told the ground is *not* checkered, unless we expect it to be so because we have Finch's poem in mind? (It may also be relevant that Milton's "L'Allegro" uses the image of "checkered shade" [line 96], although not as a night setting.) The verbal echoes of Finch's poem in particular are even clearer when one notes that in the eight lines that form the epiphanic climax of "A Nocturnal Reverie" one finds the words "the mind," "disturb," "musings," and "solemn" (not to mention a description of "quiet" and "sedate content," which the spirit "feels" just before the soul "Joys"). In "A Night Piece," the final four lines return us to "*the mind* / Not un*disturb*ed," which "*feels*" *delight* and then "*peaceful calm*," which leads to "*mus[ing]*" on something "*solemn.*" It seems that Wordsworth repeats Finch's language, and in particular he borrows from lines where Finch's poem is also describing an internal response to night. Even if one doesn't accept that "joy" and "delight" (or "sedate content . . . quiet" and "peaceful calm") are related, there are five of Finch's words in four of Wordsworth's lines (and at least nine of her words and images throughout his short poem). This is surely not coincidence.

   True, Wordsworth is describing a response that comes *after* what is called a vision, not the vision itself (which seems to be Finch's topic). Still, Wordsworth brings Finch's poem to his readers' minds (or seems to have had her language as well as her landscape and journey in his own mind; so the differences we see are meaningful, or, in other words, given the common framework, the differences between "A Night Piece" and its predecessors – the very absence of what is expected – make meaning. Why the differences appear is still open to interpretation, of course. I have already mentioned that there is critical debate on how to understand or describe such differences (where a later poem revisits and revises an earlier poem). This may, for example, be Wordsworth's way of correcting "A Nocturnal Reverie," even of unconsciously rewriting what did not seem quite right to him (or perhaps to anyone in 1798) about Finch's vision, having simply to do with shifts in cultural assumptions or with Wordsworth's own beliefs (about the source and nature of spiritual realizations, for one thing). To take the example further: Wordsworth has his traveler *begin* by looking down, as Finch's soul ends and as her gaze is directed through most of the poem. Wordsworth thus indicates that looking down is the wrong direction to look, revising Finch's implied view that what she seeks is at best, and maybe imperfectly, *reflected* in nature – as her moon is reflected in the water, or as she characterizes the natural world as an "inferior world," one that only mirrors the spiritual when the soul "thinks it like her own."

One could further suggest Wordsworth's poem is correcting Finch's in indicating that for him the spiritual can be seen unmediated, or that looking to nature can give you the real thing rather than a reflection; in other words, for him, the spiritual is immanent, not transcendent. Because of such gestures critics like M. H. Abrams have called Wordsworth's spirituality "natural supernaturalism" (and, as I hope is obvious, I have drawn on Abrams's suggestion – testing it against the poem – in arriving at my suggestions here). Others might agree that Wordsworth's poem rings changes on Finch's, but add that this is not because his assumptions or theological commitments are different but because he has ambitions to out-night her (and ultimately Milton), a theory about poetic influence developed most fully by Harold Bloom in the book listed at the end of this chapter. Which interpretation (based on which underlying assumptions about intertextual conversations) you choose will depend on what makes most sense to you, although you might beware that if you adopt one critic's vocabulary (Bloom, for example, is associated with the phrase "the anxiety of influence" and with proposing that later poets creatively "misread" the work of their predecessors), you will be understood to have adopted the critic's assumptions unless you clearly state otherwise. This is why I have tried to be clear about how I use the term "intertextuality" as a general description of all kinds of relationships between texts.

I began the above excursion into how one might understand the relationship between "A Nocturnal Reverie" and "A Night Piece" in an attempt to answer the question of how to understand the image of the moon in Wordsworth's poem. You will note that the more culturally based interpretation I flesh out in most detail above suggests that Wordsworth's moon is not allegorical, despite the brief personification ("she sails along" and "she drives") in lines 14 and 17. I want to pursue this matter further. Most basically, the question is whether the moon in this poem is a **symbol**, a **metaphor**, or a **synecdoche** (itself a kind of **metonymy**). I want briefly to pause again to discuss what is at stake in making such distinctions, a way of talking about **figurative language** or language whose semantic meaning is not primarily literal (also called **tropes**, from the Greek for "turns"). At the same time, I would emphasize that these technical terms have been defined in a confusing number of ways. Least theoretically, and most broadly, a symbol (the word comes from the Greek for "putting together," originally referring to two pieces of a broken coin reassembled) is a sign: one thing stands for another. Ultimately, all language is symbolic, in that words stand for objects or ideas. In most modern thinking, however, symbols are seen as **polysemous**, which is to say they are not fixed in their reference; they mean more than one thing. If one says that "roses" stand for "love" (or the moon for God's presence on earth), one is suggesting that moons and roses are not only symbols, but fixed symbols; most critics these days would say that symbols do not work so tidily, although one can still say we see symbolic systems formed in allegories (I have heard allegory defined as "a system of symbols strung along a narrative," as when Milton gives Melancholy her companions).

In the modern use of the term, then, Wordsworth's moon is clearly a symbol because he is using the word "moon" to stand for something or some things. But this does not get us very far: does "moon" refer to the satellite that daily circles the earth? Or to something more allegorical, which is to say, here, something less material? If the moon stands for the higher spiritual realm invoked by both Milton's and Finch's poems, we could say the moon in "A Night Piece" is metaphorical, leading to yet another sometimes confusingly defined term. Traditionally, and most basically, metaphors are distinguished from similes: they often are said to make comparisons without explicitly or tacitly using "like" or "as." Some critics propose that metaphors do not simply compare two things but create a new, composite entity. For example, if I say "a poem is like a pheasant disappearing into a bush," I might be trying to characterize poetic inspiration as difficult to pin down and, perhaps, as able to take flight. (Presumably, I would add, I am not interested in having my readers think that inspiration can be hunted, shot down, cooked and eaten; the likeness I am proposing is limited in scope.) If, on the other hand, I say "A poem is a pheasant disappearing into a bush" – I take this statement from the poet

Wallace Stevens – I am (on some people's account) not just proposing that one thing (a poem, my main subject or what some would call the **tenor** of my metaphor) is *like* another (a bird running away, or the **vehicle** that which helps me explain what a poem is like). I am inventing something new: a poem that *is* an escaping pheasant (although, of course, on further consideration it seems clear that my poem-pheasant is still a figure of speech).

So: is Wordsworth's moon a metaphor in this sense? If so, with what is the moon merged or associated? One could reasonably argue that, yes, given the high diction of lines 14–22 (beginning with the description of the moon as "the glory of the heavens" one line earlier), this moon is metaphorical, in that it is described as **numinous**: evincing the spiritual or divine, giving figurative attributes to a noun that remains nonetheless concrete (the actual moon is not just a figure for something else, the way – say – Milton's personified Melancholy is). At the same time, one could as reasonably argue that Wordsworth's trope is metonymic, specifically a synecdoche, where the figurative meaning comes from replacing a subject by one of its characteristics (calling military officers "the brass," for example), more particularly with synecdoche substituting a part for the whole, the general for the specific or the specific for the general. If Wordsworth's moon is metonymic, it is so because it is one part of the natural world standing in for the whole (which, in turn, metaphorically, would be something more numinous than mere physical matter). This, again, is to read "A Night Piece" as revising Milton's and Finch's more orthodox theology (wherein the natural world reflects but is not the same as the spiritual realm). Indeed, at the close of "A Night Piece," we are not really told what has been revealed to the speaker. We know it is interior, having something to do with "the mind" (and that there is no personal pronoun suggests the traveler or speaker has in some way been taken out of the personal self). However, we are left with an image of a mind musing on a "solemn scene" (which may be the moon in the sky or may be the traveler moved by the moon in the sky); the precise significance of the scene is not specified and we ourselves may be invited to "muse," to speculate rather than to explain away or translate into other terms the feeling of significance found in what is, prosaically, simply a scene of someone seeing the moon at night.

I have mentioned that some critics would argue that Wordsworth's revisions mark his ambition to out-night his predecessors, in the process of which he may need to misread them (so he can repeat without feeling overshadowed by what they have written). One could, alternatively, propose that "A Night Piece" is both a double tribute to and an argument with

Finch's "A Nocturnal Reverie" and, in a more distanced way, with Milton's kind of night piece. That is, one could say Wordsworth revises or argues with Finch and Milton. But if Wordsworth, as it were, corrects Finch by putting her high "something" back into natural elements – albeit elements like stars and moons – rather than situating spirituality "too high for syllables to speak," he still implicitly builds on her poem for his meaning. That is, once he reminds me of Finch's landscape and her "higher" project, I find significance in the places where "A Night Piece" refuses to follow "A Nocturnal Reverie." Finally, too, one could argue that it is Finch's distinctive descriptions of the natural world in lines 7–37 of her poem (which for her describe a prelude to or an inferior reflection of something higher) that Wordsworth's poem takes most seriously in not marking the world of physical sight as inferior (a second form of tribute).

I have pursued here only one possible interpretation of "A Night Piece," as an example of how poems can make meaning by positioning themselves next to other poems, suggesting how the transcript, as it were, of such intertextual conversations can be illuminating. I also hope to offer some sense that working within a tradition is not simply a matter of superficial repetition. In English, the words "treason" and "tradition" come from the same Latin root (meaning "to hand over"). Just so, one could say that the most interesting version of tradition is treason – a handing over, a handing on, recrafting or reconceiving of earlier poetic gestures in a way that culturally or personally, deliberately or not, renews them but also changes them. Without necessarily agreeing with Harold Bloom that Wordsworth misreads his predecessors, showing in particular his anxiety about Milton's influence, you might find that "Wordsworth's reading of Finch's poem" is different from a plausible eighteenth-century reading or a more current reading of Finch's poem. Your interpretation of Wordsworth's poem as in conversation with Finch's need not assume he understood Finch's work the way you would. Indeed, for me, reading "A Night Piece" entails in part trying to hear where Wordsworth's conversation with Finch surprises me (in a way that may or may not affect how *I* interpret Finch's poem in its own right), just as my reading of Finch's poem clearly influenced my reading of Shakespeare's dialogue between Jessica and Lorenzo.

I want to end this chapter by noting that night pieces do not disappear after Wordsworth's day, although poems of reverie, set in a natural world at night, leading to moments of revelation, continue to change. To illustrate, I want to leave you with a final poem, James Wright's 1963 poem, "A Blessing." The title, of course, already suggests some form of spiritual encounter. However, Wright's poem, I will suggest, leaves open the possibility that his epiphany is as much psychological as theological; although Wright certainly knew both Milton's and Wordsworth's (if perhaps not Finch's) poems, what he inherits from or makes of the language of epiphany or contemplation is new. Here is "A Blessing":

Just off the highway to Rochester, Minnesota,
Twilight bounds softly forth on the grass.
And the eyes of those two Indian ponies
Darken with kindness.
They have come gladly out of the willows   5
To welcome my friend and me.
We step over the barbed wire into the pasture
Where they have been grazing all day, alone.
They ripple tensely, they can hardly contain their happiness
That we have come.   10
They bow shyly as wet swans. They love each other.
There is no loneliness like theirs.
At home once more,
They begin munching the young tufts of spring in the darkness.
I would like to hold the slenderer one in my arms,   15
For she has walked over to me
And nuzzled my left hand.
She is black and white,
Her mane falls wild on her forehead,
And the light breeze moves me to caress her long ear   20
That is delicate as the skin over a girl's wrist.
Suddenly I realize
That if I stepped out of my body I would break
Into blossom.

By now I know I do not need to rehearse at length the ways in which "A Blessing" moves as a night piece moves: (literal and figurative) darkness is everywhere in this poem that gradually unfolds for us an increasingly metaphorically charged landscape (note the synecdoche in "tufts of spring," for instance, or the increasingly anthropomorphized ponies), leading to an explicit epiphany ("Suddenly I realize"). The retreat from the everyday, working world is metonymically figured, as well, from the move "off the highway" in the first line (and gradually off the map of named towns, as well) to the speaker stepping "over the barbed wire" that fences in the ponies in line 7.

One can note, too, that the diction of the poem is far less formal than that in any of the other poems treated in this chapter, as is the form, which is to say that the poem uses no end rhyme, nor is there any regular metrical pattern; the poem is in what is called free verse. One could say that the poem's freedom from any regular sound patterns places its speaker and readers outside of any rote or directed scheme (just as the poem seems to be about retreat from the world of daily routines). Such a suggestion would not be wrong, although I would add that in the mid-twentieth century, particularly by 1963, Wright's plain speaking voice and avoidance of traditional form would have been more common than not. Readers would still have heard Wright's poem as being a "sincere," unaffected voice, which is to say readers of poetry in the early 1960s in the United States heard what sounds like everyday speech, without rhyme or metrical schemes, as more sincere, less artificial, than blank verse or rhymed couplets, an analog of freedom from social or larger cultural forms. Still, I'd point out that the rhetoric of sincerity is culturally determined: earlier periods would have found free verse (as opposed to blank verse) simply a sign of bad craftsmanship.

That said, on closer inspection, Wright's language is not actually the language of casual speech: ponies' eyes do not "darken with kindness" (nor would we say they do unless we were waxing poetic). Nor are the similes – the ponies "bow shyly as wet swans" and the ear of one is "delicate as the skin over a girl's wrist" – everyday language. As in "A Night Piece," the landscape seems to be charged with the projected emotions of the speaker. The imagery of the poem, also, forms an arresting pattern. We, as readers of night pieces, may well recognize the move off a highway and over a fence as a familiar retreat from the world of human affairs; similarly, the details offered as the speaker moves into an uncluttered, natural world (the munching horses, the mane, the light breeze, the pony's ear) are not unlike those in Milton's or Finch's or Wordsworth's nightscapes. The lack of any sky (even twilight is brought down to earth, "bound[ing]" up to the speaker) is more surprising. And, even more unexpected, we find a repeated motif of loneliness: we are told the ponies have been grazing all day "alone" (although there are two of them); "There is no loneliness like theirs" (again, although there are two of them and they are said to be "At home" in line 13, which suggests not only that they live in the pasture but also, idiomatically, that they are in their element, comfortable with where they are and what they are doing). By implication, the speaker of the poem – who sees loneliness everywhere, even though we are told in line 6 that he, like the ponies, has a companion with him – is looking for a way to feel at home.

In Wright's poem, too, it could be said that absence speaks. Earlier night pieces (even Wordsworth's) led the speaker and readers to an epiphanic moment, a moment in which something apparently spiritual was fleetingly made present. Wright's speaker moves out of the quotidian (the workaday) world, but he seems not to experience the presence of some other, higher realm, the absence of which is almost palpable if we know we are in a night piece and know, thus, the choreography of such pieces. One could even say that the poem figures in various ways the speaker's and even the world's separation from that "something" experienced in earlier night pieces. For instance, the ponies "can hardly contain their happiness" that they have contact with humans, without whom they were lonely and alone, but they do not seem to evoke or yearn for anything clearly higher; the speaker describes one of the ponies as if she were a lover being courted (that the ponies "love each other" but are lonely already prefigures this apparent need to unite with something other than one's own kind). Both animals and speaker, however, have desires for "something" that is not the lofty "something" of earlier night pieces; in a night piece that reiterates images of loneliness and of love or desire, what is conspicuous by its absence is any reaching toward a higher or transcendent realm in which the speaker's (and the ponies') yearnings will be fulfilled.

It is true that the final sentence at first reading feels as if it does offer such fulfillment to the speaker (as well as fulfilling our expectations as readers). However, like Milton, if to a different effect, Wright performs a bit of verbal legerdemain. Line 22 appears to yield the awaited epiphany: "Suddenly I realize." Yet the realization is conditional: only "*if*" the speaker could step out of his body would he be able to "break / Into blossom." And the line breaks further complicate the emotional effect of the ending. Line 23 breaks at the word "break," and the enjambment for a moment leaves us with the image of someone not only bursting out of himself (literally, stepping out of his body) but also breaking, which in the context of the language of love and images of courtship brings to mind (just for a second) something closer to heartbreak than to breaking into bloom. The last line works, then, something like a punch line, especially since for someone to blossom is for that person to flourish and to open. Both connotations work well with the poem's thematic concern with openness to the world, to other creatures, to some kind of awaited union that takes one out of the narrow bounds of self. At the same time, of course, the speaker does not (and, being embodied, presumably will not) break into blossom. Wright's poem does offer an epiphany, but what is finally present seems far more modest, more conditional, and more psychologically rooted, than Milton's or Finch's or even Wordsworth's visions. Although Milton also ends by acknowledging he has not yet been offered the vision he nonetheless seems to present in the poem, although Finch concludes with an acknowledgment that morning will "break" (the word is hers) and close down the soul's higher perspective, and although Wordsworth leaves us with an image of what happens after his "Vision closes," Wright qualifies what he comes to see far more quickly and more emphatically than do his predecessors, almost as if his epiphanic realization is of the impossibility of experiencing an epiphany. The modesty of Wright's epiphany (most visible by contrast with what other nights have offered other poets) leaves us with a more guarded, almost bittersweet – perhaps a more modern, secular – version of the night piece.

This chapter has discussed and tried to exemplify some ways in which poems make meaning in relation to the larger conversations in which they participate (and which, I would add, have presumably given shape and language to poets' views and feelings). Some such conversations involve widely shared poetic gestures; others are more pointedly aware of individual earlier poems. In the next chapter, I will turn to discuss a specific form in which poems have been written – the sonnet – bearing in mind that set forms, like subgenres or motifs, involve intertextuality. Moreover, there is nothing that would prevent a sonnet from being in conversation with a night piece; the languages poets speak (unlike the textbooks introducing poems) are not compartmentalized.

Terms used

anaphora	metonymy
apostrophe	motif
blank verse	numen (numinous)
deictic	panegyric
emblem	parataxis
encomium	personification
epiphany	polysemy (polysemous)
figurative language	prolepsis
hemistich	quatrain
imagery	refrain
internal rhyme	stepped line
invocation	symbol
locus classicus	synecdoche
metaphor	tenor

trope   vehicle
valediction   verse paragraph

Other poems that might be read

John Keats, "To Autumn" (1819)
Walt Whitman, "Out of the Cradle Endlessly Rocking" (1859)
Emily Dickinson, Poem 249 ("Wild Nights—Wild Nights!") (*c.*1861)
Wallace Stevens, "Sunday Morning" (1915)
Robert Frost, "Acquainted with the Night" (1928)
Muriel Rukeyser, "Night Feeding" (1951)
Ted Hughes, "The Thought-Fox" (1957)
Mark Strand, "The Prediction" (1970)
A. R. Ammons, "The City Limits" (1971)
Robert Pinsky, "A Long Branch Song" (1984)
Li-Young Lee, "Ash, Snow, or Moonlight" (1986)
Yosuf Komunyakaa, "Sunday Afternoons" (1992)

Useful further reading

M. H. Abrams, *Natural Supernaturalism: Tradition and Revolution in Romantic Literature* (New York: Norton, 1973).

Harold Bloom, *The Anxiety of Influence: A Theory of Revisionism* (New York: Oxford University Press, 1973).

Rosalie Colie, *The Resources of Kind: Genre Theory in the Renaissance* (Berkeley: University of California Press, 1973).

Jonathan Culler, "Presupposition and Intertextuality," in *The Pursuit of Signs: Semiotics, Literature, Deconstruction* (Ithaca, NY: Cornell University Press, 1981): 100–18.

Stuart Curran, "Of Form and Genre," in *Poetic Form and British Romanticism* (New York: Oxford University Press, 1986): 3–13.

Tony Hoagland, "The Slipperiness of Metaphor," *The Writer's Chronicle*, vol. 33 (2001): 46–50.

John Hollander, *The Figure of Echo: A Mode of Allusion in Milton and After* (Berkeley: University of California Press, 1981).

Christopher Miller, *The Invention of Evening: Perception and Time in Romantic Poetry* (Cambridge: Cambridge University Press, 2006).

David Miller, "From Delusion to Illumination: A Larger Structure for L'Allegro and Il Penseroso," *PMLA: Publications of the Modern Language Association of America*, vol. 86 (1971): 32–9.

David Miller, *John Milton: Poetry* (Boston: Twayne, 1978).

Mark L. Reed, *Wordsworth: The Chronology of the Early Years, 1770–1799* (Cambridge, Mass.: Harvard University Press, 1967).

Michael Riffaterre, "The Poem's Significance," in *Semiotics of Poetry* (Bloomington: Indiana University Press, 1978): 1–22.

Chapter 3

The Gestures and Subjects of the Sonnet

in Thomas Wyatt's "The long love that in my thought doth harbor" (1557), Sir Philip Sidney's "Loving in truth" (1582), William Shakespeare's Sonnet 18 (*c*.1595), and John Donne's "Batter my heart . . ." (*c*.1621)

Most readers of poetry have encountered sonnets, especially love sonnets. Moreover, any form book will tell you about at least two, sometimes more, variant forms of the sonnet, all with fourteen lines and in iambic pentameter (or in some cases iambic **hexameter**, that is, with six iambic feet in a line). The name of the form comes from the Italian meaning "little song" or "little sound." In the Renaissance or early modern period, Italian court culture was famous for its polish and what we might now call conspicuous consumption in both the visual and the literary arts. Petrarch's sonnets – written in Italian – were particularly admired, especially by slightly later poets of the English court who were intent on showing that English poetry could vie with Italian. In both cultures, I'd add, writing courtly poetry was a way of displaying the author's prowess as a writer, a skill newly valued in the early modern period among other things because courts needed people who could not only write but write with wit and diplomacy, diplomacy being a skill important in the negotiations between emerging and contending centers of power at the time. The sonnet in English was first part of English court culture, and a polished sonnet was in some ways a writing sample; that is to say, an elegantly written poem showed off usable skills that could secure patronage or status at court.

Despite these origins and despite the apparently set structural features of the sonnet, however, poetic forms are living things. True, we now can memorize the sonnet's various fixed and expected features. A Petrarchan sonnet has two sections, an octave formed of two quatrains rhyming *abbaabba* and a sestet formed of two **tercets** (or groups of three lines), usually with the rhyme scheme *cdecde* or *cdcdcd* or *cdedce*. There is a **turn** (also called a **volta**) between the octave and sestet, often marked by a conjunction such as "yet" or "however" or "but," words that mark the point at which a train of thought changes direction. The Miltonic sonnet is related to the Petrarchan, with more variation in the rhymes of the sestet; usually without the emphatic thematic turn between the octave and the sestet, although there often is a turn somewhere between lines 9 and 11, and making frequent use of enjambment (that is, the lines are not **end-stopped**), the Miltonic form may allow a more unified thematic or emotional development. The most frequently found type of sonnet in English is called the English (or Shakespearean) sonnet: three quatrains (rhyming *abab cdcd efef*) and a final couplet (with the rhyme *gg*). The Spenserian sonnet (rhyming *abab bcbc cdcd ee*) is often considered a variant of the Shakespearean, with interlocking quatrains balanced against a final couplet; its intricate rhyme scheme and a quick turn between lines 12 and 13 make it perhaps the most difficult to write. Yet to list these "rules" is like parsing the grammar of a sentence without noticing the tone or content of what is said. You need to know the grammar, but you will do best at hearing what is being said if the grammar is internalized, not something you need consciously to puzzle out.

The forms I just rehearsed are named after the poets who are best known for writing in them: Petrarch, Milton, Shakespeare, and Spenser. These writers most probably had themselves internalized how sonnets work, and variations almost certainly did not arise because some poet sat down and decided to be different; in the Renaissance, in fact, originality or difference for its own sake was not valued. One of the reasons the form changed as it passed from Italian into English probably has less to do with any individual's desire to be innovative than with the fact that rhythm and rhyme work differently in English and Italian; among other things, English is a rhyme-poor language, so the two rhymes (*abbaabba*) of the Petrarchan octave are more difficult to make work smoothly in English. What the poem is presenting will also affect how it moves. It may at first be frustrating to consider how flexible (to use Ellen Bryant Voigt's word) the sonnet is, but if you approach sonnets with the idea that they must all doggedly follow some preset structure, you will miss what is most interesting about these poems. On the other hand, if you read a sonnet without knowing what expectations most sonnet-readers have – that is, without some sense of the expected underlying structures or conceptual syntax – you will also miss part of how sonnets convey meaning.

You might think about sonnets as being like musical forms: they have a time signature (the basic contract of the piece), but of course a piece of music in four-four time that never used half-notes or rests as variation would be dull. Perhaps a better analogy is with dance: here too variations are what make a dance performance impressive. If when you waltz you are still counting to yourself and watching your feet (as it were), you are still a beginner and certainly not very polished. In the case of the sonnet, however, it is not just a time signature – or the way your feet move – that forms the underlying contract. At the most basic level, a reader or writer of sonnets has internalized a number of features. A metrical pattern, a set series of rhymes, lines organized in quatrains and a couplet or an octave of two quatrains and a sestet of two tercets, often marked by syntactical structures, all work together within a small, fourteen-line space. Moreover, as I say above, thematic concerns are also relevant. In Petrarch, the form begins as a sometimes spiritualized love poem. In English, especially in Milton's hands, it eventually becomes a forum for political topics; and by the early nineteenth century Samuel Coleridge was describing the sonnet as "a small poem in which some lonely feeling is developed." Throughout, the sonnet was and still is a place in which to argue with or ring changes on earlier sonnets, and in this sense, like the poems discussed in chapters 1 and 2, sonnets participate in larger intertextual conversations.

The best way to hear this conversation is to enter it yourself, first by reading a good many sonnets. In this chapter I want to consider four sonnets, starting with Thomas Wyatt's "The long love that in my thought doth harbor," which was already a reworking or loose translation of one of Petrarch's Italian sonnets. You might look also at "Love, that doth reign and live within my thought" by Henry Howard, Earl of Surrey, written about the same time and reworking the same Petrarchan sonnet ("Rime 140"), to see the latitude each poet has taken with Petrarch's work. That is, although it is a translation, the poem written by Wyatt seems less interested in literal fidelity to Petrarch's poem than in showing that the English "tongue" (and Wyatt's in particular) can produce poems as "praiseworthy" as those in Latin or Italian. The words in quotation marks are actually from the period, from an introduction by the printer Richard Tottel who collected and circulated poems by Wyatt and others in his 1557 *Songs and Sonnets,* usually known as *Tottel's Miscellany* (and published after Wyatt's death).

While Wyatt was alive, his poems circulated primarily in manuscript among aristocratic readers; as I mentioned, the sonnet in English was born at court, a setting that is reflected in the sonnet's concerns. Here then is Wyatt's "The long love that in my thought doth harbor":

> The long love that in my thought doth harbor,
> And in my heart doth keep his residence,
> Into my face presseth with bold pretense
> And therein campeth, spreading his banner.
>
> She that me learneth to love and suffer,
> And wills that my trust and lust's negligence
> Be reined by reason, shame and reverence,
> With his hardiness taketh displeasure.
>
> ....
> Wherewithal, unto the heart's forest he fleeth,
> Leaving his enterprise with pain and cry;
> And there him hideth, and not appeareth.
>
> What may I do when my master feareth
> But in the field with him to live and die?
> For good is the life, ending faithfully.

First, I should point out that by breaking the poem into sections – two quatrains followed by two tercets – and marking the turn between the octave and the sestet with a dotted line, I am providing you with something like those footprints painted on the floors of dance-school studios so you can follow the underlying pattern in a way the usual printing of the poem – fourteen lines without spaces or lines between sections – would make less visible. You might notice, however, that Wyatt's use of syntax (and punctuation) more subtly does exactly what my breaking of the poem into sections does: lines 4, 8, 11, and 14 each end with a period; the turn of thought (or volta) at line 9 begins with the word "wherewithal" used as an adverb, meaning "following, out of, or by means of which," and the image is of the poem's speaker responding to a lady's advice by changing direction, specifically by running away from the field of battle.

In fact, the whole poem uses a consistent image, drawn from **medieval romances** or the tropes of **courtly love**. The conventions of courtly love, like those of medieval romances, did not realistically reflect life, certainly not life in Renaissance courts, but they (perhaps like pop songs or soap operas these days) provided well-known plots and images. While thus not unusual in the period (and taken directly from Petrarch), to our minds the image of feelings – of love – in the first quatrain may seem odd: love is imaged as a small knight running around in the speaker's body. Love "harbors" or takes lodgings in thought, has his home in the speaker's heart, and sets up camp in the speaker's face. The image of "press[ing] with bold pretense" into the speaker's face and planting a banner there is an image of taking over or claiming victory on a battlefield. More literally (if talking about your feelings in terms of a small knightly figure running around your body counts as literal), the image is probably of blushing, that is, of the speaker showing his feelings on his face. The first quatrain, then, sets the stage: we are in the world of courtly love; love is a knight victoriously (and a bit boastfully) claiming his territory. The rest of the octave (indeed, the entire poem) continues this extended metaphor, almost a miniature allegory, known as a **conceit**.

The second quatrain of Wyatt's poem introduces a second character: "she." In part because of the early modern English usage, these four lines can be difficult to parse, although the quatrain is also the second full sentence of the poem, with syntax and rhyme and image coinciding to mark the poem's sections. Most clearly in this second quatrain, we are told that some "she" is not happy (she "taketh displeasure") with the knight's "hardiness," which is to say she's irked by how bold he is when he displays his banner on the speaker's face. Presumably, the "she" is a lady (we are still in the courtly setting of the conceit, with knights and ladies) loved by the speaker; indeed, line 5 says as much: she is the one "that me learneth to love and suffer," which is to say she teaches the "I" to love, identified also with suffering. It is still common to talk of suffering the pangs of love or being lovesick. For us, the oddity of the way Wyatt represents love is, first, that a love relationship is figured in terms of knights and ladies, and second, more surprisingly, that the knight is not strictly speaking identified with the first-person speaker or the self. Instead, the speaker's feelings are personified as that knight living, taking up temporary lodgings, and camping in the speaker's heart, thoughts, and face. In this context, and given that the gist of the second quatrain seems fairly clear, we can more or less puzzle out the syntax of lines 6 and 7, which say that the "she" of the poem not only teaches the speaker about love but also "wills that [his] trust and lust's negligence / Be reined by reason, shame and reverence."

The first time I read Wyatt's poem, I found I was not certain whether trust and lust were neglected (that is, whether the speaker says he was told he was not paying sufficient attention to trust and lust) or whether the speaker says he was told that lust led to negligence. The latter seems more plausible, given the lady's "displeasure" mentioned at the end of the first quatrain, although precisely how to understand the position of "trust" in the sentence is still murky. Most likely, the lines describe how the lady desires ("wills") that the man stop neglecting proper etiquette, that he use his reason and draw on a sense of virtue rather than think (or "trust") his show of passion will gain him some presumably physical reward. I am not pretending that this reconstruction of the meaning (indeed, the grammar) of the sentence is obvious. I am, however, suggesting that my initial difficulties might not be difficulties that would have beset sixteenth-century readers, and that we can still figure out what the poem is saying. It is a matter of context: the context of courtly love conventions, the context of the rest of the octave in which the lines are placed, and – finally – the context of other versions of the same poem. You might look at the Surrey poem (or, if you read Italian, you could look to Petrarch's original). Such a comparison indicates that other Renaissance readers heard a reference to something like unseemly hopes and desires; where Wyatt talks of "trust and lust's negligence," Surrey writes of "doubtful hope and . . . hot desire." It is not that Surrey provides us with a crib sheet, precisely, or that Renaissance readings necessarily provide the final word on the meaning of Wyatt's poem. However, Surrey's parallel translation does give us an added sense of the contemporary range of possible meanings for these lines. I would add that if Surrey's phrasing seems less convoluted, he also sacrifices the kind of verbal wit that appears in Wyatt's poem when Wyatt playfully introduces the image of reining in untoward, runaway passions and so further animates the conceit. Knights, after all, tend to come with horses, and so the image of the knight galloping into the speaker's face is fleshed out in the image of the lady's wish that the knight slow down by using reins (although there is also a probable pun on passions needing to be "reigned" or ruled by reason, a commonplace description of moral behavior in the period).

Wyatt's poem also playfully deploys rhyme. He keeps the expected Petrarchan pattern throughout the octave (*abbaabba*), but notice how the import of the words unfolds over the course of the first two quatrains: "harbor" and "banner" describe manly, which is to say knightly, behavior; however, the rhyme words in the second quatrain ("suffer" and "displeasure") at least in retrospect associate the knight's brashness with less positive states: suffering and displeasing his lady.

The turn in Wyatt's poem at line 9 is then marked not only by a change in the rhyme pattern (*cdc* or "fleeth – cry – appeareth"), but also by a switch of perspective and a turn in what we might call the expected plot line. In courtly romances, knights tend to prove themselves by being bold. Wyatt's knight, on the other hand, apparently listens to his lady and runs away. At very least, two systems of value (knightly brashness and courtly love) seem to have come into conflict, although it is far from clear that Wyatt or his contemporaries could have framed the cultural pressures informing or on display in the poem in quite this way. Indeed, I suspect Wyatt's poem most self-consciously draws on his audience's familiarity with the plots of medieval romances, or tales of knights and ladies from the Middle Ages. Although you don't really need to read numbers of medieval romances to understand the poem's conceit, nonetheless, it helps to know poets borrow also from other genres and, in some romances, knights do disappear into forests, spending time as uncivilized wild men, often in gestures of atonement, before they are returned to civilization. Wyatt's knight, you will notice, runs home (in line 2, we are told the heart is his "residence"), but there is also a probable pun on "hart" (meaning deer) and "heart" in line 9 where the knight runs away "unto the heart's forest." So the knight's retreat – while a clear change of direction and of knightly bearing – probably did not seem all that surprising to Wyatt's first readers.

So where are we? As the poem has unfolded to this point (midway through the sestet, to the end of the first tercet), it wittily traces love in what would have been terms familiar to early sixteenth-century courtly readers who would not necessarily have understood the knight's retreat at the turn as untoward, although they might have expected the knight to emerge, stronger for the experience, from that retreat. Something interesting happens, though, in the last tercet: there is, it seems, a second turn.

On the one hand, a poem that portrays the ethics of love (the "she," after all, is said to have counseled a sense of shame and the curbing of passion) and that ends using the words "good" and "faithfully" seems at first, if read quickly, to take a familiar course. Even the rhymes of the sestet – "cry," "die," and "faithfully" rhymed in Wyatt's day – suggest the poem reaffirms being faithful forever to the lady. And at least some Renaissance readers understood the poem as conveying just this moral lesson. Printers (Tottel, for instance) often felt free to add their own titles to poems they collected. When reprinted, Wyatt's poem was entitled "The lover for shamefastnesse hideth his desire within his faithfull hart." However, if you read carefully (and I've already suggested one thing all poems do is to position us to read carefully), and if you further bear in mind that verbal wit, including both the elaborate conceit and the puns, has been part of the poem's tone throughout, I think you can see what I've called a possible second turn.

Let me describe this turn by looking more closely at the final tercet. First, the first-person ("I," which forms an internal rhyme with "cry," "die," and "faithfully") reappears. And the fidelity sworn is *not* to the lady, after all, but – using a different convention of the feudal culture informing medieval romances – to a "him," called "my master," and linked by the third-person masculine pronoun to the knight. The military imagery is continued, too, when the speaker says he must stay "in the field" with his master. (The image here becomes a bit difficult to visualize – we were in a forest, not a field – so it seems that staying "in the field" means staying at the knight's side in a battle.) Yet, if the knight represents passion, the "I," contrary to the lady's stated will, does not quell his passion or forswear his lust, but declares his loyalty to just those feelings, which are represented by the knight. True, there's a suggestion that the speaker may die (when his love is banished or forbidden). As I mentioned, some sixteenth-century (and some modern) readers would thus claim that the fidelity is indeed to the woman. But one could equally argue that the speaker is rather defiantly saying he will not reform.

While this is hardly a feminist stance (and you could think more about Renaissance appeals to male bonding or the meager descriptions of women except as objects of desire in Renaissance lyrics), Wyatt's poem probably was also intended to be and probably was read as a seductive poem, not least because it coyly and wittily reaffirms lust, the wit being in what I have described as a surprise ending, one that causes a reader to do a kind of double take. The cartoon version would be the "I" saying to the lady who has asked him to tone down (or rein in) his advances, "I can't; passion is my master and I'm sticking with *him*." I suspect that the poem is intended to provoke a smile or chuckle at the wit, even at the sly honesty, and is in that sense an appeal to the loved one's intelligence (and perhaps her vanity), although it is also a kind of curriculum vitae or sample of the kind of rhetorical skill Wyatt shows he could bring to the court. Indeed, Surrey's 1542 epitaph entitled "Wyatt Resteth Here," written after Wyatt's death, praises Wyatt's "tongue that served in foreign realms his [that is, Wyatt's] king." I would add that this display of his skills does not mean that the cleverness and the wit with which the conceit and turns are played out in the poem were not heard at the same time as seductive.

Certainly a similar use of wit and certain assumptions about the sonnet's form, content, and tone can be heard in Sir Philip Sidney's "Astrophil and Stella" (that is, translated into English, "Starlover and Star"), a long sequence including 108 sonnets written almost fifty years after Wyatt and Surrey showed what English could be made to do in the sonnet. Sidney's sequence (again, as with most court poetry) circulated in manuscript to a limited audience, one that would have known who Sidney was (the eldest son of an aristocratic family) and would have assumed the sonnets alluded to Sidney's relationship – the exact nature of which is unclear to us – with Penelope Devereux, who married someone else in 1581, the year before the sonnets are thought to have been written. The following poem, then, is the first of a long series of poems, although it can be read (as I propose to read it here) independently of the sonnets that follow in the sequence.

Loving in truth, and fain in verse my love to show,
That she dear she might take some pleasure of my pain,
Pleasure might cause her read, reading might make her know,
Knowledge might pity win, and pity grace obtain,
I sought fit words to paint the blackest face of woe:
Studying inventions fine, her wits to entertain,
Oft turning others' leaves, to see if thence would flow
Some fresh and fruitful showers upon my sunburned brain.
But words came halting forth, wanting Invention's stay;
Invention, Nature's child, fled stepdame Study's blows;
And others' feet still seemed but strangers in my way.
Thus, great with child to speak, and helpless in my throes,
Biting my truant pen, beating myself for spite:
"Fool," said my Muse to me, "look in thy heart, and write."

Although I want to save a detailed discussion of rhythm and meter in sonnets for the next chapter, I will pause here to note that Sidney is using iambic hexameter – with six stresses in each line – rather than Wyatt's iambic pentameter line. Indeed, I did not discuss meter in Wyatt's poem, because it is difficult to do so. The English language and in particular the pronunciation of English changed over the course of the century in which both Wyatt and Sidney wrote. Chaucer's much earlier English was in fact often indecipherable to the sixteenth-century reader, but even some of Wyatt's understandings of English may not have been readily available to the next generation of English speakers . . . or to us. If you say Wyatt's first line ("The long love that in my thought doth harbor") out loud to yourself, it may not sound as if it is alternating stressed and unstressed syllables to form an iambic line. It probably sounds more like the following (in which I've marked stressed syllables with a slash mark and unstressed syllables with a "u"):

u / / u / u /   u / u
The long love that in my thought doth harbor

Current scholarship suggests that "long" (sometimes, in fact, written out as "longe") was probably pronounced as two syllables at the time, which would make Wyatt's line well-behaved iambic pentameter (the final unstressed syllable in the line would be perfectly normal). The problem for us is that some of our speculations about pronunciation come from poems like Wyatt's. So the reasoning is a bit circular: the line is iambic pentameter because "longe" was pronounced

```
/    u
longe
```

but we know this because Wyatt's line is in iambic pentameter. Since Wyatt was *inventing* the sonnet in English, this dependence on a norm that was not really yet a norm seems unwise.

However, we can say that by the time Sidney was writing certain norms had been established, and I think you can hear how Sidney's first line is metrically less problematic:

```
/   u   u   /    u   /   u   /    u   /   u   /
Loving in truth, and fain in verse my love to show.
```

The inversion of the first iamb (not an unstressed syllable followed by stressed syllable but a stressed syllable followed by an unstressed syllable: a foot called a **troche**) is found frequently in sonnets by Sidney's day; the line then not only sets for us as readers a time signature or metrical contract, it also is quite smooth, all the smoother for the slight (if conventional) fancy footwork of the trochaic opening.

Since poems unfold, and since sonnets unfold in ways that are not only expected but often marked by rhyme, syntax, and image, it makes sense to begin discussing Sidney's poem by examining not just the first line, but the first quatrain (rhymed *abab* – already a departure from Wyatt's Petrarchan rhyme scheme), which is half of the first sentence. It is, obviously, a complicated sentence; indeed, lines 2 through 4 develop a rather elegant rhetorical figure, moving from pleasure to reading to pity to grace (in the process, imagining moving a loved one through the same progression). This figure has a name: that is, it is recognizable as a classical rhetorical device, although what it is called depends on which rhetorician you consult. The Greeks, the Romans, and the Renaissance itself had treatises cataloguing rhetorical tropes and the movement traced by Sidney has alternatively been called **anadiplosis**, **gradatio ascensus**, or, most simply, a **marching figure**. I would add that you, as a modern reader, need not memorize all names for every figure of speech or figure of thought (there are form books you can consult). What *is* important is to recognize that the poem opens sounding skilled, clearly marking the speaker (and writer) as well versed in classical rhetorical techniques.

At the same time, the very first line of this sonnet emphasizes sincerity; the speaker (the character Astrophil, to judge by the sequence title) says he loves "in truth," which seems to mean he truly is in love; as noted above, the opening line even metrically stresses the word "truth." In short, in terms of both sound and rhetoric, we (and certainly early modern readers who knew their rhetorical devices) know we are listening to a rather smooth-tongued speaker who says he wants his verse to (as it were) just tell the truth. While, in Sidney's day as in Wyatt's, eloquence and polish *were* courtly virtues (that is, skills admired and useful at court), there were nonetheless debates – not unprecedented, but renewed – about whether the language of the heart would be slick and fast-talking, or whether sincere language was marked by what was called **plain style** – a style that avoided obvious rhetorical devices and one to which Wyatt himself turned, disclaiming the courtly style found in his sonnet, after he left court. We still, I think, have something of the same prejudice, believing that plain speaking is more "honest" or "sincere," although in the early modern period plain style was far less colloquial or conversational than what we might hear as plain speech. I don't, however, want to apply our assumptions about language to another period's ways of using language. My point here is, first, that Sidney and his earliest readers already knew that the kind of language heard as the language of sincerity is itself a cultural (and rhetorical) convention and, second, that the tendency to hear plain speaking as speaking truthfully is not foreign to us.

Thus, when Sidney's speaker says he wants to show his love, this intent seems a bit at odds with the very polished rhetoric he uses. Indeed, there is already a slight sense in the first line of the poem that the poem's speaker is saying two things at once: the word "fain," which literally means "eager" – the speaker presents himself as eager to show his true love – also carries a faint echo (orally) of the word "feign," which of course means "to pretend." The grammar of the sentence makes this secondary or double meaning implausible, but it nonetheless resonates with the slight tension between the self-professed truthful lover and the elegant language of a fast-talking, polished courtier.

That what is imagined through the marching figure is also an elaborate seduction plot further underlines the questions raised about the speaker's sincerity. We know the imagined audience for the speaker's poetry (or "verse") is a loved one: the "she" is specifically "dear she" in line 2. But what is imagined is that a poem expressing pain will be clever enough to please her (not unlike the use of cleverness in Wyatt's sonnet). Sidney's speaker takes further or makes more explicit what I (perhaps because I already knew Sidney's poem when I first came to read Wyatt's) heard in "The long love that in my thought doth harbor." More specifically, lines 3 and 4 in Sidney's poem imagine the loved one, presumably enjoying the poetry, will keep reading, and so will come to believe that the speaker really is suffering from unrequited love and will take pity on him. Here the speaker even becomes a bit sleazy: he imagines that pity might "grace obtain," which suggests he thinks the lady will grant him her favors, that is, again at least on one reading, that she will yield to him.

The second quatrain completes the octave (rhymed *ababbab*) and the first sentence, and continues the speaker's self-presentation; he is imagining "verse" that will show his love and seduce the listener. When I talked about the first quatrain, I suggested that "fain" (coupled with the rhetorical showmanship on display and the seducer's machinations) might make a reader question the speaker's intentions – even if by line 4 those intentions are explicitly (and elegantly) stated. In short, I suggested he imagines he might "entertain" the lady's "wits" and thus seduce her. To be honest, I suspect my reading of "fain" in line 1 came to mind only on a *second* reading of the poem, because I heard a pattern (that I could see as a pattern) of double meanings, of self-conscious anxiety about whether smooth language is the language of the heart or of sincerity, a pattern most evident only after I had read line 5: "I sought fit words to paint the blackest face of woe." Not only does "woe" rhyme with "show" (in line 1) – and "show" emphasizes outward appearance over inner truth (as when we say something is "just for show," meaning it is not substantial) – but the image of *painting* a face also suggests putting on a mask (or applying make-up) for effect, implying that the speaker's "show" of his feelings may not be heartfelt. The image expanded in the second quatrain may further suggest that the smooth style and classical tropes ("inventions" from "others' leaves" in the image of leafing through the pages of other writers' work) we have read in the first quatrain may *be* the "fit words" the speaker sought . . . and that they may be not only not his own words but also insincere.

In most of the octave we hear or overhear the speaker describing how (and why) he wants to write a love poem, which may indeed be the very poem we are reading; further, in this first movement – the octave – of the sonnet, the speaker shows himself to be a master of discursive and perhaps manipulative elegance. At the same time, however, he uses few images, at least until the last two lines of the octave, which begin to introduce more figurative language, closer to (although not quite consistent enough to be exactly like) the conceits found in Wyatt's and others' earlier sonnets. That is to say, describing how he turns others' leaves may simply suggest that the speaker pages through books, but when he then adds that he does so "to see if thence would flow / Some fresh and fruitful showers upon [his] sunburned brain," the image of leaves seems for a moment to become a botanical image (of the leaves of a plant), given the extended image of rain flowing on the parched ground of the speaker's brain to yield "fruit" (meaning that he hopes reading other poets' work will inspire him).

I have mentioned that the ninth line (beginning the sestet) in a sonnet typically contains a turn, and Sidney's sonnet certainly fulfills a sonnet-reader's expectations by beginning line 9 with the word "But." Specifically he says he wants to write an effective love (or seduction) poem and reads other poems to help him do so, "but" (the first tercet suggests) his reading of others has not yielded fruit: he claims (most literally) that no words flowed, that he was uninventive, that studying others both stifled him (invention flees) and tripped him up or caused him to suffer writer's block (with "others' feet" described as "strangers in [his] way"). Actually, I have just paraphrased the first tercet rapidly – although I think reasonably – for the most literal reading, the gist of the tercet. But these lines are anything but literal statements. My paraphrase, in other words, ignores what may be the most salient feature of these three lines, namely that they shift tone, becoming highly metaphorical, and they verge on what we might call **mixed metaphor**, by which I mean that the images in the tercet are resonant, but are also disconcerting. Most people would define mixed metaphor as a defect in writing, when incongruous or illogically connected metaphors (or parts of metaphors) are used together. In Sidney's poem, I think you can see that the images do not seem to sustain one conceit or any unified extended metaphor of the sort found in Wyatt's poem. Instead, the metaphors keep changing. It is not only that the images shift from line to line, but also they seem first to suggest one thing and then another, the way that "leaves" initially suggests just "pages," but then (on rereading) resonates with the following more agricultural or natural imagery.

Similarly, as we move into the tercet, we are told that words come "halting forth," and do not have invention's "stay." Are words then fruit? No, it seems they are crippled (since a stay would be a support, like a cane) and the image of trying to walk is extended with line 11's image of "feet" (which are, of course, also punningly poetic – iambic – feet). You could try to extend the image of natural growth and view words as plants needing support. But this won't work, not only because plants in need of support are precisely *not* stunted but because line 10 does not extend the image of plants but instead offers us the figure of invention as a child fleeing a wicked stepmother: the stepmother "Study" is, also, beating the child, "Invention," who runs from her "blows," which makes the earlier image of a cane – a support or "stay" for Invention – as what was lacking seem a bit disconcerting (which is the effect mixed metaphors have). On top of this, we are told that "Invention" actually is "Nature's child." So, the image of fields and fruit returns (almost), although it rests uneasily with the image of a schoolroom or family drama. Certainly, if this is not mixed metaphor, it is a failed conceit.

I am not, though, proposing that Sidney's is a failed poem. Quite the contrary. Given what happens when I read the multiple metaphors (expecting a smoothly extended conceit following Petrarch or Wyatt), I would propose that the tercet is a demonstration of what it is about: the speaker says he cannot write smoothly; when I try to make sense of what he is saying, I no longer hear an elegant rhetorician at work as I did in the octave. Notice that I am proposing you take seriously the images and the ways in which they resonate with one another, the ways in which they can be seen to almost but not quite form extended metaphors (of plant growth, then of schooling . . . no, of natural growth . . . no, of walking . . . no, of writing as giving birth). There certainly are times when teasing out the implications of images (as in Wyatt's poem) *does* suggest a consistent set of references, an extended, coherent metaphor. And it may be that I have simply missed some field of reference that would make Sidney's images coalesce. But it seems most likely that the poem is demonstrating how using a series of familiar images (from "others' leaves") has not allowed him to write smoothly: he keeps switching metaphors in mid-stream (to mix my own metaphor), as a demonstration of how others' "feet" just get in his way. Throughout, the mixing of metaphors is carefully underlined; specifically, Sidney won't let us drop one possible set of images (say, that the images of vegetation) and move to the next, as when he reintroduces "Nature" in line 10, just when we were no longer thinking of fields and fruit but of a schoolroom. Similarly, the image of the cane (or is it a "stay"?) keeps reappearing, even while used in different ways; the child is brought back in line 12, although again in a different way from how it appeared in line 10; and the image of a schoolroom (also found in line 10) reappears – along with the idea of being beaten, although no longer by stepdame Study – in line 13. This demonstrates the speaker's loss of eloquence rather eloquently.

The final tercet, or at least the first two lines of the final tercet, continue the flamboyant and purposeful mixing of metaphors. Notice that even the rhythms of lines 12 and 13 are irregular. That is, line 12 is in iambic hexameter, but it has two caesurae which at very least make the line sound "halting" (recalling how at the start of the sestet's turn we are told that "words came halting forth"):

u [caesura] /   u   /   u / [caesura] u   /   u / u   /
Thus,   great with child to speak,   and helpless in my throes,

Line 13 then opens with the conventional trochaic inversion ("Biting" is a trochaic foot). However, instead of continuing as iambic hexameter, at the caesura the trochaic meter reasserts itself in "beating," which also echoes the "b" and "ing" sounds in "biting," which is to say the **alliteration** or repeated consonant sounds (repeated vowel sounds would be called **assonance**), make the words sound alike. Read out loud, the meter makes the voice seem to peter out and start again mid-line, again emphasizing the emotionally distraught state the speaker claims.

In some ways, certainly on first reading, the final line of the poem appears to solve the dilemma that has unfolded over the course of the poem: our smooth-talking speaker, reduced to sputtering when he tries to write a love poem, is told he need not try to be polished or to put on a show; he needs only to copy what's in his own heart. The trochaic opening of the previous line is repeated in line 14, but this time the rhythm sounds less awkward. That is, although the meter is in some ways a repetition of that found in line 13, we tend to hear a less fraught and more conversational voice in the repeated meter coupled with the replacement of a medial caesura by two pauses (one after "Fool," a second after "me") and the replacement of the hard "b" sounds (known as **plosives**) by the softer "r" and "l" sounds (called **liquids** or **glides**). In much the way we are relieved when we return from dissonance to harmony in a musical resolve, the sound alone is reassuring. And notice too that, although Sidney's poem is a Petrarchan sonnet, it also resolves with a rhymed couplet (as "spite" is re-sounded and resolved with the final word, "write") at the same that a sudden second turn between lines 13 and 14 lands us on what first seems solid ground (in terms of sound, in terms of the problem posed and worked through in the poem's story or narrative, and in terms of the movement – the desire voiced in the octave; the problem posed in the sestet – of the poetic structure). There is the further implication that this solution is not plotted by the speaker or derived from others but rather inspired: it is the speaker's Muse, we are told, that offers advice; indeed, the muse is given the last word, presumably as an image of the kind of inspiration the poem all along implies would trump study or calculation.

I have already mentioned that a second reading suggested to me part of the speaker's problem: he was trying to put on a show, a problem apparently solved at the end of the poem where he is told he should simply be himself. There is, however, a disingenuous quality to this resolution. The octave has shown us that the speaker can be quite eloquent and smooth talking, and it has drawn our attention to the speaker's self-consciousness about the possible duplicity of elegant speech. If those first eight lines seem less than sincere, the question is raised: is the problem that they just do not sound sincere even though the speaker does love "in truth," or is the problem that they are not effectively seductive? As I've already mentioned, Sidney's audience would have known as well as we do that the language of the heart may not be that effective unless it is well crafted, and part of the question is how we are to take the final injunction simply to write his feelings. I don't know about your heart, but I do know that in moments of heightened emotion I tend to fall back on cliché; that is, phrases such as "Oh, my," or "Oh, no," or less printable expletives spring to mind or tongue. We can imagine (to use another, contemporary cliché) Sidney's speaker carving on a tree his and his lover's initials flanking a picture of a heart: "A hearts S." Presumably this could communicate sincere feelings, but it would be nowhere near as effective as the fourteen lines we have just read. The question remains: effective at doing what? In other words, it is the building tension in the previous lines that makes the final line work as a compelling and (at first reading) apparently simple declaration of love. Without the rhetoric rejected as too smooth (in the octave) or too halting (in most of the sestet), that last line would sound nowhere near as "heartfelt." Thus, in some ways, the final line is as much a matter of artifice as the marching figure in the octave.

Sidney and his contemporaries might not have used exactly the vocabulary I have just used, but, as I mentioned, writers and thinkers in the period were well aware of the problems involved in writing "what you feel." Literary critics these days might agree that writing what you feel may change feelings – objectifying them or chastening them or even calling them into being by writing them down. Or language may simply be inadequate to feeling. In any case, sounding sincere is no guarantee of actual sincerity. Sidney's sonnet, at least on a second or perhaps third reading, is clearly self-conscious about this feature of language. That is, even as she is reading "look in thy heart, and write," a reasonably sophisticated reader would recall the self-consciousness of Sidney's speaker evident in the possible pun on "feigning," the underlined distinction between the artifice of showing or painting and the sincerity of speaking "true" feelings, the fact that the speaker has alternately shown himself to be highly polished, even calculating, in the octave, and then, in the sestet, unable to write polished verse, perhaps craftily "showing" this inadequacy that he might "pity win." The questions again arise: is writing from your heart possible? If so, how would a *reader* be able to tell what is written from the heart and what only appears to be heartfelt? Do we take the last line to cancel what the speaker says in the previous lines of the poem, which thus simply document how the speaker arrived at his final revelation and which could and perhaps should have been erased after the speaker sees they are beside the point? Or is line 14 the final step in a seduction plot, with the cleverness (we have, after all, potentially been warned in the very first quatrain of what the speaker hopes to accomplish) itself a seductive pose, as in Wyatt's sonnet?

I have no answers to the above questions. However, I would say that the very polish as well as the courtly setting and the Petrarchan subject – love – of the Renaissance sonnet made it a form in which the opposition between artifice and sincerity or inner feelings – and so the limitations of elegant language – became obvious thematic concerns. This feature of early sonnets in English surely also draws on the cultural contexts in which this kind of poem evolved, which included considerations not only of the styles appropriate to what are sometimes called "court" and "country" (classical elegance and plain style) but also of religious debates in the period: the crown's break with the Roman Catholic Church (and so the theological commitments of being at court) and, ultimately, the Protestant Reformation fueled discussions about the uses and limitations of conventional language and about the language of the heart (or of the conscience, that is, of inner voices not unlike the voice of Sidney's muse). If Wyatt showed off how polished English poetry could be, even he already knew the potential cost of elegant speech.

The two poems with which I want to conclude this chapter are equally self-conscious about the limitations and possibilities of language, although the self-consciousness is played out in different registers. The first, by Shakespeare, also helps to show how, when the structure of the sonnet varied in English, the unfolding (what T. S. Eliot called the "felt thought") of the poem shifted as well. Although scholars debate the dating of Shakespeare's sonnets – with conclusions often dependent on how both formal and thematic developments in the poems are interpreted – most would place the eighteenth sonnet that follows as a relatively early poem, from around 1595, which is to say within a few years of the publication of Sidney's poem in 1591.

> Shall I compare thee to a summer's day?
> Thou art more lovely and more temperate.
> Rough winds do shake the darling buds of May,
> And summer's lease hath all too short a date.
> Sometime too hot the eye of heaven shines,
> And often is his gold complexion dimmed,
> And every fair from fair sometimes declines,
> By chance or nature's changing course untrimmed.
> But thy eternal summer shall not fade
> Nor lose possession of that fair thou ows't.
> Nor shall Death brag thou wand'rest in his shade,
> When in eternal lines to time thou grows't.
> So long as men can breathe or eyes can see,
> So long lives this and this gives life to thee.

You may have noticed that, like "The long love that in my thought doth harbor," Sonnet 18 is written in iambic pentameter. Shakespeare's poem also resembles Wyatt's in that it uses an extended metaphor or conceit, namely that of seasonal change. However, the poem unfolds a bit differently from Wyatt's Petrarchan sonnet. The rhyme, for one thing, does not link the first eight lines together: the lines rhyme *abab cdcd*, rather than *abba abba*. There are still ways in which Shakespeare's poem does work as a Petrarchan sonnet would: sound and sentence structure still hold the first two quatrains together (note that lines 4, 6, and 7 all begin anaphorically with "And"); the syntax also clearly signals a turn at line 9 of the very sort a reader of Petrarchan sonnets would expect: the first word of the line is "But." However, the rhyme in lines 9 through 12 (as well as the fact that lines 10 and 12 are end-stopped while line 11 is not) suggests we have not turned some corner into a sestet composed of two tercets, but have instead a third quatrain, rhyming *cdcd*. Wyatt's and Sidney's sonnets both have second turns – what I called a double take when discussing "The long love that in my thought doth harbor" – but Shakespeare's poem has a more clearly marked second turn, one signaled by the rhymes and anaphora of a final couplet.

Before jumping to the end of the sonnet, though, it makes sense to follow the poem's unfolding thought from the first quatrain in which, beginning with a question, the speaker considers whether or not his loved one (the "thee" of the poem) is like "a summer's day." The answer in the first quatrain seems to be, no, in terms of beauty and temperament the loved one is better because not intemperate (presumably not making people uncomfortable as a hot day would) while also, as the poem says, "more lovely." The poem seems to trace the speaker's mind at work, as he moves from associating summer with beauty and comfort to noticing that summer is a season . . . and seasons pass. Spring, after all, is brought up in line 3, and the brevity of any season (even the most desired) in line 4. That is, spring buds may bloom in summer, but then summer is (or so the metaphor of a lease suggests) itself borrowed time, the image suggesting that the lease of summer will expire, having "too short a date." In fact, the diction in the first quatrain is full of words that suggest questions of time: it is not a season but a "day" to which the loved one might be compared; "temperate," meaning "moderate," is derived from the Latin *tempus*, meaning "time," "May," of course, is a month, and the final word of the quatrain is "date." The quatrain, indeed, closes with the pointed phrase "too short a date."

The second quatrain, then, continues what already seems as much a meditation on temporality as a love poem, even as it slightly shifts the way in which summer is considered. That is, the nature of time is again signaled in the very first word of the second quatrain. "Some*time*" almost subliminally underlines the suggestion that seasons are temporally bound while more literally pointing out that summers are not all of a piece; they vary. Most flat-footedly, although recalling the suggestion already present in the second line of the poem where the loved one's temperate nature is praised, the second quatrain opens noting that the sun – "the eye of heaven" – can be unpleasant "sometime." It is worth underlining, too, that an argument (an emotional or associational argument, at least) is unfolding. The second quatrain, in short, does not simply repeat the first even if it does continue to use the metaphorical comparison between the loved one and summer.

Most obviously, the sun (an icon of summer) is loosely personified: it is the "eye" of heaven; the sun has a gold "complexion"; and we are told the sun (like everything "fair") does not maintain its fairness. Notice also that "sometime" is repeated in line 7: "And every fair from fair sometime declines." This both echoes the "sometime" (and the theme of time) in line 5 and also has a slightly shifted meaning: it is not that those who are fair stop being fair every once in a while (in the way the sun is said to be "too hot" every once in a while in line 5); it is more reasonable to read "sometime" in line 7 as meaning "at some point," which is to say all fairness eventually becomes less fair. I say this is a more reasonable way to read "sometime" because of the generalization ("*every* fair . . . sometime declines") and the statement about how it is either by chance or just in the nature of things ("nature's changing course") that fairness is "untrimmed," that is, "stripped of its ornament." You might notice finally that even as the summer sun is personified – imaged as a person with eyes, a complexion, fairness – the diction and especially the rhymes in the second quatrain are also making us think of sunset, so that it is not just the passing of a season but of a day that is subtly suggested when we read the progression figured in the verbs: "shines," "dimmed," and "declines."

At this point, we do find a turn: the loved one reappears and is contrasted with the changes (and decline) attributed to seasons and days and beauty or fairness: "But thy *eternal* summer shall not fade." Not only is the first word of line 9 marking an expected turn in the argument ("But"), but a new kind of summer – an "eternal summer" – is mentioned, and the word "fade" (which would otherwise mark the obvious end of the sequence implied in the movement from "shine" to "dimmed" to "declines" to "fade") is negated. In fact, the return to addressing the loved one is not that surprising: the personification of the sun has kept a person (eyes, complexion, fairness) in the back of our minds. Moreover, while the meditation on temporality or the lack of permanence seems the central concern of the second quatrain, the personification of the sun means we probably have been thinking as much about the fact that people do not live for ever as about literal sunsets. Given that we are reading a sonnet (and so, if we are versed in the grammar of sonnets, we are expecting not simply a love poem but potentially a seductive love poem), other expectations are raised as well. In love poetry in particular, going back at least to Horace, there is a conventional way of mentioning how quickly time passes, whereby the poet reminds his love that she will not be beautiful for ever and so should enjoy life and love while she can. This common theme is called **carpe diem**, literally – in Latin – "seize the day." While Shakespeare's speaker does not quite make this argument, it is loitering in the background. It is an intertext. Especially in a sonnet, where if you have read Wyatt and Sidney you might expect clever seductive arguments to appear, when a speaker says to his lover that she is lovely but fair things do not last, the obvious next step should be to tell the lover to seize the day, to make love while loveliness lasts, or (as we still say) to make hay while the sun shines.

However, although the turn from praising the loved one and meditating on how things do not last is extended in the third quatrain, the expected carpe diem argument is not quite what we get; the surprise, the foiling of expectations, is part of the poem's "plot." If earlier *every* fair is said to become less fair, in line 10 the speaker proclaims that his loved one will *not* be claimed by death or "lose possession of that fair thou ows't." "Ows't" is a word for which most anthologies provide a note of some sort, suggesting that it is a older usage meaning "own." In the late sixteenth century (as you can find by looking in the *Oxford English Dictionary*) "ows't" could most straightforwardly mean "own," with the "n" elided (that is, omitted). In short: line 10 may simply say the lover will not become less fair, but rather owns (that is, permanently possesses) "fairness." At the same time, the idea of the fleeting nature of beauty or fairness is kept in motion in a reader's – and, narratively, in the lover's – mind: "ows't" puns on "to owe," echoing the earlier image of a lease, precisely of not owning something. The implication (or undertone) is that the loved one is fair, but fairness will need to be given back, even as the line more literally says the loved one's beauty will not be lost. In any case, the primary movement is still a denial that the speaker's loved one's attractiveness will fade or even, in line 11, that the loved one will die (as the poem's language echoes the image of the valley of the shadow of death found in Psalm 23): "Nor shall Death brag thou wand'rest in his shade." Admittedly, echoing a psalm is not the most effective way of seducing someone (with the reminder of religious tenets presumably counteracting exhortations to seize the day). And the final line of the third quatrain is a bit puzzling when it names the conditions under which the loved one will escape the passing of time: "When in eternal lines to time thou grows't."

I say line 12 is puzzling, but it is only puzzling before you have read the final couplet. By the end of the poem, the "lines" mentioned seem rather obviously to be lines of poetry, the lines we are reading. But we encounter line 12 before lines 13 and 14, so there is a moment in the unfolding of the poem, at first reading, when the "lines" seem more to present an image of ropes or cords, possibly the ropes that were (and are) used to graft branches onto root stock (used with fruit trees, for instance). Or it may be that the threads of fate found in classical mythology – threads cut by the Fates when your time is up – are being called to mind. I take these suggestions from Stephen Booth's commentary on Shakespeare's sonnets, and that some commentary is required shows how the lines stop us for a moment, especially since they seem to return us to the image of time but not quite to carry forward the gesture – the exhortation to seize the day – we might be expecting. This makes the final couplet stand out further (because we have paused at the image of growing in lines to time), but I do not think it stops us in our tracks. Even if we are not yet certain what kind of image these "lines" form, we are told they are "eternal," and the image of growing to time in eternal lines for a moment almost assuages the apparent anxiety we have been hearing as the speaker is haunted by how quickly time passes. More specifically, the image suggests that the threads of life will not be cut or that the lover will become one with time the way a graft is bound to an older tree stock. In both cases, the images seem to speak of generation or of being fruitful – even of genealogical trees or family lines – which surprisingly turns the expected carpe diem theme (for a moment) into something more like a marriage proposal (complete with the suggestion of having children) than a seductive proposition.

But there is another and sharper turn in the last two lines, which are set off from the preceding quatrains not only because we have to pause to make sense of line 12; the lines are set off as well by the rhyme of "see" and "thee," by the fact that they form a separate complete sentence, by the anaphora ("So long . . . So long"), and indeed by the elegance of the final line, which uses a trope called **chiasmus** – from the Greek for "crossing" – as the words "lives this" are repeated and reversed at the end of the last line in "this gives life." What the couplet does, it seems, is not seduce or woo a beloved but promise to use poetry to make the loved one live for ever. Or at least for as long as people continue to read or recite poetry ("So long as men can breathe or eyes can see"). That is, while the rhythms and the chiasmus seem at first further to resolve the problem of how short life is, which has informed the poem from the very beginning, the actual claim is interestingly limited. The poem does not counsel facing the brevity of life by living it to the fullest, as a carpe diem poem would do. Nor is there some higher eternal realm to which the poem turns. The speaker does not even claim that poetry is eternal, although the sonnet does claim it will carry on the life of the loved one as well as having children would do, and will do so at least as long as people continue to read (silently or out loud) "this."

Since we as readers are, presumably, reading "this" (that is, the poem to which the deictic points), the poem does surely continue to live in *our* present, even if we might question what kind of life it gives to the loved one, who is even less clearly described than the "she" in Wyatt's or Sidney's poems. In this sense, as with the Wyatt and Sidney poems, Shakespeare's sonnet is as much about its own powers (or about the power of language) as about the one loved . . . and, indeed, it seems that from one perspective Shakespeare has expanded on what was already implicit in the earlier sonnets discussed here – namely, their focus on speech, on the speaker, and on language.

The same is also true of the last sonnet I want to consider here, a poem from the early seventeenth century, which takes Wyatt's, Sidney's, and Shakespeare's considerations and presentations of language and love in yet a new direction. The following is the fourteenth of a series of sonnets entitled "Holy Sonnets" by John Donne in which the language of love is used to address God, a mixture of the spiritual and the erotic that, as I already noted in chapter 2, was not in itself new:

> Batter my heart, three-personed God; for You
> As yet but knock, breathe, shine, and seek to mend;
> That I may rise and stand, o'erthrow me, and bend
> Your force to break, blow, burn, and make me new.
> I, like an usurped town, to another due,
> Labor to admit You, but Oh, to no end.
> Reason, Your viceroy in me, me should defend,
> But is captived, and proves weak or untrue.
> Yet dearly I love You, and would be loved fain,
> But am betrothed unto Your enemy:
> Divorce me, untie or break that knot again,
> Take me to You, imprison me, for I,
> Except You enthrall me, never shall be free,
> Nor ever chaste, except You ravish me.

I hope that by now the movements of various types of sonnets are familiar to you, and that you can feel (even before counting syllables or making a schematic representation of the *abbaabba* rhyme scheme of the octave) that Donne's is a Petrarchan sonnet, with what Ellen Bryant Voigt calls the "bivalve structure" of such sonnets. I also hope that by now you have seen it is useful to begin with the first quatrain (after quickly reading through to the somewhat shocking end of the poem) in order to hear how the poem unfolds on a second reading.

"Batter my heart" clearly is using the language of love poetry, but in it we overhear a speaker addressing God; indeed, the first quatrain is an apostrophe to a Christian ("three-personed") God. The conceit in the first quatrain might seem opaque to a modern reader at first because it draws on the image of a tinker, telling God not to fix the speaker's heart but, in effect, to melt it down and make something new. We still use the word "to tinker," meaning to make small but not major changes in something, but for most of us the image of an actual tinker, a traveling repairman who mends broken things (such as metal household utensils), is no longer familiar. Thus, the image of someone using a small forge or banging dents out of pots and pans may not come to mind when we read Donne's speaker telling God to stop fiddling around and instead "batter" his heart. Perhaps because a small restaurant near where I live and teach advertises "hand-battered halibut," I and my students have sometimes joked about the culinary image that comes to mind when speaking of "battering" a heart – an image that in context is clearly out of line with the rest of the poem's tone, imagery, and subject matter. Even ruling out such stray and ultimately not useful connotations of "battering" a heart (but recalling the heart Sidney's muse tells him to "look in"), the tone of Donne's poem may seem a bit odd. That is, it may seem untoward of the speaker to tell God what to do or to berate God for just tinkering: "for You / As yet but knock, breathe, shine, and seek to mend." Still, once you have a tinker in mind and consider the conceit – the speaker's heart is a vessel or pan; God is the maker or fixer of pots and pans – the images are not all that unorthodox, even if the tone is unusual.

In fact, the tone is even more peculiar if you think a bit more about what precisely God is being told to do. When we speak of **tone** we usually mean the speaker's attitude toward his or her subject – as when your mother says, "Don't take that tone of voice with me!" Word choices – about which I'll have more to say in chapter 5 – and, even more, context usually give us our sense of tone, whether bossy or sarcastic or affectionate and so on. In Donne's sonnet, it is the use of the imperative when speaking to God that in the very first line of the poem marks the tone as noteworthy; I can imagine God replying, "Don't take that tone with me, young man!" If you read through the first quatrain line by line, I think you can see that even the line breaks – in combination with what's being said – show the oddity of the speaker's tone and perhaps suggest the speaker's desire is quixotic or misguided. For instance, given most theological assumptions about God's power, you would think that God could easily fix what He "seeks to mend." Instead, our speaker implies that God is not doing a good job.

And look at the use of enjambment. There is a semi-colon – a near if not a full stop – at the end of line 2, but we are nonetheless tempted – deliberately, I think, since the temptation reoccurs throughout the poem – to ignore the stop and read straight through from line 2 to line 3 before the next imperative verbs – "o'erthrow me, and bend" – force us to tinker with our understanding of the syntax. That is, we are tempted to read the poem as saying God should mend the speaker so that he (the speaker) might "rise and stand." Among other things, "rising" has clear theological resonance in a poem about a "three-personed God," calling to mind Christ rising from the grave. Instead, however, upon encountering the verb "o'erthrow," we have to go back to note the semi-colon at the end of line 2, to understand that line 3 opens a new independent clause, inverting the usual word order (perhaps as its tone inverts the usual hierarchy between God and petitioner) to command God to *vanquish* the speaker so that he (the speaker) can rise and stand. Leaving aside the second peculiarity suggested by the enjambment between lines 3 and 4 – people usually bend before God; they do not usually command God to bend – there is a kind of paradox in asking God to undo or overthrow the self so that it might rise (since being overthrown and rising or standing are usually antonyms, that is, opposites, especially if you encounter the image of rising and standing before you encounter the image of overthrowing, as a reader of Donne's poem in fact does).

Theologically, it is not at all unusual to figure conversion or grace as putting away the old self and being made new (in Christ), but to *command* God to overthrow your "self" is new: among other things, issuing commands is not precisely the tone to take if you wish to subdue the self. Indeed, we might ask what "I" would rise and stand if the self – the "I" – were overthrown. The movement into and at the end of the octave might suggest that the speaker is self-conscious about the inadequacies or misguidedness of the first quatrain's tone (although starting the second quatrain with the first-person singular "I" does not bode well for the speaker's apparent quest to get God to overthrow the self). In any event, the second quatrain's continued rhyme and even the slightly more humble conceit – the self as a town taken over by "another," clearly not God – suggest that the speaker, on the one hand, continues to confront the problem of how to position or represent himself (a self he wants to have remade) before God. That is, the new conceit (of the town) suggests the speaker is trying a new approach, a new way both of presenting himself to God and, in the course of trying new conceits (that is, by the very act of shifting the images, as in Sidney's poem), of representing the inner conflict he is experiencing. The conceit in the second quatrain, I'd add, is less opaque for modern readers, especially those who have read poems like Wyatt's in which inner faculties or desires are personified. In "Batter my heart," the image is of the self as a town that should be run by Reason (God's second-in-command), but that is instead paying tribute to someone else (the devil, I assume) because Reason is not doing his job ("is captived, and proves weak or untrue"). This seems slightly more orthodox than the first quatrain's tacit indictment of God.

I have already suggested that there is an almost painful self-consciousness in Donne's poem, painful because of what seems to be at stake in representing this self who wants not to be the self it is. In light of this, it is worth pausing again to ask about the nature of the self in the second conceit. Who or what part of the self is the "I" who unsuccessfully "Labor[s] to admit" God, that is, to let God back in to take over the self? There is, I'd add quickly, no single answer I can see that is proposed. Nor should we expect a firm answer, since the very problem that the poem enacts for us is the difficulty of representing the self without asserting it. Still, the ways in which this problem is figured are interesting. Clearly, there is an "I" who is distinct from "Reason." Moreover, the same "I" is still asserting itself. Indeed, we could see this poem as a battle of pronouns (so the fact that there are fourteen uses of the first-person singular – "I" or "me" – but only nine uses of the second-person singular – "You" or "Your" – seems significant). You can hear what I might call a fracturing of self in the poem; it is (as the first quatrain implies) in ways about the desire to fracture the (old) self, by a speaker well aware of the difficulty of communicating the desire not to be himself. The rhyme words in the octave further underline this dilemma as the sounds of "You" and being made "new" in the first quatrain are echoed and perhaps deflated when the speaker describes himself as to another "due" and his Reason as "untrue" in lines 7 and 8.

Word choices also emphasize the self's uncertainty and uncertain allegiances. "Viceroy," if you consult the dictionary, means the governor of a country or province who rules as the representative of his or her king or sovereign, drawn from the old French words *vice* ("deputy") and *roi* ("king"). In fact, appropriately enough for Donne's poem, the prefix "vice," meaning "instead of," or "in place of," is originally from the Latin word *vicis*, meaning "change or turn." I say "appropriately" because conversion (for which the speaker seems to yearn) is precisely a turning or change. And the sonnet is an appropriate form in which to consider a turn, as well. Yet there is surely also a resonance, an undertone, where we are made to think for a moment of "vice" in the moral sense as well.

The expected poetic turn at line 9 should, or so a reader of sonnets might expect, be the place where the problem posed in the octave is addressed; certainly, the syntax tells us we have a turn when we read the word "Yet." You might even see the poem's enacted thought as making a wide turn, since lines 8, 9, and 10 open with "But," Yet," and "But," in what sounds like a series of turns. Or perhaps false starts. In context, the repeated conjunctions seem to enact the unending labor figured in the second quatrain, which we are told is "to no end." That is, the poem may suggest that the speaker is unable to turn himself around – or perhaps the poem is about a kind of turning around of the self that may not be subject to the will (in which case neither commands, labor, nor pleas would presumably accomplish much). We cannot, after all, will not to will.

I may be getting ahead of myself here, however. As we first move into the sestet, to the first tercet, the speaker yet again repositions himself, with a new conceit (perhaps suggested by the word "untrue" at the end of line 8). Beginning in line 9, the speaker presents himself anew, this time as a lover betrothed to the devil (or so God's "enemy" would seem to be) but one who truly loves God, even if God is again commanded to break the self's engagement or marriage to the enemy. Actually the tone of line 11 – "Divorce me, untie or break that knot again" – sounds less presumptuous than the tone of "Batter my heart . . . o'erthrow me, and bend." For one thing, the way in which the speaker represents himself has changed. Although the image of the soul as feminine (as God's bride) is quite traditional both in the Bible and in earlier poetry, in this sonnet it also serves to reposition the speaker in a subservient position (again, something to consider further if you are interested in the implications of how male and female roles are imagined in early modern poetry and culture). The sestet also moves the language of the poem back to the language of love more familiar in sonnets. Finally, because (as in Sidney's poem, too) the inner conflict enacted in the octave shows us that the speaker may not be as self-assured as a reading of the opening commands to God might first have suggested, line 11 seems more a cry of frustration than simple self-assertion, especially as we move into the final tercet, where the speaker says to God, "imprison me," ironically telling God to curb the very self asserted with the imperative verb and the use of the first-person "me." In some ways, on this understanding of the poem, the last two lines of the poem simply continue the conceit of the speaker as a lover, although in other ways the images of violence – unnervingly coupled with the elegance of the chiasmus ("Except You . . . never" in line 13 is repeated and reversed in line 14, with "Nor ever . . . except You") and the rhyme ("free" and "me") – suggest we may have another turn and a final couplet. In other words, the structure and rhymes and tone of the poem inform its meaning.

I have just said that the rhymes guide our understanding of the poem, but actually it is difficult to be certain what rhymes with what in "Batter my heart": most linguists who study shifts in the pronunciation of English say that by the late sixteenth century "I" would have been pronounced "ay" (perhaps even "ayee"). So, although "enemy" would rhyme with "I," it might still also faintly echo the sound of "me" and "free" (a thematically interesting echo that demotes the sound of "enemy" in our ears at the very end of the poem). Both modern linguists and Donne's own contemporaries suggest that spoken English continued to have wide dialectical variations, something that might be particularly true of the mixture of persons and voices in London, where Donne wrote and presumably listened to what one contemporary, George Puttenham, author of a 1589 treatise, *The Arte of English Poesie*, called "auricular figures" (figures that are heard); Puttenham also writes about "slipper[y] volubility in utterance," which implies that the pronunciation of words varied.

Ultimately, how you hear the poem's rhymes will probably be influenced by how you understand the tone and thematic implications of that final couplet. And how we interpret that couplet is informed among other things by the gestures we are expecting, that is, by the poem's overall form. Yet it almost seems as if a Petrarchan form is played against a Shakespearean form. For example, the rhymes of the first eight lines form a perfect Petrarchan octave (rhyming *abbaabba*) even as the grammar and images give us what seem more like two discrete quatrains. Line 9, as you would expect in a Petrarchan sonnet, begins with an apparent if problematic turn: "Yet." We also begin here a third conceit: after the images of the tinker and the besieged town, we turn to images of love (an appropriate Petrarchan move). That this conceit follows through line 14 could then suggest we have a Petrarchan sonnet, that we are moved in the way a Petrarchan sonnet moves its readers. But the rhyme scheme seems to do something else: *abbaabba cdcd ee* looks as if what began as a Petrarchan sonnet suddenly is changed around line 12 into a different form. This formal tension may, in fact, resonate with the thematic tensions in the poem, which is after all about change. In any case, something interesting happens thematically if you align the "I" of line 12 with "enemy" (line 10) by hearing them as rhyming, while the "me" of line 14 is (with that second, conspicuous, Shakespearean, turn) set off from the "I" and the "enemy" in terms of sound. The first person of line 14, in other words, may be associated by rhyme only with "free." I wouldn't rule out, I'd add, that there's a kind of tug-of-war going on as we try to decide what the rhyme scheme is. "Free" and "me" could rhyme with "enemy" for a "*cdc edd*" pattern. I don't think so, but it's possible. Certainly there's at least a possible indecision proposed, which thematically would raise again what seems to be the poem's central question: is this self ("me") capable of being redeemed ("free") or not – that is, does it rhyme, still, with "enemy"? Whichever way you read the rhyme, it seems significant that the rhyme is "slippery," that the use of the first-person "me" in the couplet is (grammatically) an object, not a subject, and that, for almost the only time in the poem, God ("You") is not *commanded* as God is, if with increasing desperation, in the earlier lines.

When I first presented Donne's poem, I noted that the ending was somewhat shocking. I want here to return to the images of rape in the final couplet, which are and I believe we can say are intended to be shocking. Grammatically, of course, we do not have a discrete couplet; what we read in lines 13 and 14 is part of a dependent clause ("for I,") that acknowledges the preconditions of salvation in two prepositional clauses: "Except you enthrall . . . / . . . except you ravish." In some ways, then, the couplet may offer a kind of paradoxical resolution, or at least a momentary respite from the tension built earlier in the poem, between a new self, the one that would be reformed or remade by or absorbed into God, and an old self that cannot will not to be (presumably beset by the sin – of pride – with which all humans, in this Protestant view, are born). Another way of putting this is to say that Donne is trying to defer to God, and yet, given his beliefs about whether he can will to be unwillful, his quest is both impossible and necessary.

The unsettling image, and in particular the word choices, in the couplet may help further this theme. Earlier, we have a speaker at odds with himself as his self-assertiveness belies his stated desire to submit to or be taken over by God, in short, to lose the self. Both "enthrall" and "ravish" are words that merge or unite these two gestures; "enthrall" can mean "imprison," but also "delight." "Ravish" means both "to rape" and "to fill with joy or to enrapture." Both words carry the implication that being taken over by something larger violates the self, even if loss of self is desired. The richness of language may thus just encapsulate or repeat the tension found throughout the poem: the old self resists (being taken over is violation; being enthralled is imprisonment), while another side of this self longs to be subsumed by God, understanding on some level that this would be delight, joy, rapture. In another sense, however, perhaps the word choices work much the same way as the final resolution of the meter (line 14 is straightforward iambic pentameter), the shift away from the imperative, and the second turn in the final couplet work. That is, perhaps this is an arrival at just the right words, and an image that finally rightly—or, in Donne's terms, righteously—positions the speaker; after all, the speaker has been desperately looking for the right image of his relationship to God. Still, even if this is true, the use of "again" in line 11 suggests this battle or struggle is not one that the speaker (or by implication anyone with Donne's beliefs) ever finally puts to rest.

Ultimately, I am less interested in insisting you must take the end of the poem either as resolution or as an indication the struggle presented will continue than I am in trying to show how various interpretative decisions – responses you may first make almost subliminally but that are invited by the rhymes, the images, the tone, the formal gestures, and the diction of the poem – will affect your final interpretation of the poem. I would add that I find Donne's poem moving, both in the sense of its representation of the speaker's movements of thought and feeling and in the sense of its ability to present us with the emotional feeling of a spiritual dilemma (even if the speaker's perspective is foreign to us).

I have mentioned the meter in "Batter my heart," as well as in the other sonnets presented here, but there is much more to say about the rhythms and meter of these poems; so much more that I want to devote the next chapter to how people talk about meter and rhythm in poetry, including a return to consider how the rhythm and meter in Donne's sonnet contribute to its effect.

Terms used

alliteration	liquids
anadiplosis	marching figure
assonance	medieval romance
carpe diem	mixed metaphor
chiasmus	plain style
conceit	plosives [or glides]
courtly love	tercet
end-stopped lines	tone
gradatio ascendus	troche [trochaic]
hexameter	volta [turn]

Other poems that might be read

Henry Howard, Earl of Surrey, "Love, that doth reign and live within my thought" (1557)
John Milton, "When I consider how my light is spent" (*c.*1652)
William Wordsworth, "London, 1802" (1802)
Percy Bysshe Shelley, "To Wordsworth" (1816)
Ralph Waldo Emerson, "The Rhodora" (1834)
e. e. cummings, "ladies and gentlemen this little girl" (1922)
William Butler Yeats, "Leda and the Swan" (1923)
Countee Cullen, "Yet do I marvel" (1925)
Muriel Rukeyser, "To Be a Jew in the Twentieth Century" (1944)
Marilyn Hacker, "Elektra on Third Avenue" (1974)
Seamus Heaney, "Glanmore Sonnets" (1979)
Michael Palmer, "Of this cloth doll which" (1984)
John Ashbery, "Rain Moving In" (1984)
George Starbuck, "Sonnet with a Different Letter at the End of Every Line" (1999)

Useful further reading

Stephen Adams, *Poetic Designs: An Introduction to Meters, Verse Forms and Figures of Speech* (Peterborough, Ont.: Broadview Press, 1997).
Stephen Booth, *Shakespeare's Sonnets* (New Haven: Yale University Press, 1977).
Stuart Curran, "The Sonnet," in *Poetic Form and British Romanticism* (New York: Oxford University Press, 1986): 29–55.
Richard Lanham, *A Handlist of Rhetorical Terms*, 2nd edn. (Berkeley: University of California Press, 1968).
George Puttenham, "The Art of Poesie," *Representative Poetry OnLine*, <http://rpo.library.utoronto.ca/display/displayprose.cfm?prosenum=17> (7 July 2006).
Ellen Bryant Voigt, "The Flexible Lyric," in *The Flexible Lyric* (Athens, Ga.: University of Georgia Press, 1999): 114–71.

Chapter 4

The Uses of Meter and Rhythm in the Sonnet

in Charlotte Smith's "To Dependence" (1784) and
Percy Bysshe Shelley's "Ozymandias" (1817), while
revisiting briefly Sir Philip Sidney's "Loving in
truth" (1582), William Shakespeare's Sonnet 18
(c.1595); and John Donne's
"Batter My Heart . . ." (c.1621)

As the previous chapters suggested, there are numbers of ways in which poems work on or in you when you read. While many poets and readers simply "speak poetry," which is to say they have internalized what we might call the grammar of poetry, as a critical reader you can also more explicitly analyze the features of poems that make meaning or affect you. Cognitive psychologists suggest that when we read we cannot or at least do not process (or bring to bear on what we read) too many things at once, although they also say that people who are practiced readers of the kind of thing they are reading (this could include anything from instruction manuals to history books), or who have ready to hand the background information required by whatever they are reading, can process what they read more quickly. This may be true. However, poems in general may ask us to slow down and dwell more on the nuances of language than we usually do when reading (and perhaps to think less instrumentally, that is, without rushing to extract usable information for some other end than the pleasure of reading). At the same time, what cognitive psychology tells us suggests that the more practiced a reader of poems you are, the more readily you will hear various gestures, tones, and nuances in the poems you read. I hope it's clear that I do not believe the act of analysis blunts the pleasures of reading poetry. Poems are not fragile things; most are quite capable of surviving whatever readers say about them; moreover, paying conscious attention to the technical features of poems has many benefits. For one, if you harbor the ambition of becoming a writer yourself you will want to know how poems accomplish what they do; in the same way magicians learn how magic tricks are done, so too writers or aspiring writers – moved by a poem – often want to know "how did that poem *do* that?"

As importantly, even if you are not an aspiring writer, once you have attended to rhyme or diction or line breaks or images or syntax, or the culture in which a poem was written, or to how the expected movements of a particular form work or are refused in a given poem (just to name a few of the ways poetic language affects readers), you will begin to hear more in all poems that you read. On this, I suppose I agree with what cognitive psychology has recently proposed, although I want to offer a more down-to-earth analogy. Before I came to live in my current home, I would take walks in small suburban neighborhoods like the one in which I now live and pass quickly by yards to which I paid little attention. I thought the view was dull. Or I would sometimes admire the view in a distanced way. Once I began to tend a yard, however, I came to know the names of shrubs, flowers, ground covers, and trees. My eyes came to focus on plantings in other yards in an entirely new way and to notice details I previously had not really seen. So, too, knowing the details of how language is used in poems will make you hear more, even when you read or reread a new poem without stopping consciously to consider the form, stanzaic structure, tropes, sounds, tone, or the ways in which a poem responds to or draws on the work of other writers (to mention a few more features of poetic language).

The above is a long preface to a discussion of meter and **rhythm** in poems, but perhaps a useful preface since the vocabularies for talking about rhythm and meter are technical in ways that might make this chapter feel like an excursion into things mathematical. I wanted, then, to start by explaining why I think it is useful to learn how to discuss the metrical and rhythmic qualities of poetry, namely because, as with other features of poetic language, such knowledge helps you to listen more carefully and to hear more when you do so. Ultimately I want to offer you two alternative vocabularies, although there are many ways in which people talk about patterns of emphasis in lines of verse, or the rhythms of spoken English (involving pitch, force, loudness, even duration, all sometimes called **accent** or **lexical stress** and distinguished from **meter** or the codified patterns – as in the sonnet's iambic pentameter or hexameter – we associate with **versification**).

It may be useful to start with a brief sketch of some terms you will encounter in form books that focus on poetic meter. Greek poetry used **quantitative meter**, a metrical system based on the duration of a syllable rather than on the stress it is given. Anglo-Saxon poetry used **alliterative meter** (where lines were divided into half-lines, each containing two stresses and with at least one of the stressed words in the first half of the line alliterating with the first stressed word of the second half). Modern English poetry that uses set metrical patterns is more typically **accentual-syllabic verse**, in which patterns of stressed and unstressed syllables forming poetic feet are used. (**Accentual verse** would be poetry that pays attention to stressed, but not unstressed, syllables.) Since I have been talking about sonnets, and since sonnets typically have a set meter – iambic pentameter or (as in Sidney's poem) iambic hexameter – I will concentrate here on the metrical and rhythmic features of sonnets, their **prosody**, beginning with some lines from two sonnets already discussed in chapter 3.

Consider first the opening line of Shakespeare's Sonnet 18: "Shall I compare thee to a summer's day?" The poem is often cited as an example of perfectly smooth iambic pentameter. Metrically, we would then mark line 1 as follows, with five iambic feet:

```
        u  /  u  /  u  / u /  u    /
(a)   Shall I compare thee to a summer's day?
```

This way of scanning (**scansion** being the graphic representation of patterns of stress) would be uncontroversial for most readers. However, you might note two problems. First, in English, verbs and nouns (indeed "content" words in general) typically are said with more force, more emphasis, than what are sometimes called "function" words such as prepositions or articles. So the stress on "to" deviates from standard English speech patterns, that is patterns of lexical stress. Spoken English, in short, may not come in Greek feet. Second, depending on how you hear the poem's emotional content, you might think that a voicing of the line – say, in a dramatic reading of the poem – would be inclined to stress the word "thee," suggesting that the person addressed is beyond comparison (that is, "shall I compare *you*, who are incomparable?"); or perhaps a performer would emphasize the word "Shall," suggesting that the act of comparing is audacious ("How *could* I do that?"). We do use emphasis to underline meaning when we speak, after all.

One can express these senses of how the line would be performed using traditional scansion, as follows:

```
            u / u   /   /  u u /   u    /
(b)   Shall I compare thee to a summer's day?
```

or

```
      /   u u  /   u u u /   u   /
(c)   Shall I compare thee to a summer's day?
```

or even

```
      /   u u  /   /  u u /   u   /
(d)   Shall I compare thee to a summer's day?
```

None of the above would be improper or implausible ways of scanning the line. The first, (a), marks the expected, conventional metrical contract as iambic pentameter; (b), (c), and (d) pay more attention to the accents of the spoken language and indicate slightly different interpretations of what is important in the poem. This does, however, raise questions about the relationship between metrical stress and the rhythms of speech.

Metrically, poems tend to set reader expectations – to establish a metrical contract, in this context – in the first lines, although metrically the further question arises: why assume that this is a poem in iambic pentameter? Looking at example (d), for instance, you might ask why it is not a line with four feet, as follows (where I have separated the feet by the mark | and given you the names of the feet above the scansion)?

dactyl	**spondee**	**pyrrhic**	**amphimacer**
/ u u	/ /	u u	/ u /
(d′) Shall I com	pare thee	to a	summer's day?

Example (d′) is not one any practiced reader of poetry, let alone of Shakespeare's sonnets, would find reasonable, I hasten to add. It is not that the feet I have named are unknown, although the amphimacer is rarely found in English verse. (I would add that the one common foot I have not yet mentioned is formed of two unstressed syllables followed by a stressed syllable, as in the word "understand," and is called an **anapest**.) However, although there's nothing on the page that tells you what the underlying metrical contract is, readers know that sonnets – certainly in Shakespeare's day – almost always use **duple** – that is, two-syllable – poetic feet like the iamb or troche. We might say the metrical contract was already established before Shakespeare began to write this particular sonnet. He could vary the contract without breaking it even in the first line, especially since the rest of the poem maintains five stresses per line (and most of these lines are, even when scanned as they might be spoken, well-behaved iambic pentameter). For example, you might think of line 4 of Sonnet 18:

```
iamb    |   iamb  | iamb  | iamb  | iamb
u   / | u   /  | u   / | u   / | u  /
And summer's lease hath all too short a date
```

In chapter 3, I mentioned that a trochaic opening is a fairly standard deviation within the sonnet's iambic pentameter (or hexameter) meter, so – returning to example (d) – it would not be out of line, so to speak, to hear a stress on the word "Shall" at the beginning of Sonnet 18. The line would thus be heard as primarily iambic pentameter with two variations, the first conventional, the second, not so conventional:

```
        troche |   iamb   | troche | iamb  | iamb
          / u |   u   /  | /   u | u   / | u    /
(d")  Shall I   compare   thee to  a sum mer's day?
```

It is not the case that meters should not vary. I was once asked to test a computer program that beeped, signaling an error, when I deviated from iambic pentameter. Had such a program been available in the Renaissance, we would have few interesting and certainly none of the best-known sonnets in English, not even Sonnet 18, which is unusually regular metrically. Most practiced readers of poetry, knowing this, would understand that example (d") does not suggest there is anything wrong with the line, although a sensitive reader might complain that the scansion in example (d") does not show us the ways in which the rhythms of speech compete with the metrical stress, the latter setting an underlying series of beats something like the way a metronome marks a time signature for musical performers.

With this in mind, I want to introduce an alternative way of analyzing rhythm and meter that I take from Derek Attridge, to whose books you might turn should you wish to pursue further a study of **Attridge's system of beat–offbeat scansion**. I would add that generative linguistics also offers ways of marking the rhythms of poetry and of spoken English. Here I will only mention that there are alternative systems available – and, as one might expect, scholarly debates about these systems. If you are interested in investigating how generative linguistics has been used or in trying your hand at using the Attridge system, go to the interactive on-line program called INTRA listed at the end of this chapter (a computer program that I would not mock, unlike the above mentioned sonnet-writing program).

For now, I want to return to the first line of Shakespeare's sonnet to sketch briefly the virtues of Attridge's system, especially when analyzing iambic pentameter lines. First, to use Attridge's system, you mark how you might say a line, noting the stressed and unstressed syllables. This is not prescriptive; you simply mark stressed syllables with "s" and weak or unstressed syllables with "w." In the following example I use Attridge's notation to mark the lexical stresses in Shakespeare's line – using examples (b) and (c) – first with "Thee" stressed and then with "Shall" stressed:

(1)   w   s   w   s   s   w w   s   w   s
(2)   s   w w   s   w   w w   s   w   s
      Shall I compare thee to a summer's day?

Remember that the above ignores the underlying rhythm or expected metrical pattern in a sonnet, which consists of alternate beats and offbeats (that is, stressed and unstressed syllables). For Attridge, the underlying or standard rhythm of iambic pentameter verse is represented (using "B" to indicate a beat and "o" to indicate an offbeat) as: o B o B o B o B o B. Attridge then offers three "deviation rules," which are ways in which deviations from the standard contract occur. Interestingly, these also have less to do with prescription (that is, they aren't rules that dictate how you *must* hear a line) than with how English works, which is to say the rules are derived from the ways the ear negotiates between the rhythms or accents of spoken English and the underlying metrical contract in lines of duple meter. Another way of putting this is that Attridge's system graphically represents the relationship between the metrical pattern and the rhythmic stress in a line (rather than attending to individual feet).

The above may sound abstract, but it is relatively simple in practice. Before giving you a more concrete example, though, I need to rehearse a short version of Attridge's "deviation rules" and tell you a few things about what he calls "conditions." The first rule is the "promotion rule." An unstressed syllable may realize a beat when it occurs between two unstressed syllables or between the end or beginning of a line and an unstressed syllable. Although Attridge is not thinking of performance or voicing *per se*, one way to think of this is to consider how rarely we say three unstressed syllables – all equally unstressed – in a row. In spoken English, stress is hierarchical and relative. In a line of iambic pentameter, the promoted syllable – represented by Attridge as a "B" with a line over it ($\overline{B}$) — would normally be the middle syllable (with line boundaries forming special cases) because of the way the underlying metrical contract gives us certain rhythmic expectations. The second rule is the "demotion rule," which specifies that a stressed syllable may realize an offbeat – represented as an "o" with a dot over it (ȯ) – when it occurs between two stressed syllables, or after a line boundary and before a stressed syllable. Again, think of three strong stresses in a row, and consider how the stresses will almost certainly not all be equal; one stressed syllable will be "demoted" and, in an iambic pentameter line, the middle syllable will be the one demoted (again with line boundaries forming special cases and again because of how we are aware of that metronomic underlying pattern where beats and offbeats alternate). The final rule is the "implied offbeat rule": an offbeat may be implied between two stressed syllables. The implied offbeat is represented as ô. Once more, while Attridge is not discussing actual performance, you might think of this almost as a pause, considering that it takes longer to say sequences of stressed syllables because you must pause to take a breath between them.

Finally, Attridge notes that strict duple meter will also impose "conditions," including an "implied offbeat condition" where an implied offbeat occurs only if immediately preceded or followed by a non-final double offbeat (a double offbeat is represented as ŏ; a triple offbeat would be ŏ). Double offbeats would then occur in strict duple meter only when offset in this way by an implied offbeat or in what Attridge calls an **initial inversion condition**, which would include what in chapter 3 I discussed using a more traditional vocabulary as a trochaic opening. Flat-footedly, this is to say that if a line opens with a troche and then moves back into an iambic meter, you will get what Attridge represents as B o (what conventionally would be a troche) followed by o B (which is to say, more conventionally, an iamb). Attridge then represents this as B ŏ B. It is not that Attridge just substitutes "o" for "w" or "B" for "s" (or "o" and "B" for the more standard "u" and " / "). It is that this system shows you both the complexity of a line (including where it is least predictable) and the ways our sense of rhythm tends to move speech patterns in standard sonnets toward the underlying iambic pentameter contract.

Here, then, is an example. Going back to example (b), which scanned line 1 of Shakespeare's sonnet as having "thee" stressed, and using Attridge's system to mark under the line where the line deviates from the underlying o B o B o B o B o B pattern, you would get the following:

(1)   w s w s   s ww s   w   s
       Shall I compare thee to a   summer's day?
       o   B o   Bô B   ŏ   B   o   B

Attridge's scansion, then, shows the two places where the line deviates (albeit in an orderly or rule-bound fashion) from the underlying contract, and it shows how we do hear the rhythms of poetry in lines (not just in phrases or syntactical units). The line above maintains five stressed and five unstressed syllables; you might think of this as working something like the way a blues line works. If you slow down, adding an unexpected second, sequential, stress on the word "thee," you will not only pause between the two stressed syllables ("—pare [pause] thee"), but you will make up for lost time with the unstressed syllables ("to a") that follow, to preserve or acknowledge the underlying time signature of the line.

The line moves differently if you emphasize "shall":

(2)   s   w w   s   w   w   w s   w   s
      Shall I compare thee to   a summer's day?
      B   ϫ   B   o B̄   o B   o   B

Again, the relationship between the pattern of accented syllables and the underlying rhythm – still with two orderly deviations, here including an initial inversion or trochaic opening – is graphically represented, although the deviations occur in different places from those in example (1).

You might think of this form of scansion as marking places where an imaginary inner foot tapping out the underlying rhythm of a sonnet does some fancy footwork, marking almost a kind of syncopation. Or you could think of it more mathematically. An iambic pentameter line is going to have five stressed and five unstressed syllables. If the lexical stresses fall so that you have two stressed syllables in a row – as in example (1) above – you might expect this to be offset by two consecutive unstressed syllables somewhere in the line, given that you are working with only ten syllables and that half the syllables would normally be stressed. Similarly, there is what you might think of as a conservation of the underlying five-beat rhythm in the promotion of the unstressed syllable "to" in example (2).

Attridge's system thus gives us a way to represent what we actually hear. Sonnet 18 is, indeed, a sonnet in which only lines 1, 2, and 11 seem obviously to have more than one deviation from the basic contract or rules, and even those lines are relatively uncomplicated rhythmically. Nonetheless, the sonnet is not relentlessly unvaried, and the Attridge system allows us not only to acknowledge this feature of the poem, but also to specify where we hear the variations (or, to use Attridge's vocabulary, the deviations). Many scholars – I draw here on Richard Cureton and Ellen Stauder, whose works are cited at the end of this chapter – have noted that in the Renaissance, especially by Shakespeare's day, poets were increasingly interested in representing speech patterns, and the rhythms of the speaking voice often operate in tension with the metrical constraints of (to stick with the example I have been using) the sonnet. For some, this leads to a rhythmic complexity that is found interesting in its own right. My own tendency, I would add, is to think more about the affective clout (and thematic implications) of the ways the sense of a speaking voice works with and against the underlying metrical rhythms in sonnets. Yet even I would hasten to add that rhythms do not have "automatic" thematic implications. That is, even relative rhythmic complexity or simplicity might be used to different effects, depending on context.

It is useful to consider here how an attention to prosody using Attridge's system might be illuminating if we turn to the sonnet by Donne that I discussed in detail in chapter 3. To further illustrate both how Attridge's system works and how complicated even Donne's first line is, let me begin with line 1. I have noticed that when people begin trying to mark how they hear a line, they often resemble the centipede who, asked which leg he uses first, becomes overly selfconscious about the process and suddenly cannot walk. All I can do is to assure you that you *do* know how to speak English (if you are reading this book) and that you do know how to read lines of poetry out loud. You would not, for instance, say the word "batter" with the stress on the second syllable, if you were unselfconsciously reading Donne's first line. So, if you find yourself flustered when trying to write down how you hear a line, try first simply reciting the line (perhaps to a friend) before you try to transcribe what you have said.

Here, then, is how I would scan the first line of Donne's sonnet, marking above the line how I hear the lexical stress (which need not be the same way you hear the line) and marking below the line how the spoken sense of the line works with and against the standard o B o B o B o B o B rhythm of iambic pentameter:

```
s   w  w   s    s   s  w   s   w  s
Batter my heart, three-personed God; for You
B   ʊ̌     B ô B   ̌ʊ     B   o  B
```

What we have above is, first, an initial inversion condition or trochaic opening. How or why I hear "three-personed God" as I do is more complicated. You will note that I have a double offbeat (balancing the preceding implied offbeat), but one of the unstressed syllables in the double offbeat has been demoted (which is why the symbol combines a double offbeat with a demotion). I have had students ask why I would not demote "three" to indicate a less complicated line:

```
s   w  w   s       s    s   w      s    w   s
Batter my heart, three-personed God; for You
B   ö̆     B     ȯ  B   o      B    o   B
```

My answer is twofold. First, the Attridge system is not prescriptive, and we might simply disagree. Second, however, in spoken English (I draw here on generative linguistics), we usually place more relative stress on nouns, especially those that fall toward the end of phrases. So, as everyone reading the line probably would agree, the word "God" receives more lexical stress than any of the syllables in "three-personed" (something that makes both rhythmic and thematic sense). "Three-personed," however, is a compound word, and in English, in compound words, stress tends to move to the "front" of the compound. In other words, "three" would normally receive relatively more lexical stress than the first, stressed syllable of "personed." To demote "three" relative to the first syllable of "personed," then, does not represent as well the normal rhythm of the spoken line, even as the underlying metrical contract does move us toward a five- (not a six-) beat line, so one syllable – I would say the "per" in "personed" – will be demoted.

When I discussed Donne's sonnet in chapter 3, I noted his use of the imperative: "Batter," "o'erthrow . . . and bend," "make me new," "Divorce . . . untie . . . break," "Take me," "imprison me." These all *say* the speaker wants to be taken over or to lose himself in God; however, they voice this wish as a command, hardly the way to lose your self. With this context in mind, you could then also say that the predetermined metrical pattern of the sonnet, into which the language tries to, but does not easily, fit echoes the theme of trying to submerge the ego or individual within a larger pattern, namely God's pattern. Thus, it is interesting to look again at the places in Donne's poem where the perturbations of the voice and its deviations from the underlying metrical pattern are most obvious. I stated earlier the probably obvious fact that iambic pentameter lines involve ten syllables (that is, five alternations of unstressed and stressed syllables). However, if you count the syllables in the lines of Donne's poem, you will note that an unusual number of the lines have eleven – and in the case of line 9, possibly twelve – syllables. Sometimes lines of poetry just will not accommodate the underlying rhythmic pattern, but there are standard ways in which critics and poets move eleven- or twelve-syllable lines back to ten syllables by using **elision**, which is where two syllables occupy a single metrical position (normally where an unstressed vowel precedes a consonant or where one syllable ends with and the next begins with a vowel). Often anthologies (and even poets themselves) mark where this is done by using an apostrophe, as when "to another" becomes "t'another."

It is highly unlikely that Donne sat down to map out elisions (and he certainly knew nothing about Attridge's system). Still, in chapter 3 I mentioned that you might hear the whole sonnet as an attempt to subsume the "I" of the poem in the "You" of the poem, or as a struggle between pronouns. And "I," "me," and "You" are all single syllables that end in vowels, which is to say where a line using these words has "extra" syllables, these words are obvious candidates for elision. The attempt to emphasize "You" and de-emphasize "I" or "me" would in context reflect the speaker's purpose in the poem, and I assume that Donne, more famous in his lifetime for his sermons than for his poetry, would have had an ear for how this works rhetorically. The Attridge system simply allows us graphically to represent what I assume Donne would have heard without such scansion.

That said, let me turn to line 9, the volta, which is also a line where we (and the speaker) become increasingly aware of the difficulty of fitting the voice of the poem into an underlying metrical – and perhaps theological – pattern: "Yet dearly I love You, and would be loved fain." It is almost automatic that "loved" should become "lov'd," but that would still leave a line with eleven syllables. There are two places where you might elide: "dearl'I" (for "dearly I") or "Y'and" (for "You, and"). Assuming, again in context, that one would not slur over "You," the first is more likely. Listen, though, to what then happens to the line:

```
(1)  w    s w s    w    w    s    w s    s
     Yet dearl'I love You, and would be loved fain.
     o    B o B      ŏ         B    o  B ô B
```

Or you might want to represent how the speaking voice interacts with the underlying contract as follows:

```
(2)  w    s w s    w    w    s    w s    s
     Yet dearl'I love You, and would be loved fain.
     o    B  ŏ·    B̄    o    B    o  B ô B
```

I suspect example (1) is more likely – although it does not "promote" the "You" – since example (2) has the line deviating even more than example (1) from the standard underlying rhythm with an elision, a double offbeat (and one involving a demotion) followed by a promotion, and an implied offbeat. Further, the more time between the implied offbeat and the double offbeat, the more "off kilter" the line sounds. (Notice that Attridge's conditions suggest an implied offbeat will be immediately followed or preceded by a double offbeat.) In either case, however, there is a large amount of fancy footwork needed to realize the underlying contract. At very least, the distress in the voice seems audible. I will not scan more of the lines of this poem here, but I would invite you to consider the complexity of the rhythms of lines 6–10 and the relative smoothness of the last two lines of the poem (lines 13 and 14 fulfill the underlying contract without deviation except for one elision – "Y'enthrall" – in line 13) in light of my earlier question about whether at the end of the poem the speaker does or does not seem to resolve the dilemma posed in the sonnet.

I hope what I have just said gives you some idea of how the relationship between the sense of a speaking voice and the metrical contract in a poem may affect how we understand the meaning of a poem. If this were a book on prosody or rhythm I might continue to look at the textures of sound in more poems or in lines of increasing rhythmic complexity, but here I am more interested in introducing you to the multiple ways in which poems make meaning or affect us. So I want to turn to discuss two more sonnets, not in order to illustrate scansion in any systematic way (I hope the above discussion has begun to do that), but to add scansion to the other features of poems to which you can pay attention.

The first of the final two sonnets I want to examine is "To Dependence," published in 1784 in a volume called *Elegiac Sonnets* by the English writer Charlotte Smith. I am, then, looking forward in history (Smith wrote roughly a century and a half after Donne), among other things to see how later writers understood and used the sonnet. As one might expect, by the late eighteenth century some of the features associated with early modern sonnets had changed, although I think you can imagine how Smith's description of sonnets in the preface to her book – she called the form a "vehicle for a single sentiment" – could grow out of Sidney's consideration of the language of sincerity (not to mention his injunction to write from the heart), or even from Donne's use of the sonnet to represent the self's internal struggle. Smith may also look back to earlier women's sonnets. Not surprisingly, given the representation of women (loved or not) in earlier sonnets, women well before Smith wrote their own sonnets, often in response to men's representations of love and ladies. For example, Lady Mary Wroth, Sidney's niece, wrote a sonnet sequence from a woman's point of view, responding to Sidney's sonnets in *Astrophil and Stella*. Smith's audience, however, would have been a bit different from Lady Mary's. Part of why Smith's sonnet interests me is that she is a writer not only from a different period and gender but from a different walk of life than most of those whose work I discussed in the previous chapter, and I think her poem invites us to take note of this. By doing so, "To Dependence" positions us as readers a bit differently from how earlier sonnets do, and it yields to slightly different kinds of questions.

To ask these questions, it helps to know that Smith was not a court lady or an aristocrat or even well off (although she was well educated for a woman of her day). Indeed, her husband (to whom she was married at age fifteen) was imprisoned for debt and ultimately fled to France, leaving Smith to support herself and her children (she gave birth to twelve), which she did by writing not only three books of poetry but also novels and children's books. Then as now, prose sold better than the poetry, but poetry had more cachet. In any event, when in her poem Smith describes "Dependence," she is talking about economic relations and, as the prefaces she wrote made certain her readers knew, when she spoke of hardship or fraud she was speaking from personal experience, since her husband's estate was in litigation through Smith's lifetime while she, being a woman, was unable to represent herself in the ongoing lawsuits.

In general in the period, to call someone dependent most often referred to his or her status not as a minor or a woman (although married women, even if they earned money, were by law financially dependent), but as someone who had to work for a living as opposed to those with inherited money. These days, we might call someone who earns his or her own money "independent," but in the late 1700s someone of "independent" means would not have had to work for wages or a salary. Before giving you the poem, I would also note that only in the past decade or so have Smith's poems come back into print, although she was well read in her own day (many editions of *Elegiac Sonnets* appeared in her lifetime, including French and Italian translations), a circumstance that may have to do with an historical prejudice in favor of male writers, but may also – perhaps relatedly, but more subtly – have to do with Smith's thematic concerns and our modern sense of what makes a theme "important." Before saying more on this subject, though, let me give you Smith's poem:

> Dependence! heavy, heavy are thy chains,
>> And happier they who from the dangerous sea,
> Or the dark mine, procure with ceaseless pains
>> An hard-earn'd pittance – than who trust to thee!
> More blest the hind, who from his bed of flock
>> Starts! – when the birds of morn, their summons give,
> And waken'd by the lark – "the shepherd's clock"
>> Lives but to labour – labouring but to live.
> More noble than the sycophant, whose art,
>> Must heap with taudry flowers thy hated shrine;
> I envy not the meed thou canst impart
>> To crown *his* service – while, tho' pride combine
> With fraud to crush me – my unfetter'd heart
>> Still to the Mountain Nymph may offer mine.

It makes sense, as always, to begin with a closer look at the first quatrain and even the first line of this sonnet (while noting that the quatrain forms a clear unit in terms of the images, the syntax – lines 1–4 form a sentence – and the *abab* rhyme scheme). The poem opens with or as an apostrophe to dependence, which is personified, and it from the start slightly challenges some assumptions readers of earlier sonnets might bring to the poem. First, although the exclamation mark and the title ("*To* Dependence") might incline you to hear this as a poem offered to or in praise of dependence, the initial quatrain and especially line 1 quickly suggest otherwise. Dependence is imaged as a jailer (using chains). Notice, too, the smoothness of the meter; there are no deviations, nor is there rhythmic complexity in the first line we read. Obviously, my sense of the meter is drawn from my reading of the tone and content of the words, but still I might say that the voice at the start of this sonnet almost trudges through the standard iambic pentameter, before we get lines with more variation. In other words, smoothness of meter does not always indicate polish or elegance; here, the rhythm instead works well to introduce a speaker who sounds familiar with and tired out by "dependence."

If the meter at first does not necessarily bespeak elegance, some of the language in the first quatrain nonetheless sounds a bit flowery. There is the inverted syntax in "happier they," and the diction seems a bit high-flown, if verging on cliché with "ceaseless pains" and the elided "hard-earn'd pittance." The actual images, however, are curiously down-to-earth. We're told that those who work hard for low pay – seamen or fishermen (those working the "dangerous sea") or miners – are happier than those who suffer a different kind of dependence, or so it seems the speaker says when telling the personified Dependence that even manual laborers are happier "than [those] who trust to thee."

Although the celebration of independence seems a kind of commonplace to us, two more things do stand out, at least given when the poem was written. First, as I mentioned, sailors and miners would not have been considered independent in the parlance of the time. So it seems some other, more dire, form of dependence is at issue for the speaker. Of course, in earlier court cultures, courtiers were also technically dependent, and someone reading without a sense of when Smith wrote might think she is talking about the tension between the need to please court patrons and the desire for artistic freedom (or maybe even moral integrity). However, this would be a bit of a stretch since, as I mentioned, Smith's preface made clear she was anything but a courtier. We, and I suspect even more Smith's first readers, are thus invited to readjust our sense of the kind of dependence that might be at issue in this (or any) sonnet; specifically, we are, even without Smith's preface, invited to notice that a woman has written this poem. (By law married women in 1784 had no claim to their own earnings, which belonged to their husbands – placing them, indeed, in a kind of double dependence.) Alternatively, a reader unaware of who wrote this sonnet or when it was written might be tempted to think of Smith's dependence as like Wyatt's or Sidney's, that is, as the psychological dependence of unrequited love. Again, however, this seems unlikely. Smith made certain her name (and so gender) as well as her circumstances *were* known when she published her poems. Unrequited love would have been considered generally inappropriate for a female speaker, and certainly for one identified, as Smith was, as working first to pay her imprisoned husband's debts and then to support herself and her children while separated from her husband. Moreover, unrequited love hardly seems like the emotion that would affect someone in Smith's position.

I want briefly to return to my argument that the speaker's is presented as a unique form of dependence (and of labor, presumably as a writer) and is claimed as harder to bear than even the least of occupations. This is a claim we might treat with a bit of skepticism – Smith's life was arguably hard, but arguably not as hard as that of a seaman or miner – although I would note that it is surprising to find seamen and miners in a sonnet at all; they are not courtly, and they do not seem to be allegorical figures (even if Dependence is). England did, of course, have sailors and miners. Both in fact worked in economically important industries of the day, but neither economics nor lowly workers were considered poetic subjects and especially not subjects for sonnets. In sum, Smith's diction may at times be literary, but what she is describing in the first quatrain is (historically) actual physical labor, closer to home, if you will, than our references to such occupations might be, and it could be said that even as the poem deplores the speaker's "dependence" more than that of those who work for a "pittance" (the words are associated by near rhyme), it also draws on or invites an unusual (for the time) recognition of the harshness of those occupations, which gives force to the comparison.

The second quatrain, then, in some ways continues this argument, although it may be puzzling in other ways. I noted that the language of the first quatrain sounds a bit formal, even flowery, given its content. The language of the second quatrain can be seen to underline this slight tension between what is said and how it is said. Actually, for many modern readers, even the meanings of some words in lines 5–8 may be unclear: "hind," for instance, is now a little-used, formal, even poetic, term for a kind of deer; "flock" usually refers to a gathering of birds or mammals; and similarly, if "meed" (looking ahead to line 11) is now used at all, it is as a poetic or rhetorical term, usually referring to praise for excellence. Without having the whole of Smith's poem, if someone told me they were reading a poem containing the words "flock," "hind," and "meed," I would guess the poem to be a highly artificial or high literary presentation of rural existence, a conventional trope or mode I will discuss further when I talk about pastoral in chapter 7. But when I read the clause Smith has actually written in lines 5–6, I see it is unlikely that she is describing a deer sleeping on a group of other animals when she writes of "the hind, who from his bed of flock / Starts!" And when I consult the *Oxford English Dictionary*, I find that "hind" can mean a servant or agricultural laborer and "flock" can mean tufts or particles of wool or hair, or serve as a type of what is valueless or contemptible or lowly (while "meed" earlier meant "wages"). Interestingly, to judge by the quotations offered in the *Oxford English Dictionary*, the meaning of "meed" shifted to its more elevated current definition just around the time – and perhaps fostered by what – Smith was writing. Even more interesting, again to judge by the sources from which the *Oxford English Dictionary* quotes, "hind," "flock," and "meed" are words not primarily found in literary sources in Smith's day. And it useful to know where words have lived – in what kind of documents or speech they tended to appear – to hear the realm or register which a poem's use of these words invokes.

Hearing tone (and I will have more to say about tone in the next chapter) is not an exact science; for now I simply want to point out how reconstructing the way Smith's diction might have been heard in 1784 is useful if you are, as I am here, interested in how an act of historical imagination might help you to hear the poem. You might, then, put together the images of laborers in the first quatrain with the second quatrain's use of what first seemed formal or even overly elegant words. On closer inspection, we've found that in the 1780s these words would have continued the references to actual physical labor, and even to yet another economically important industry in England in the period, namely the production of wool. With all this in mind, we might reread Smith's second quatrain with a different ear. Most literally the quatrain seems to describe a farm worker, sleeping outside or at least not in a bed, waking up with the birds. In this context, living "but to labour – labouring but to live" may not sound romanticized; it seems more to say the hind earns no more than what is needed for subsistence and has no time for anything except keeping himself fed (although even so he is "more blest" than women who are dependent). That is, although there is no independent clause in the second quatrain – it is neither a full sentence nor part of a full sentence – the sentence fragment apparently continues the thought in the first quatrain, so that I might paraphrase the whole octave as saying: "Seamen and workers are happier than dependents like the speaker. Farm laborers too."

As usual, though, paraphrase does not seem to do justice to the poem. I do not think the meaning I have just proposed is wrong. And the reconstruction of words like "hind" and "flock" as bringing to mind images of ill-paid workers sleeping in the rough seems right as well. However, there are other features of this quatrain that are more rhetorically polished and sound almost courtly (although, as such, they are in tension with the subject matter). For one thing, the poem itself tells us it is quoting the image of the lark as "the shepherd's clock," and by the third printing of her book Smith added notes, one of which says the phrase is from Shakespeare. There seems also to be a slight echo, one Smith does not single out, of Shakespeare's Sonnet 29, where thoughts of a loved one change the speaker's despondent state of mind, "Like to the lark at break of day arising." And looking ahead, or drawing on a second reading, the "Mountain Nymph" in Smith's final line comes from Milton, who uses the nymph as a figure of liberty. All of this reinforces the sense that "To Dependence" draws on the language of earlier poems, the sense that the speaker sounds educated. Returning to the quotation from Shakespeare in line 7, I would say further that it is probably less important to know precisely where the phrase comes from than to know, as the quotation marks tell us, that it is a literary quotation. As an aside, I'd add that it does not *hurt* to find out – as I did, turning to Stuart Curran's notes in his edition of Smith's poems – that Shakespeare's line is from Act V, scene ii, of *Love's Labour's Lost*, and is slightly misquoted; Shakespeare describes the lark as the "ploughman's clock." My point here, however, is that line 7 has a kind of elegance suggesting a speaker who knows Shakespeare sufficiently well to wear that knowledge lightly; and line 8 also is elegantly phrased, with that chiasmus making living and labor (repeated and reversed) sound pleasing to the ear, even as what is described is no cause for celebration.

The question is: Why? Why, that is, do we have increasingly literary descriptions of not-so-literary subjects – forming a discrepancy between the language used and the subject – in the octave? Does the tone elevate the content as a kind of homage to honest if brutal work? Or do the references to work suggest that previous sonnets have thoughtlessly, as metaphor or allegory, used images of real work without considering what (thinking of Donne, for instance) a real, historical tinker's life was like? I confess I have no fully satisfactory answer, although the poem clearly gives rise to the question. I do, however, have one or two ideas about the kind of answer I might propose. The first of these might return to the idea that we are listening to a speaking voice, in a poem called "To Dependence," which – if it were by a male courtier in the sixteenth century – would most likely be a voice fretting about the difficulty of securing patronage without sacrificing integrity or artistic freedom, or about the "chains" of love. Instead, this voice surprises us by being fully capable of elegance (as capable as Wyatt or Sidney or Shakespeare) even as it talks about harsher economic realities than the earlier writers do. It may simply be that (consciously or no) Smith felt her skills as a writer needed to be displayed, not to gain patronage at court but to ensure she as a non-aristocratic woman writer would be taken seriously. This comment, of course, is not an interpretation of the poem *per se*, but a turn to cultural pressures that might explain an otherwise puzzling feature of the poem's language.

At the same time, I do think the elegance of style set against the harshness of the subject matter may work in a way more internal to the poem, although to describe how this works I need to talk about the sestet, noting first how the poem turns at line 9. I might point out that I am tacitly here suggesting that, despite the reference to Shakespeare and the *abab cdcd* rhyme scheme in lines 1–8, the end of the poem indicates we have a Petrarchan sonnet, as does one of Smith's prefaces in which she acknowledges she is trying to write "on the Italian model." I would hasten to add, though, that this is of interest not because I have a passion for classification but because Smith effectively toys with the expectation of a turn or shift in line 9, an expectation set by the form of her poem. First, the rhymes of the sestet (*efefef*) ultimately knit the last six lines together. But until line 13 one might think one has entered a third quatrain (and so be poised for a second turn into a couplet, an expectation that is not fulfilled). Second, the anaphoric openings of lines 5 and 9 ("More . . . More") work much the same way, apparently knitting together the second quatrain with the lines following line 8, for a moment suggesting they will form a similar unit, a third quatrain. However, the *sense* of lines 9–14 and the kinds of references that enter the poem (what you might call the register or range of the voice) do shift at line 9.

The comparisons in the octave are framed so that we are told who is "happier" or "more blest" before we know than whom seamen, miners, or agricultural workers are happier or more blest; indeed, the less blest (who trust dependence) are not even mentioned in the second quatrain, which as I mentioned says in essence "Farm workers too." Syntactically, then, we are prepared to read the next sentence fragment (lines 9 and 10 are set off by a semi-colon) as "Sycophants, too." But of course that is not what the lines say, and we need not only to shift registers (sycophants – servile flatterers and a common topic in works about courtiership – would seem to re-place us in the court setting the octave refused us), but also to rethink how the syntax works. Who, we might ask, is more noble than the syco-phant? The laborers of the octave, presumably, although for a moment (if we read lines 9–11 as a tercet), we might also think that line 11's "I" (the first use of the first-person singular in the poem) is the subject of compari-son: "More noble than the sycophant . . . I." The semi-colon at the end of line 10 rules out this reading, but surely we are invited to contemplate the possibility, given that the syntax is fractured; line 9 is, after all, a sentence fragment and flirts with but finally does not continue the pattern of telling us who is "happier" or "more blest."

In short, the grammar of lines 9–10 is confusing. The rest of the sestet similarly gives the impression of a voice that is less polished than that heard in the octave, despite the turn to references that, at least until the final line of the poem, seem to recall courtly settings. It is the coherence of this shift, in part, that inclines me to see the elegance of the octave's style (but not content) as purposefully balanced again the elegance of the sestet's setting (but not style). Moreover, the image of a flatterer's art bringing flowers to the "shrine" of dependence seems in ways self-referential. That is, the image suggests that the courtier's flowery language (in sonnets, for one) presumably paid homage to dependence, either on a lover (a traditional Petrarchan conceit) or more tacitly on a patron. The speaker in "To Depen-dence" dismisses that form of ambition (the shrine is explicitly "hated" and the "flowers" – metaphorically, flowery language – are explicitly "taudry"). "Taudry" (or "tawdry") is an interesting word here: literally, it means "tastelessly showy," "shoddy," or "cheap." My etymological dictionary tells me the word comes from a contraction of "St. Audrey's lace," a form of cheap lace. Smith certainly did not consult an etymological dictionary; however, the connotations of the word "taudry" still come packaged with the word, which is thus a mark of class (this is cheap lace, tasteless, even if showy) and also feminized (not only does it refer to lace, but buried in the word is St. Audrey's name).

Let me pause here to take stock of what the above discussion has done to my understanding of the poem's unfolding meaning or gathering argu-ment through line 12. I have a speaker who obviously can write flowery poetry (or so the elegance evident in the movement from the negative apostrophe to Dependence to the chiasmic description of the farm worker would suggest). The speaker's elegance is not, however, being used in any obvious way to seduce a lover or impress a patron, and the subject matter – hard, underpaid physical labor, which is a form of economic dependence but is nonetheless said to be better than the speaker's dependence – is sur-prising both because it is unusual in a sonnet and because it seems not to be in keeping with the polished writing. In the sestet, then, it seems that the kind of elegance traditionally used by male lovers and courtiers is explicitly imaged as cheap, feminized finery. If so, the poem uses something like sarcasm. That is, the elegantly posed images of "lowly" occupations (seamen, miners, agricultural laborers) are set against an image of a "higher" occupation (placing flowers on Dependence's shrine is at least in part an image from courtly life and perhaps courtly love), but the use of the adjective "taudry" implies that what seems "higher" is actually cheaper – and less "manly," to use the vocabulary of the period – than what is usually more socially or publicly despised.

Further, when the voice of the sonnet shifts at line 9, and begins using syntax that is increasingly difficult to parse, the speaker appears to be casting about for what to say. That is, the *content* of the sestet seems more traditionally sonnet-like, with flowers, shrines, service, perhaps court intrigue or some civic analog of that (with "pride" and "fraud" and "sycophants"), but the *voice* seems less courtly. Again, there is almost a conceptual chiasmus in the poem: an elegant treatment of economic hardship is repeated and reversed with a more stumbling treatment of what would usually be more refined or literary images: art, flowers, and shrines (not to mention mountain nymphs). This is not to deny that the sestet's individual images and phrasing are still quite polished in places. For example, to say that Dependence a "meed . . . canst impart" is more formal than, for example, saying Dependence pays a "pittance," although both line 4 and line 11 are about wages paid. Formal diction or no, however, it is difficult to parse the grammar. In addition to the sentence fragment in lines 9 and 10, the use of pronouns is confusing. I take it the "thou" of line 10 must be Dependence, who is addressed throughout the poem, although the pronoun's distance from the last mention of the noun to which it refers is grammatically awkward (the last use of "thee" is six lines earlier and the noun, "Dependence," appears a full nine lines earlier). The reference of "*his*" ("*his* service" is crowned by what Dependence gives him) is also at first difficult to figure out, although the word is underlined by Smith, presumably both to distinguish the "thou" from the "he" and perhaps – since on consideration "his" can only refer us back to "the sycophant" – further to dismiss flatterers, as when we say "Oh, *him*" (using emphasis when we speak in order to dismiss or elevate, depending on the context).

The meter, I would add, underlines the awkwardness or perhaps the speaking quality of the voice by line 12, as well:

```
w    s     s    s w    w     w     s    w    s
To crown his service – while, tho' pride combine
o    B ô  B ô B        ᵛ̆                B    o    B
```

The emphasized *"his"* makes it implausible that we will demote the stress on that word (or promote the relatively unstressed "while"), resulting in a good deal of negotiation between the voice and the underlying o B o B o B o B o B meter (as the line involves not only an implied offbeat between the stressed syllable "crown" and the explicitly emphasized *"his,"* but also a triple offbeat following). I am given a sense of a speaking voice, and I hear the voice as less elegant and the speaker as casting about for what she wants to say, then, through the metrical deviations, the difficult-to-assign pronouns, the pause before the voice begins a dependent clause that is interrupted by an aside ("while, tho' pride combine / With fraud to crush me –"), and the puzzling placement of the dashes, the first of which seems as if it should come after, not before, "while."

Moreover, the last line and a half of "To Dependence" does not make it any easier for us to untangle the syntax. I think you can see that an "unfetter'd heart" is one without chains, which satisfyingly returns us to the opening image of Dependence's chains, now – equally satisfyingly – apparently cast off. And a knowledgeable reader of poetry might recall that Milton includes a "mountain nymph, sweet Liberty" in line 36 of "L'Allegro," his poem praising the active life and the companion poem to "Il Penseroso." Those hearing the echo of Milton will presumably then further hear the speaker's claim that she is at liberty, not chained by Dependence. At the same time, I assume it would take *any* reader of the sonnet a minute or so to figure out the reference of "mine," the last word of the poem. Obviously, since the speaker's heart is offering something to the Mountain Nymph (she says, "my . . . heart / . . . to the . . . Nymph may offer mine") one needs to go back three lines and past the interpolated mention of what is crushing the speaker to realize that "mine" is opposed to *"his* service." It is presumably her service the speaker offers (or may, that is, is free to, offer) to the Mountain Nymph, but it takes a moment to see this. The obvious question is "why?" or "to what effect?"

First, it seems that despite the apparent proclamation of freedom and the resolution of the problem – namely, dependence – the poem does not ultimately allow us a sense of a comfortable solution or resolution; we've had to work too hard to figure out what is being said. Notice I am not saying that the poem is badly written but that there is a point to the awkwardness (as there was in both Sidney's and Donne's poems). More generally, instead of being frustrated by or dismissing passages that make you work to figure out what is being said, you might step back to ask why this happens. Second, if you do step back and think about what has been said (such reappraisals being rather familiar gestures in sonnets from Wyatt to Donne), Smith seems to leave what kind of freedom she can claim deliberately unclear. It is not a life or person that is unchained, just a heart. Moreover, Mountain Nymphs, whether they come from Milton or from mythology, are not the kind of creatures you meet every day. More seriously put, in a poem that opens with references to historically concrete occupations – at sea, in mines, with pains and labor – the allegorization of "Liberty," unlike that of Dependence, places us outside the very real historical world mentioned in the octave ... a world that is probably also invoked in the references to "pride" and "fraud," given Smith's frustrations with the legal complications that would not release her father-in-law's money to support her or her children. To put it bluntly, nymphs rest uneasily in law courts. And that may be the point.

In short, Smith has taken the gestures and subjects of previous sonnets to heart; in particular, she might be said to translate the consciousness of thought and feeling in early love poems, eventually figured as inner, spiritual turmoil in sonnets like Donne's, when she ends her sonnet distinguishing the outer world of chains and labor from an inner world of art, which (thematically) she is claiming as an aesthetic world, or perhaps a therapeutic world – in any case, a world in which her art (aligned with her heart, or inner self) serves nothing outside itself. Someone looking for activism in poetry will not find it in Smith's sonnet, or not straightforwardly, although there is arguably a form of realism involved in the tacit recognition that sonnets, like nymphs, probably will not win lawsuits or put food on the table (even if they may, nonetheless, affect feeling, which is to say that if one's life is lived in chains there may be some value in feeling one's heart is "unfetter'd"). Indeed, although in this imaginary argument I am constructing over the politics of Smith's poem someone could counter that she in fact sold her writing precisely to feed herself (serving not patrons or a lover but the market), the fact remains that her poems did not make money in the way her novels did. So it is not really disingenuous of Smith to offer her poem (from the heart) to an imagined figure of inner freedom (the Mountain Nymph); the very act of imagining the nymph illustrates the power claimed for imagination. I suppose an even lengthier and more clever reading might in turn consider whether – the Nymph being originally Milton's – there is not also in Smith's poem some ambition, some bid for continued literary fame or life, for which she indicates she does not need a Shakespeare, being able to write her own lines (unlike the women loved in earlier sonnets by male poets).

I was once told that a good analysis answers three questions: "What do you know?" "How do you know it?" and "So what?" Most of this book concentrates on how to answer the first two questions when reading poems. The previous paragraph, however, begins to broach the last question, namely, what is entailed by what you have read. Such questions may be the most interesting questions we can ask. And asking them may ultimately be part of why we read poems, which is to say we think what they have to say matters or has significance, although I hope it is clear I think that, before asking what is at stake or raising more theoretical, political, or psychological questions about a poetic statement, you should listen carefully to precisely what is said.

Such listening might also include thinking about the historical context in which a poem was written. I began discussing Smith's poem by noting that her work has only recently come back into print or favor. This may be because the relatively recent fashion of reading poetry in its historical context has given us tools with which to ask the questions that reveal what is most interesting about sonnets like "To Dependence." That is, rather than dismissing Smith's poem as soft-minded or overly sentimental, or awkward, we can notice that she interestingly bears witness not only to the condition of non-aristocrats and of women in the late eighteenth century, but also to her period's increasing interest in psychology and in feeling (to what is sometimes called "the cult of feeling or sentiment"), which not coincidentally arose on the eve of the industrial revolution. Smith's poem, in short, gives voice or body to such abstractions of intellectual and literary history.

Whole books could be written on the kinds of questions to which Smith's poem gives rise. Here, however, I want to turn to and conclude with the discussion of another, slightly later sonnet, "Ozymandias" by Percy Bysshe Shelley, a poem that also includes history and also yields interestingly to questions about the historical pressures of its time. We know Shelley wrote his sonnet in late December 1817, in friendly competition with a friend, Horace Smith, who also wrote a sonnet entitled "Ozymandias." Both poems may have been prompted by a magazine review of a book on travels in Egypt (although Shelley read a great many travel books, several of which may inform the poem). While there has been much ink spilled over the exact sources for the poem, to start it suffices to know that Napoleon invaded Egypt in 1798, ostensibly to liberate the Egyptians from the Ottoman Empire but certainly also to make British access to India difficult, and that he left, after being defeated by the British navy, in 1799. Napoleon's venture into Egypt, though short-lived and unsuccessful in military terms, nonetheless yielded a flood of information about the country from the scientists and artists who accompanied the French forces, and, although Egypt did not officially become part of the British Empire until well after Shelley's death, England did maintain a presence in Egypt that continued the flow of information and plunder from Egypt to Britain, including Egyptian antiquities acquired and still owned by the British Museum.

The title of Shelley's poem, "Ozymandias," however, refers not to the Ottoman, French, or British empires, but to the earlier (thirteenth-century BCE) reign of an infamous Egyptian pharaoh, Ramses (sometimes known as Ramesses) II, whom the Greeks called Ozymandias or Osymandias (as the Greek is usually rendered in English). Simply reading the title, then, alerts us to the poem's interest in political leaders (Shelley, whose radical politics were well known, might have said "tyrants" rather than "leaders") and, although we might not notice at first, alerts us as well to how even those whose reigns were long (as Ramses' was) are subject to being renamed by other or later cultures. Here, then, is the poem:

> I met a traveller from an antique land,
> Who said – "Two vast and trunkless legs of stone
> Stand in the desert . . . near them, on the sand,
> Half sunk a shattered visage lies, whose frown,
> And wrinkled lips, and sneer of cold command,
> Tell that its sculptor well those passions read
> Which yet survive, stamped on these lifeless things,
> The hand that mocked them, and the heart that fed;
> And on the pedestal, these words appear:
> My name is Ozymandias, King of Kings,
> Look on my Works, ye Mighty, and despair!
> Nothing beside remains. Round the decay
> Of that colossal Wreck, boundless and bare
> The lone and level sands stretch far away." —

The opening of this sonnet seems relatively straightforward, at least semantically, syntactically, and metrically, although within the first two lines we can tell there is an **embedded narrative** and a **frame narrative**, which is to say we are being told a story of how (in the frame narrative) the speaker was told a story (the embedded narrative), which we are then told, second-hand (or perhaps third-hand). The choice of the word "antique" is also interesting; as opposed to the apparent synonym "ancient," "antique" has the connotation of something long gone (not just long-lasting), as well as of something perhaps out-of-date. The story thus raises a few questions from the start. On the one hand, the speaker seems to lay claim to first- (or second-) hand knowledge, saying he got his story from someone who was there. On the other hand, the traveler almost appears to be a time-traveler. At least, the land he is said to be from may no longer be around; it is "antique."

To say all this is not even to mention the fact that the story is clearly fictional, even if it invites us to think otherwise. That is, despite the poem's references to an historical figure (Ramses) and its use of a country (Egypt) very much part of current events in 1817, there could have been no such traveler whom Shelley as author met, because there was no statue of the sort described standing in Shelley's day (a statue of Ramses found across the Nile from Luxor had, according to the Napoleonic army sources, no legs left by the early nineteenth century; in any case, most Egyptian statues were of seated figures and none would have had detailed facial expressions). In 1817, the best-known statue of Ramses had no inscription (the one quoted later in the poem is something about which Shelley could have learned, directly or indirectly, only from classical sources); indeed, had there been an inscription, it would have been indecipherable, since the Rosetta Stone, which allowed later scholars to read Egyptian hieroglyphics, had only just been discovered and not yet decoded. It is even unclear whether we are to imagine the inscription as being in Egyptian hieroglyphics, given the Anglicized Greek form of Ramses' name. Whose inscription we are to imagine, in short, is increasingly in question. For the moment, though, looking at the first quatrain, we can say we have an author (Shelley) telling the story of a speaker ("I") telling the story of a traveler (about whom we know only that he is "from an [ambiguously] antique land"). *Our* information is thus fourth-hand. Yet if we know little of the traveler, his is the primary voice we hear, and what we hear in the first quatrain continues to sound at first relatively straightforward: a description of parts of a giant statue reduced to legs, a face, a frown.

True, the rhymes throughout the poem are complicated (not least because Shelley uses half rhyme, as in "stone" and "frown"); still, just as the traveler seems able to decipher the lineaments of Ramses' (that is, Ozymandias') statue, we can see we have the lineaments of what most critics agree is a Petrarchan sonnet. The half rhymes in the first quatrain are counter-balanced by the full and internally repeated rhymes of "land," "stand," and (surprisingly, given the apparent solidity of sound and reference in "land" and "stand") "sand." We then hear "command," which sounds not just solid but intimidating (as the description is of a "wrinkled lip, and sneer of cold command"). The continuation of the rhyme from the first quatrain initially sets our expectation that we have a Petrarchan sonnet, as well, although the second quatrain unexpectedly launches a new rhyme scheme after line 5. In this way, if we think we know how sonnets work, or are accustomed to the gestures and movements of sonnets, we are thrown off balance because "things" (at the end of line 7) refuses to rhyme with "command."

At the same time, you could argue that thematically the poem thus makes us align Ozymandias' command with the "lifeless things" of line 7, suggesting, as does the condition of the statue, that such command is no longer living. (Nor, perhaps, are the structures of sonnets, although most readers find themselves poised waiting to find what rhymes with "things," an expectation not fulfilled until line 10 in the sestet.) This sense of waiting to see what will happen or how something left unresolved will resolve is fostered also by the syntax. Notice, for instance, that we have a single sentence, albeit one with multiple dependent clauses, that runs from line 1 through the end of line 11. At least through line 8, moreover, most lines are heavily enjambed, so that we are left hanging (if also compelled forward) by the lack of syntactical closure at the end of the lines. Similarly, the ellipsis in line 2, as if the traveler pauses to think about what to say next, for a second almost visually suggests that the parts of the reconstructed story are as dispersed as the parts of the statue.

Indeed, discussing the first quatrain, I noted we have a poem that seems not just to tell a story but to be in part *about* telling stories: Shelley tells us of a speaker who tells us of a traveler who tells us a story. By the second quatrain, we see the traveler's story is not just his story; the embedded narratives continue, at least to judge by the prevalence of words that keep our attention on the act of fiction-making. Notice that in the second quatrain, the statue's facial features "tell" us something about a sculptor who "read" something (namely "passions"). In other words, what we know is actually sixth-hand: we have the sculptor's story of passions told by his statue, about which we are told by a traveler, about whom we are told by a speaker, who is given to us by Shelley. Since the poem underlines this telling and re-telling, the act of storytelling seems indeed central. It may even be that the narrative drive of the poem (the way we are moved from one thing to the next, as we are by riveting stories) is also emphasized by the way we are invited to keep reading to find what rhymes with "things," by the long single sentence that spans the usual turn at line 9 (which here begins with the word "and," instead of the usual "but" or "yet"), and by the use of enjambment.

Yet by line 8, and perhaps throughout lines 6, 7, and 8, the syntax is also difficult. Most scholars agree that "hand" and "heart" in line 8 are the direct objects of the verb "survive" in line 7. I cannot see how else to make grammatical sense of these lines, although it is clear that the lines do trip us up or at least stop our forward reading. We are clearly told that the sculptor was a good reader of the passions he sculpted (the passions he "stamped on these lifeless [that is, shattered stone] things"). However, I suspect most of us will first assume that these passions survive in their artistic recreation, perhaps thinking back to the familiar trope used in Shakespeare's Sonnet 18, about how art makes things and people last. Reading "Ozymandias," however, we then have to pause as we read line 8 – "The hand that mocked them, and the heart that fed" – and to go back to line 7 to see that "survive" means not "to last" but "to outlive" (and hands and hearts are what the passions outlive). "The hand that mocked" the passions (and which the passions outlive) is presumably the sculptor's hand. I say this both because the face of the pharaoh sketched in Shelley's poem suggests a less than flattering portrait (what with the wrinkled lip and the sneer) and because "to mock" in 1817 could mean not only "to ridicule" but also "to create an imitation of reality." So the sculptor's hand "mocked" Ozymandias in both senses of the word, even as the ridiculed passions survive the "mock-up" or statue of them. When I first read this poem I found myself confused by what it would mean for Ozymandias' passions to survive him (taking, as I still take, the heart in question to be Ozymandias' heart, which fed his passions). I am not certain I have yet wholly understood the implications of this claim, but I think I can say at least that the poem indicates the kind of passions Ozymandias presumably felt (contempt for others, a sense of superiority, a desire to dominate) did not disappear from the world when Ozymandias died.

You might notice, too, that in light of earlier sonnets – about how love does not die or about how the soul does not die – this is a new claim for a sonnet to make (if not a new claim about human nature). Still, the claim is not simply that tyrannical passions persist (even if this claim is brought to mind, and probably begins to implicate the Ottomans, and perhaps Napoleon and the British as well). The larger claim seems to be that artists know how to read these kinds of passions, which in turn (in the context the poem provides) means not just that artists can reveal or celebrate feeling (as in Charlotte Smith's poem) but that artists know how to judge feelings, in this case judging them unattractive or (and by) mocking them. Moreover, this point seems to be what lines 9 through 11 (the first tercet) build upon. That is, I assume we are to imagine the words said to be on the statue as commissioned by the pharaoh (and, indeed, we have a classical source telling us there was once an inscription that read "I am Ozymandias, king of kings. If anyone would know how great I am and where I lie, let him surpass any of my works"). Historically and fictionally, Ozymandias' inscription clearly was intended as a boast about his power and greatness being both unsurpassable and long-lived. In Shelley's poem, however, the ironies imposed on this boaster by history are clear and are hammered home by the slant rhyme of "appear" and "despair" as well as by the way the rhyme of "kings" with "lifeless things" recalls for us the ruins – the new appearance – of those boasted "Works." We can presume Ozymandias thought other, less mighty, rulers would despair of reaching the height of his power. In light of the demise of not only his kingdom (now "antique") but even of his monument (by line 13, a "colossal Wreck"), however, his words have come to have almost the opposite of their (presumably) intended meaning. They now suggest that anyone hoping for such power should despair because it does not last. In other words, not only is this a (sixth-hand) story about how well the anonymous sculptor read and criticized the passions of the powerful, it is also a story about how history is not a story with an unchanging or predictable plot line. Ozymandias' pride and certainty about the reach of his power are ultimately "mocked" in lines 9–11 by Shelley, who thus positions himself as another artist who reads well (and unmasks the false pretensions of) tyrannical passions.

Let me digress for a moment to talk about what some students who have read this poem with me have proposed, namely that biblical echoes in the phrase "King of Kings," and the formality of "ye" in "ye Mighty," made them think the poem invoked religious matters (perhaps juxtaposing earthly power with higher power). I simply want to say here what I have said to those students, namely that this is not a dumb or even an anachronistic suggestion. After all, in Donne's poems (and indeed in Petrarch's) higher powers *were* at issue. However, Shelley's simple declarative statement, "Nothing beside remains," seems not to allow us to do much with that possible religious register. If you read biographies of Shelley, as well, you will find that he at several points in his life publicly declared himself an atheist (and indeed was expelled from college for that reason). In short, to think there might be a biblical reference seems at first plausible. It is finally ruled out (I believe) simply because it does not carry through in any other way in the poem, and reading more of Shelley's works further weakens the idea that there is a religious theme in or informing the poem. In short, to consider the apparent echo is a digression – one that seems not to lead in interesting directions. I still mention it here, however, because this is a book about how to read poems. And when reading poems, given the richness of reference typical in poetic language, even the most practiced reader will on occasion set off down a blind alley. It seems to me dishonest to pretend that some questions do not come to mind which turn out to be unpromising or uninteresting in the long run. In fact, this is why I frequently pause to run through (or take stock of where asking questions about specific word choices or passages leaves me in) a broader view of a poem's gathering meaning.

I want in fact to try just such an exercise after raising a final question about how to read the tone or voice and implications of the final tercet of

Shelley's sonnet. Lines 12 and 13, I would add, are fairly complicated metrically; line 12, for instance, despite the simplicity of the syntax, does not easily accommodate the usual underlying metrical contract:

```
s    w   w s   w   s     s    w   w s
Nothing beside remains. Round the decay [enjambed line . . .]
B    ŏ   B   o  B ô   B     ŏ    B
```

Line 13 is slightly less complex, but still not simple (and still strongly enjambed):

```
w    s   w s   w   s      s    w   w   s
Of that colossal Wreck, boundless and bare
o    B  o B  o   B ô   B     ŏ    B
```

The final line of "Ozymandias," however, is perfectly regular. Moreover, the diction is simple, as well, with most of the words being monosyllabic and not Latinate. In terms of sound, then, the poem ends soothingly, as if the voice has resolved whatever difficulties it had. Yet it is not clear that "Ozymandias" has a speaking voice – or a characterized speaker – in the way that most of the other earlier sonnets discussed have had. It appears from the closing quotation marks that we are to understand the last tercet as part of the traveler's reported story; and yet, as I noted earlier, the traveler is in some ways the least realized character in the poem. Finally, too, the apparent moral (and the moral many readers draw from this poem) is not all that soothing, whoever its source. That is, on one reading, the poem simply widens its angle of vision to suggest that nothing on earth lasts, that the sands (as with the sands of time) will finally level everything, perhaps even Shelley's poem and the remaining fragments of the sculptor's art, along with Ozymandias' less savory works.

I could stop discussing the Shelley poem here, leaving it as a poem about how everything – the bad but perhaps also the good – will pass, a kind of riposte to or recasting of the claims of poems like Shakespeare's Sonnet 18. But this seems to me to ignore two important features of the poem that I mentioned above. First, there is that comment about how the sculptor could read well, which seems to make a claim for art somewhat at odds with the above interpretation of the poem's ending. That is (taking stock of the whole poem's movements and assuming there is a turn in line 11, as there seems to be), it is not clear to me why history's falsifications of

Ozymandias' claims would lead the speaker to revise his earlier claim that the sculptor's images survive: the sculptor, unlike Ozymandias, is said to have truths to tell that have not been eroded or changed. More importantly, the poem really does seem as much about storytelling as about the lust for power by tyrants, although the two subjects may be related. Indeed, the word "level" in the last line, which may to us seem an image of the razing of all human structures or endeavors, was a far more politicized word in Shelley's day, when it was used in political treatises about democracy (going back even further than the debates over the French Revolution to which Shelley, although born too late to have been part of that upheaval, paid close attention). In other words, the image of the leveling sands is at least as plausibly an image of the specific downfall of social and political hier-archies (including tyranny) as it is an image of the ephemeral nature of all human creations.

One way, then, of reinterpreting the end of "Ozymandias" is to suggest that those bare sands are more like a blank slate than a vision of apocalypse. Given the poem's emphasis on how stories on the one hand seem to catch us by the throat, leading us inexorably forward, and on the other hand can be told and retold with quite different meanings (Ozymandias', the sculptor's, the traveler's, Shelley's . . . and ours), one could hear the poem as unmasking the apparently given nature of all stories that seem as if they were set in stone (including literary histories and the official histories of social or political orders). While this still sug-gests that no poet could control the way his or her work would be read in the future, it also underlines how we as readers have voices of our own. Indeed, as we interpret poems we in effect are retelling them or making them our own (as I am here rereading the thematic center of "Ozymandias").

Of course, it is not quite this simple. Shelley *is* using a set form (the sonnet) to question set forms. He even seems aware that this may simply re-inscribe the set patterns, patterns which (in what is said as much as in the de-formation of the sonnet) he challenges. After all, there is a claim made that some readings are better than others (the sculptor, we are told, read "well"). And presumably if Shelley thought all inscribed meaning could be changed (by future readers and by shifts in historical contexts), the thematic claim for the open-endedness of stories would be at odds with an apparent desire to have *that* claim read "well." Most simply, the tension might be put as follows. If Shelley insists on the importance of not thinking messages or authorial intentions or set patterns of meaning endure for ever, should we as readers believe him? If we do believe him – taking this as his message – do we not disprove the very point being made, in that his message seems indeed to have endured? At very least, my attention to the historical contexts (such as British expansion and the currency in the circles Shelley frequented of the radical ideals of the French Revolution, despite British resistance and despite the Napoleonic aftermath) may make my reading appear at first to be most unShelleyan, in that it does not reread Shelley in light of twenty-first-century history (which, ironically, on what I take to be Shelley's account, perhaps it should).

Given this final set of puzzling issues, I obviously do not presume that every reader will happily accept what I have suggested in the two paragraphs above. Yet I would note that the kinds of questions I have raised about how poems live or are changed in history are questions that Shelley in his prose actually did struggle to address, not simply as questions about literary history but (indeed) about the larger cultural, political, and social stories in and by the light of which we live. Perhaps paradoxically, then, I conclude by suggesting that to hear the tone of the concluding line as a call for (or an opening of the possibility of) agency and change, for writing anew on those blank sands, is after all quite Shelleyan. Yet for you to retell the story of "Ozymandias" in your own way would be equally so.

I have mentioned tone several times, both as a dramatic effect of a poem's speaker and as depending on, among other things, syntactical constructions and word choices. I have not, however, said much about how we recognize tone, a nuance of language that some people intuitively seem to recognize, while others seem to be more tone deaf. The next chapter will consider three poems in which tone is crucial (beginning with yet another sonnet, but moving to other kinds of poem) to talk in more detail about ways of discussing and of discerning tone.

Terms used

accent	dactyl
accentual verse	duple feet
accentual-syllabic verse	elision
alliterative meter	embedded narrative
amphimacer	frame narrative
anapest	initial inversion condition
Attridge's system	lexical stress
beat–offbeat scansion	meter

prosody   scansion
pyrrhic   spondee
quantitative meter   versification
rhythm

Other poems that might be read

Edmund Spenser, Sonnet 15, in *Amoretti* (1595)
William Shakespeare, Sonnet 29 (published 1609)
William Shakespeare, Sonnet 129 (published 1609)
Lady Mary Wroth, "False Hope which Feeds but to Destroy" (*c.*1621)
John Milton, "To Mr. H. Lawes, On His Airs" (1645)
Thomas Gray, "Sonnet On the Death of Mr. Richard West" (1742)
Charlotte Smith, "Written in the Church Yard at Middleton in Sussex" (1789)
William Wordsworth, "Nuns Fret Not at Their Convent's Narrow Room" (1807)
John Keats, "On First Looking into Chapman's Homer" (1816)
John Keats, "When I Have Fears" (1818)
Gwendolyn Brooks, "Gay Chaps at the Bar" (1944)
Adrienne Rich, "Twenty-one Love Poems," VII (*c.*1974)
William Stafford, "Afterwards" (1993)

Useful further reading

Derek Attridge, *The Rhythms of English Poetry* (London: Longman, 1982).
Derek Attridge, *Poetic Rhythm: An Introduction* (Cambridge: Cambridge University Press, 1995).
Richard Cureton, *Rhythmic Phrasing in English Verse* (London: Longman, 1992).
Harvey Gross and Robert McDowell, *Sound and Form in Modern Poetry* (Ann Arbor, Mich.: University of Michigan Press, 1996).
Paul Kiparsky, "Stress, Syntax, and Meter," *Language*, vol. 51 (1975): 576–616.
Paul Kiparsky, "The Rhythmic Structure of English Verse," *Linguistic Inquiry*, vol. 8 (1977): 189–247.
Mark Liberman and Alan Prince, "On Stress and Linguistic Rhythm," *Linguistic Inquiry*, vol. 8 (1977): 249–336.
M. L. Rosenthal and Sally Gall, eds., "Beat–Offbeat Scansion," *Poetry in English: An Anthology* (New York: Oxford University Press, 1987): 1161–70.
Percy Bysshe Shelley, *The Poems of Shelley*, vol. 2: *1817–1819*, ed. Kelvin Everest and Geoffrey Matthews (Harlow, Essex: Longman, 2000).

Ellen Keck Stauder, "INTRA: Interactive Tutorial on Rhythm Analysis," <http://academic.reed.edu/english/intra/> (13 July 2006).

Charlotte Smith, *The Poems of Charlotte Smith*, ed. Stuart Curran (New York: Oxford University Press, 1993).

Chapter 5

The Form of the Voice:
Tone and Diction

in Robert Frost's "Design" (1936), Frank O'Hara's
"The Day Lady Died" (1959), and Elizabeth
Bishop's "Filling Station" (1965)

The sense of listening to a speaking voice is often central to our experience of poems. This is true not only of the first-person sonnets read in chapters 3 and 4, but also of poems where a character (one we are not invited to identify with the author of the poem) is presented as the speaker, as in a dramatic monologue or dramatic lyric or mask lyric – all mentioned in the first chapter's discussion of William Carlos Williams's "To Greet a Letter-Carrier." Hearing tone of voice, then, can be crucial to understanding poetry . . . as it is when you are in face-to-face conversation with a friend (where you need to be able to tell whether someone is being sarcastic or serious, for instance); tone is, after all, frequently how we gather social information (figuring out someone's attitude toward us or others). In general, we successfully hear what people are saying, parsing the tone without even stopping to consider how we do so. Indeed, the previous chapters have already mentioned tone frequently; it is difficult if not impossible to hear what a poem is saying *without* talking about tone. Still, as with scansion, we may be better at hearing tone of voice before we stop to think than we are, at least at first, when we are asked to spell out which features of language are affecting us. In the final analysis, there are no absolute rules either in life or in poetry that certify what the tone of an utterance is, although context (and a few suggestions taken from linguists' study of English usage) can help.

To begin with what linguistics can tell us about tone of voice, most linguists identify four levels of language: **formal** (this would include various forms of serious written expression or discourse), **informal** (polite but everyday conversation, for example), **colloquial** (more casual or garden variety usage), and **slang** (running the gamut from "dissing" someone to "computerese," which is to say the language of some specialized professional or social group). These levels are usually marked by **diction** or word choice and **style**, including **syntax**, which is to say how sentences are put together. (I base my discussion here on the books by Marie Borroff and David Crystal listed at the end of this chapter, to which you might turn if you are interested.) Diction is a matter of context and usage as well as word length and word origin. For instance, to say "He realized his dream" is relatively formal diction: "realize" is not often used in speech this way; it is Latinate (coming from Latin by way of Old French), and it has three syllables. However, if you say "I *realize* that" (and slam the door behind you, after someone tells you you've made an obvious mistake, for example), it is more likely colloquial, or at least informal. Similarly, contractions – by virtue of usage – are usually informal, colloquial, or slang.

Normally, and admitting context counts, as you move from longer words to shorter words, and from classical Greek or Latin roots to archaic usage (like "thou" or "whilom") to Romance roots (say, "cartel," from French and Italian) to Germanic roots (the word "back," for example) to regional ("lagniappe" [alternatively spelled "lagnappe"], used in the southern United States, from a Creole mix of French, Spanish, and Queshua) to words you make up (**neologisms** or coinages, including jargon like "spamming") you are moving from formal to informal to colloquial to slang. **Idioms** or clichés are generally colloquial or slang – in expressions like "to beat the band," or "barking up the wrong tree," or "it's the real thing." (Idioms are expressions that cannot be translated, the meaning of the phrase being different from the meaning the words by themselves might suggest.) Thinking of context again, even if you have long Latinate words, if you are using an idiom or cliché it will sound less formal, as in, for instance, "Honesty is the best policy." We tend to hear sentences composed of words derived from Germanic languages as simplicity of diction, and, as in the Sidney poem discussed in earlier chapters, we tend to hear (or read) simplicity as sincerity. Some people would also say we hear specificity or concreteness as more informal, less elevated (if you say "A monarch settled on my camellias" as opposed to "A butterfly settled on my flowers," for instance). It also matters where a word has lived before and with whom or what it has been associated. So the line "Rocks, Caves, Lakes, Fens, Bogs, Dens, and shades of Death" is elevated (it is blank verse and right out of

Milton, word length and Anglo-Saxon roots notwithstanding). Similarly, "a voice that cries in the wilderness" (which has unobtrusive Latin roots – "voice," "cry" – and the Old English-derived "wilderness" as well as primarily one-syllable words) is still formal because of where it has lived, namely the Bible.

Finally, if a poet combines words differing from each other in diction, this feature of the poem will often compete for attention with the poem's discursive sequence or narrative, sounding less like voice than like texture, as in a collage. For instance, Wallace Stevens's poem "Things of August" includes the following phrase: "The honky-tonk out of the somnolent grasses." Who is talking? Well, it doesn't sound like someone *talking*. And the mixed diction may be why: "Honky-tonk" is American slang (origin unknown); "somnolent" is Latinate; "grasses" comes from Old English. The words are of different lengths. Where you would expect to find them is in quite different contexts. "Honky-tonk" sounds like Hank Williams, which is to say American country music; "somnolent" is rarely used, but sounds a bit like nineteenth-century poetry; "grasses" is a word that might live anywhere, but it is more likely informal, although it is generic rather than specific, although there is also a slight echo of Whitman's *Leaves of Grass*, which elevates it even though it is a short word derived from Old English. You can tell this isn't an exact science – and context really does matter. Still, normal usage suggests the line from Stevens's poem mixes diction.

Style involves not only context, as above, but also elements like grammar, sentence structure (numbers of dependent clauses, for instance), and rhetorical flourishes or tropes, including inverted word order or repetition. Complex sentence structures (using compound predicates, for example), standard grammar, overt use of meters or forms associated with traditional poetry, inversions, and (depending on context) repetitions tend to sound more elevated or formal. "*What* the river *says*, that's *what* I *say*," for example, is a line from a poem by William Stafford that uses repetition; more technically, it is not only using assonance and alliteration, it is a form of chiasmus. So despite the informal, even colloquial, diction, the style is elevated. The line's meter – iambic pentameter – probably also affects how we hear the line, even though the meter is highly varied.

The proportion of nouns to verbs can also mark sentences as more or less formal. In general, the more nouns, the more formal. And the fewer **finite verbs**, or the more **stative verbs** (for example, "plays" as opposed to "is playing"), the more formal. In formal prose, nouns usually outnumber both verbs and adjectives. There are, of course, different kinds of formality, and the term itself covers everything from stuffiness to elevation. Textbooks, for example, often use many complex noun phrases (bearing lots of information) and stative (noun-like) verbs – and, unlike this textbook, they usually do not use first-person pronouns. But so too advertisements (or "infomercials" or airplane magazines) tend to use no first-person pronouns, fewer finite verbs, more stative verbs, and many nouns, although these features are often combined with quirky details, for surprise, and short, simple sentences. Thus they are not quite elevated prose, technically; neither are they colloquial: the tone of commercial language these days tends to hover between that of a conversation and that of a scientific article.

Stylistic elements can work together with or against one another. For a given sentence, you could even make a chart, listing verb:noun ratios, simplicity of sentence structure, rhetorical flourishes, literary resonances (including meter), and diction, to mark the difference between more formal and more conversational or colloquial language. I would add that I am not suggesting you chart every sentence in a poem, but if you are uncertain about the tone of what you are reading the above rules of thumb can be useful. Also, as in the example of the tonally mixed language I gave you from Wallace Stevens, in poetry tone sometimes is less a matter of characterizing or dramatizing a unified speaker than it is a way of guiding our response to what we are reading. Take the following poem, Robert Frost's 1936 "Design," for example.

> I found a dimpled spider, fat and white,
> On a white heal-all, holding up a moth
> Like a white piece of rigid satin cloth.
> Assorted characters of death and blight
> Mixed ready to begin the morning right,
> Like the ingredients of a witches' broth—
> A snow-drop spider, a flower like froth,
> And dead wings carried like a paper kite.
>
> What had that flower to do with being white,
> The wayside blue and innocent heal-all?
> What brought the kindred spider to that height,
> Then steered the white moth thither in the night?
> What but design of darkness to appall?
> If design govern in a thing so small.

I hope you have noticed that the poem is a Petrarchan sonnet, a form Frost graphically underlines, marking the turn between the octave and sestet with a visible break. The form itself elevates the tone, although *what* we are given in the octave, at least on first reading, seems a mere still life:

a snapshot of a spider that has caught a moth, sitting on a flower (the "heal-all" is a common flower, normally blue). But to say this ignores two features of the poem. One, it is a first-person report. That is, we are told that some "I" – the speaker – "found" the scene described. Why? That is, Frost could easily have omitted the first two words (or he could have written "There was a dimpled spider," without changing the iambic pentameter). It seems, then, that our attention is focused on the speaker, his attitude or perspective. If you then pay attention to the tone of voice – the second noteworthy feature of the language in the octave – you can see that the diction (especially given the regularity of the meter) is remarkably simple. This is clear even in the first line: the words "dimpled" and "fat" are more likely to bring to mind an infant or cherub than a spider. When these are coupled with words like "kite" or "froth" or with language that sounds almost like an advertisement for breakfast cereal – "Mixed ready to begin the morning right" – we have language more suited to the nursery than to the image of freakish coincidence (a white spider with a white moth on an anomalously white flower) presented. The words used (with very few exceptions) are also predominantly monosyllabic, with roots in Old English, not Latin. And there is almost a sing-song quality to the poem, with three uses of the word "white" in the first three lines. In short, the diction and style in the octave stand out for their simplicity and informality, suggesting an apparent innocence (or child-like simplicity, perhaps).

This said, there are a few moments that might give you pause if you try to read the octave as simply a kind of nursery rhyme (although, to be fair, many nursery rhymes have their origins in darker historical moments). Still, the fat, dimpled creature turns out not to be a child but a spider – and the end of the first quatrain is a bit jarring. That is, the bounciness of the iambic pentameter ("I found a dimpled spider, fat and white," reminiscent of "The itsy bitsy spider went up the water spout"), and the rather cheerful vocabulary ("dimpled," "heal-all," and – in Anglo-American culture – "white") are brought down to earth for a moment when the rhyme for "white" turns out to be "blight," and when the regularity of the meter carries us through to the end of the line "Assorted characters of *death* and *blight*." Indeed, although most of us probably do not notice the darker undercurrents until the mention of death (and maybe witches) makes us think twice, on second reading the simile comparing the dead moth to "a white piece of *rigid satin cloth*" lightly suggests that the moth is like the lining of a coffin or a pall (the heavy cloth draped over a coffin). Similarly, the spider "holding up" the cloth (and the homonyms "rite" and "right") for a moment make one think of a black mass or at least some unsacred ritual.

In fact, if we hear the octave as characterizing a speaker (and the first two words of the poem invite us to do just this), what we seem to have is a speaker who is ambivalent or perhaps not self-aware. That is, we are given a verbal picture of a "design" that seems meaningful both because of all that white on white and because the first-person narration indicates that the speaker found the scene worth reporting. However, the innocence of the perceiver, as well as of the scene according to the perceiver, rests uneasily with the undercurrents marking it as a scene of "death and blight." In fact (possibly like the speaker facing what he has seen), I at least feel buffeted by the changing tone in the octave, which is to say that my response to the poem, especially to its tone, may be analogous to the speaker's response to what he claims he found. Let me trace in a bit more detail how the poem's tone keeps shifting. We may think we have a kind of child's rhyme – the fat, dimpled spider, the heal-all, all that whiteness, the child-like diction and tropes, the regular meter – until we get to line 4. Yet if *we* "find" line 4 ("Assorted characters of death and blight") forms a kind of dark punch line or surprise turn, the second quatrain keeps the rhyme going (but now rhymes "white" and "blight" with "right"), and this as well as the advertising language ("Mixed ready to begin the morning right") probably throws our sense of tone off yet again. It seems, then, that this is either black humor or, as I said, ambivalence, or it may deliberately frustrate our efforts to imagine a fully characterized speaker. Frost, in other words, is using tone of voice to "design" a poem – and the sonnet form is surely also a design – that is less straightforward than it first appears.

The turn in line 9 is also interesting, since what changes is less the speaker's train of thought than once again the tone of voice, which becomes increasingly philosophical even as the diction remains informal – only "flower" and "innocent" have Latin roots – through the first tercet. Still, the inverted syntax ("What had that flower to do with being white, / The wayside . . . heal-all?") and, by the second tercet, archaic words like "thither" change the tone. We are not in a nursery rhyme any longer. Thematically, the three questions that form most of the sestet ask who or what designed the scene described in the octave. That is, the poem asks what active agent "brought" the white spider to the white flower and "steered" the moth. (You might note that the verbs in the sestet increasingly bespeak some kind of control: "had . . . to do with," "brought," "steered," and then "govern.") Although line 11 is not the first line where the regularity of the meter is disrupted, it is certainly a line in which the rhythm as well as the diction shifts overtly, almost as if it were spoken by someone other than the speaker heard in the poem's first line:

w   S   w   S   S   S w w w S

Then steered the white moth thither in the night?

o   B   o   B   ȯ   B   o B̄   o   B

At this point, the title of the poem might be revisited. Philosophers and theologians talk of the "argument from design" as one argument for the existence of God. And the sestet's questions about who (or rather what) designed the ambiguous convergence described in the octave bring this new register of philosophical or theological language to the fore. Frost also, I'd add, continues to use "white" as one of the poem's rhyme words rather than changing the rhyme in the sestet, as would be more usual. After that slight pause when we read "blight," "white" in the octave rhymes with "right" and then "kite." Repeated in the sestet, the word is re-associated with "height" (literally the height of the flower, but also perhaps of a higher tone and higher argument) and with "night" (literally when a moth might encounter a spider, but again suggestive of the "darker" undertones found less overtly in the octave). In other words, up through line 12, the poem uses diction, meter, rhyme, tone, images, and allusions to pose a question: what should be made of these images of death and blight? Does the feeling that such images are significant indicate anything more than a viewer's perspective? Is there one single perspective represented in the poem, for that matter?

I have deliberately not yet addressed what happens in the last two lines of the poem, in which the tone shifts yet again – and may even shift twice. Even the formal "design" of the poem becomes a bit difficult to discern in lines 13–14. The rhyme makes the lines sound like a couplet, although technically they are not a discrete unit; they are the last two thirds of the final tercet. Moreover, line 14 reads as if it is an aside while, syntactically and through the use of anaphora, line 13 is aligned with lines 9 and 11, at first apparently just raising another question: why was a normally blue flower white, and what arranged a white spider and white moth on the white flower? But in fact the "what" of line 13 asks a new kind of question, a rhetorical question, that is, a question that presupposes its own answer. "What could be responsible for such a scene other than a 'design of darkness to appall?'"

The word "of" in line 13 is also slightly ambiguous. In English, we can use "of" to form either the **objective** or the **subjective genitive**. That is, the phrase Frost uses may indicate that the design belongs to darkness (the way the poem is the poem of Robert Frost). Or the phrase may indicate that the design is made out of darkness, the way we might say "Design" is a poem of simple diction. There is also something of a pun in line 13.

"Appall" most literally means "to dismay" or "to fill with apprehension and alarm, to surprise unpleasantly" (making clear that the central scene is anything but a nursery rhyme setting). Yet the origin of the word is from a Latin verb, by way of the Old French, meaning "to become or make pale." I assume the word came to mean "to horrify" because people grow pale when alarmed or unpleasantly surprised. Yet the origin of the word subtly underlines one thematic thread found in "Design," namely the suggestion that the deathly white scene is not an omen designed by some higher power but rather involves the human tendency to find significance in the world. In short, what interests Frost is our psychological reactions, responses to which his manipulations of tone give rise in us. Moreover, the scene described is all white – literally "appalled" or made pale – which on one understanding of the phrase "design of darkness" could imply simply that in the contrast between elements (death and innocence, night and morning, light and darkness) each element makes the other stand out: darkness makes pale whiteness more visible.

Where does that leave us as readers? Have we been told that there is a malign force in the world arranging things to horrify us? (That is, is this darkness's evil design?) Or, are we simply told that we pick out contrasts – literal darkness would make the white on white on white of the scene stand out? Further, if we, like the speaker, find "innocent" elements arranged to signify death and blight to be appalling (in the sense of being unpleasantly surprising), is it then more appalling to think some evil being has arranged the world this way than it is to think that the world has no design; it just happens to be full of death and blight? This last seems to me part of the impact of that apparently throwaway last line ("If design govern in a thing so small"). In other words, it is not simply that the poem dismisses the notion that there is some orderly principle – even if one that is not benevolent – behind what we see; the tone of the last line may be even darker than that of the penultimate (that is, next to the last) line, suggesting that the world is illegible, dismaying, and without any rhyme or reason to it.

Of course, the *poem* has rhyme and reason, and if it does raise questions about whether there is any plan to the "appalling" world, it sets its own constructed poetic order against this image of chaos. The "argument from design," in this sense, is finally more like the "comforts of human design" in an unmanageable world. Interestingly, I have had students mention that the poem's scene really is not that frightening: ecology and biology tell us why there might be mutant heal-alls and why white moths and spiders might gravitate toward them. This, I trust, is true; but it does not seem to be *Frost's* point in the poem. And it is the tone of the poem that leads me to this conclusion. In other words, I am focused on a speaking voice ("I found . . ."), but the voice does not seem designed – if I can use that word – primarily to give me some sense of a dramatized speaker, a character. What character would sound so innocent (and yet so unconsciously load the dice) in the octave and then move to the more formal tone of lines 9–13, before pulling the rug out from under us with that final conditional ("if")?

To some of you who know other poems by Robert Frost ("The Road Not Taken," for example, or "Birches" or "Stopping by Woods on a Snowy Evening"), it may seem odd that I have chosen a poem in which there is no folksy speaker of the sort for which Frost's poems are best known. Yet it seems to me that in the final analysis "Design" is not really using a persona, although the poem *does* depend in interesting ways on our sense of tone of voice. It uses tone in order to position us (not to draw a character). And the position in which we are left seems finally to be uncomfortable, at best a kind of uneasy resting point, although we are made aware of why we are uncomfortable, namely because we realize we may want, but not believe in, a more decisive answer to the sestet's questions; we may similarly yearn for some sense of order larger than that provided in sonnets, without any sense such order is available. This said, I would simply add that the poem was written in 1922, although Frost did not include it in one of his books until 1936: by then, there was a civil war in Spain and the Great Depression in the United States, and even in the twenties when the poem was written almost anyone following current events in Germany was aware that the resolution of the First World War, then known as the Great War, was not going to last, that another war would break out (as it did, in 1939). Order and chaos, in other words, were pressing political and social realities, not just theoretical topics, as Frost wrote and published his poem.

I have introduced "Design" as a poem that depends on tone of voice, without necessarily using tone to give us a sense of a specific speaker. I should tell you that tone of voice can be used to develop a more unified sense of character. Robert Browning's dramatic monologues ("My Last Duchess" would be a set piece of the dramatic monologue) are the poems most often used to illustrate tone as a form of characterization. However, while I recommend you look at Browning's poem, I want here to look next at a mid-twentieth-century poem, "The Day Lady Died" by Frank O'Hara, a poet who is not known for writing dramatic monologues. O'Hara, like Frost, however, had a sensitive ear for tone and for the patterns of spoken American English, as can be seen in his 1959 elegy for the jazz singer Billie Holiday (known affectionately in her time as "Lady Day"):

It is 12:20 in New York a Friday
three days after Bastille day, yes
it is 1959 and I go get a shoeshine
because I will get off the 4:19 in Easthampton
at 7:15 and then go straight to dinner   5
and I don't know the people who will feed me

I walk up the muggy street beginning to sun
and have a hamburger and a malted and buy
an ugly NEW WORLD WRITING to see what the poets
in Ghana are doing these days I go on to the bank   10
and Miss Stillwagon (first name Linda I once heard)
doesn't even look up my balance for once in her life
and in the GOLDEN GRIFFIN I get a little Verlaine
for Patsy with drawings by Bonnard although I do
think of Hesiod, trans. Richmond Lattimore or   15
Brendan Behan's new play or Le Balcon or Les Nègres
of Genet, but I don't, I stick with Verlaine
after practically going to sleep with quandariness

and for Mike I just stroll into the PARK LANE
Liquor Store and ask for a bottle of Strega and   20
then I go back where I came from to 6th Avenue
and the tobacconist in the Ziegfeld Theatre and
casually ask for a carton of Gauloises and a carton
of Picayunes, and a NEW YORK POST with her face on it

and I am sweating a lot by now and thinking of   25
leaning on the john door in the 5 SPOT
while she whispered a song along the keyboard
to Mal Waldron and everyone and I stopped breathing

O'Hara called poems like "The Day Lady Died" his "I do this, I do that" poems for reasons I suspect are fairly obvious. The poem uses colloquial language that sounds as if it is more spoken than written to provide a casual account of a rather ordinary day. The informality of the voice is emphasized by the simplicity of diction, by the specificity of reference ("Friday," not "one day"; "Easthampton"), by the colloquial syntax ("I go get," "I will get," and "then go"), by the interpolated "yes" at the end of line 2, and also by the use of parataxis – all those clauses strung together with the conjunction "and," a word used nineteen times in this twenty-eight-line poem. Not only do the first six lines suggest we are listening to someone's list of trivial things done and to do, the paratactic construction at least up through line 26 suggests that nothing mentioned is more significant than anything else – the shoeshine, the weather, what the speaker had for lunch – although it also may suggest the pace and the onslaught of undifferentiated sensations that assault someone walking in a large, bustling urban environment (like New York City in 1959). Even the use of capital letters for the names of commercial establishments seems to mimic the design of urban signage: "NEW WORLD WRITING," "GOLDEN GRIFFIN," "PARK LANE Liquor Store," "5 SPOT." We know these names are historically accurate (there was such a magazine; those stores and that jazz club – the 5 Spot – did exist). However, if the poem's details are rooted in history and in 1950s New York in particular, at least on a first reading of the poem it does not seem that O'Hara is centrally trying to write a documentary or make a point about history. Among other things, it does not seem any more important that it is "three days after Bastille Day" than that it is a Friday. The specificity of time (12:20, 4:19; 7:15) is linked more to train schedules or perhaps the habit of watching the clock on one's lunch hour ("The Day Lady Died" appeared in a book called *Lunch Poems*) than to any sense of larger significance.

What does seem significant may in fact be the lack of significance or the fact that nothing seems connected to anything (or anyone) else, except arbitrarily (another effect of parataxis here). That is, the fragmented presentation of bits of fact (what the speaker did, what he bought, what was for sale) – the significant lack of significance – seems to be part of the point. The use of "and . . . and . . . and" does not let us (reading the poem) pause or take a breath between sentences, at the same time that the conjunction – paradoxically, since "and" is normally a word that suggests connection – really does not tell us anything about the relationship between the dinner date, the "hamburger and a malted," or the fact that "Miss Stillwagon" did not "for once" look up the speaker's bank balance. Indeed, if you stop to think about it, what the speaker tells us seems to emphasize his isolation or the fragmented way in which he encounters others in his life; again, lack of significance or a compartmentalization of experience seems to be the point. Our speaker reads of poets in Ghana (he even speaks of them with familiarity when he says idiomatically that he wants to see "what [they] / . . . are doing these days"), but, although it is suggested he sees her often, he does not know his bank teller's first name except through having overheard it "once." He buys gifts for his hosts and calls them by their proper names (Mike and Patsy are presumably the people with whom he will dine), but he says he does not actually know them, although he knows exactly when his train will arrive and what his schedule will be.

Indeed, the speaker seems to have a more intimate relationship with things (and in particular commercial things) than with people. Although we are given a list of books that might be purchased – suggesting among other things that our speaker is a cultivated person – it doesn't seem to matter if the book is by a French poet, an Irish playwright, or an ancient Greek. There is even some suggestion that the speaker is showing off (he knows there is a new translation of Hesiod, a new play by Brendan Behan), although his remarks about his bank balance and the rather ordinary lunch he eats suggest his capital is more cultural than financial. He may buy foreign liquors and exotic cigarettes (knowing brand names for which he can "casually ask"), but he does not read the *New York Times*; he reads the more popular pulp press *Post*.

Most critics who write about this poem point out that line 18 stands out, in part because its tone is less conventionally informal than what comes before. That is, the entire poem is colloquial; it is not after all "proper" English to say "I don't, I stick with Verlaine." A more formal speaker might say, "I do not purchase the other books I considered buying; I keep to my original choice (to buy a volume of poems by Verlaine)." A casual speaker, however, might well say, "I don't, I stick with Verlaine." Nonetheless, American English does not include the idiom "going to sleep with quandariness." One might go to sleep out of boredom, but having too many choices – being in a quandary, or so I take "quandariness," a word O'Hara coined, to mean – would not usually be associated with sleepiness. Yet as I've noted, the poem levels the details it includes, so that making choices such as whether to buy Verlaine, Hesiod, or Genet for someone you do not know does not seem all that important. Thus one might, faced with such a glut of consumer goods (which is what the books mentioned seem to become in this poem), nod off "with quandariness." In other words, line 18 underscores the poem's self-consciousness about the kind of culture it describes and in which it may participate.

In line with the above analysis of line 18, some readers of "The Day Lady Died" have suggested that the poem's central concern is to document – as much in its tone of voice as in the subject matter – the anomie (that is, the state of isolation and anxiety) of modern life. I would add that although mine is a book that hopes to enable you to become an informed reader of poetry, developing your own interpretations of poems, it is often helpful to look at what other readers and critics have said. Although you need not agree with others' interpretations, it is useful to know what has been said and even over which issues critics may argue. For modern American poetry, there is a website developed by Cary Nelson (listed at the end of this chapter) that provides an excellent guide to critical commentaries on O'Hara's poem (as well as on Frost's and those of many other modern American poets). I have been urging you to add your own voice to the conversation with and about poems. Here, I am simply noting that to have your own voice does not mean you are speaking or thinking in a void; you are part of an exchange that already includes other readers as well as poets. Moreover, in the same way that poems – their styles, their goals, their central concerns – shift gradually over time, so too critical approaches and critics' understandings of poems shift over time.

Above, I mentioned that some readers see the speaker of the poem – characterized by the way he sounds, his tone of voice – as embodying the way consciousness (or the self) feels or at least represents itself in a world of personal isolation, fragmentation, and consumer culture. On this reading of the poem, even the final four lines, and especially the last two lines, do not stand out; even death (according to this reading) is no more important than what to bring to a dinner party. I mention death, because the last two lines return us to the title of the poem: "The Day Lady Died." The end of the poem – finally – describes a performance by Billie Holiday. It is true that she is not mentioned by name in the poem, unless you count the punning reference to her nickname, Lady Day, in the title. Moreover, although many of you have probably heard recordings of her soulful voice, the poem itself tells us less about Billie Holiday than it does about Miss Stillwagon or Patsy or Mike (who at least have names); knowing that Billie Holiday's pianist was Mal Waldron or that she sang in 1957 at the 5 Spot (illegally, in fact, since her cabaret license was revoked after her arrest as a heroin user) is a kind of insider knowledge that the poem does not clearly assume you know or give to you.

And yet it does seem to me that something different happens, that there is a turn, in the poem's final lines, which has to do (again) with the voice of the poem. For one thing, from line 1 through line 26, the poem for the most part uses the present tense: "It is 12:20," we are told in the poem's first words. When the speaker then says "I walk up the muggy street" (line 7), we might assume it is after 12:20, since in line 3 the speaker says he is going to get a shoeshine (at 12:20), and presumably that took a few minutes. What the insistence on the highly specified present does is to locate *us* with the speaker, as if he is narrating the external events of his day in (as we would now say) "real time." But when the speaker says he is "thinking of / leaning on the john door in the 5 Spot" (lines 25–6), it turns out he is not saying that he is considering leaning on the bathroom door in yet another New York establishment he visits on the Friday on which the poem is set, but that he is remembering an earlier event.

The final lines of the poem use the past tense, and the poem for the first time presents us with an internal reality, a memory. Further, I would argue that this memory is more moving – more humanly and more fully imagined – than any of the present events mentioned in the rest of the poem.

That is, we may not know Billie Holiday by name, but we do know "she whispered a song along the keyboard / to Mal Waldron," which is an image of a singer who, unlike anyone else presented in the poem, has a human relationship. She whispered "to" Mal Waldron, suggesting both that her words were directed "to" Waldron and that her voice followed the tune he was playing on the piano, the way you might dance "to" a tune. Not only is this in distinct contrast to the speaker's lack of relationship with the people who will feed him, but the sense of having an effect – and a significance – is extended as we are told that "everyone and I stopped breathing." By contrast, Billie Holiday's breath is emphasized by the reference to her whisper, suggesting that in memory – and in O'Hara's poem – she lives on. There is thus a distant echo and slight reversal of Shakespeare's "So long as men can breathe or eyes can see, / So long lives this, and this gives life to thee." Moreover, there is also almost a pun on the phrase "breathtaking performance." Certainly the image is of time stopping, as opposed to the rushed voice and images of rushing around found in lines 1–24. The sounds of the words make *our* voices stop, as well. The plosives and stops (the "t" and "p" and "b" and "g" sounds in "stopped breathing") literally, that is, physically, require that the air flow in your vocal tract be stopped if you read the poem out loud. This as well as the fact that the poem's long run-on sentence has finally come to a close makes O'Hara's point viscerally as well as descriptively. We stop breathing. That the conclusion of the poem takes us out of time, stops us, might be said to be both an analog of and a tribute to the songs Billie Holiday sang; that is, the poem shows us how powerful an effect her voice had (all the more powerful for appearing in a world where most daily occurrences have little effect, as suggested in the body of the poem), and the poem itself may affect us similarly.

I first introduced the poem as an **elegy**, which is not a form (the way the sonnet is), but a mode or mood; most simply, elegies are poems that mourn the dead, although most people would agree that from the earliest English examples – mostly famously Milton's 1637 "Lycidas" – elegies are at least as much about mourning (that is, coming to terms with loss) as about who or what is lost. As I said, not everyone agrees that "The Day Lady Died" *is* an elegy. For some, I suppose it might be called an "anti-elegy" (in which death is not given more significance than, say, shopping). You will have to draw your own conclusions about whether or not the poem is elegiac. If, however, you decide it is a poem of loss, then it is an elegy. O'Hara uses none of the features that – after Milton – came to be expected, almost formulaic, in the English elegy: a statement of lament, a seeking of consolation, a list of mourners, a sense that the whole world is mourning. Yet one could hear the end of O'Hara's poem as all the more moving because the flatness of everyday life for the speaker makes the memory of Holiday's effect on "everyone and [the poem's] I" all the more effective – and so all the more of an elegy for her. As with what I have called the "conceptual syntax" of night pieces and sonnets, elegies can set readerly expectations and work in part by then thwarting (or extending) those expectations.

There may be another sense, too, in which the central debates critics have about O'Hara's poem revolve around readerly expectations of elegies. As I said, for some critics the poem does not cohere, even in a last moment of epiphany or memory or elegiac lyricism; the details reported all remain random and their lack of significance (to repeat what I said earlier) *is* their significance. The poem is then a kind of "anti-elegy." For other critics, the contrast between the random daily actions in lines 1–24 and the significant memory described in lines 25–8 is what makes the poem moving. There are still others who revisit the apparently random details of lines 1–24 in light of the end of the poem to propose that in retrospect these details are not so random after all. In fact, I have already proposed that the images in "The Day Lady Died" may coherently suggest the lack of coherence in modern, urban life. The details included in the poem are not figurative or emblematic in the way the details in Frost's poem are, but they may give us a sense of the speaker's significantly fragmented perspective. Pursuing this understanding of how the poem works further, you could note that Billie Holiday was what might be called an "outsider": she was African American in 1950s America (before the 1964 Civil Rights Act); she was a heroin addict who was jailed. If you think then about not only the Bastille (a prison, an icon of a revolution against oppression) but also about Ghana, even more of the poem's details seem purposeful. Ghana had its own revolution in 1957 (two years before this poem was written); previously Ghana was known as the Gold Coast, a center of the African slave trade, relevant to the social position of African Americans like Billie Holiday. Note, too, the title of one of the Genet books the speaker considers buying: Les Nègres. Moreover, Brendan Behan, Verlaine, and Genet all, like Billie Holiday, spent time in jail. The question remains, however, whether this pattern of significance means that the speaker is mourning all those who are social outcasts in some way or whether the speaker is attracted to what seems exotic or foreign to him – so that his affection for Billie Holiday is something like his choice of cigarettes, more affectation than affection.

This is an argument that is not just a matter of changing critical norms, which is to say that these days most critics would not dismiss the poem, but how they hear and respond to the significance of O'Hara's voice varies depending not only on their expectations of what a poem should do (including whether or not elegiac lyric transcendence seems desirable) but also on their assessment of whether O'Hara (a white man from a somewhat privileged background, although also a gay man in 1950s America) is trying to claim – and, if so, whether he can in good faith claim – a kind of kinship with an African American woman like Billie Holiday. I have spoken of the voice represented in the poem as "the speaker's voice" because a poem is not a journal entry; even with the sense the poem provides of overhearing an individual (one much like Frank O'Hara), the representation of a self speaking is crafted to give us this sense. In short, even if it is a self portrait of sorts, in the same way that painted self-portraits are paintings not people, the poetic speaker in "The Day Lady Died" is an effect of writing, not simply the author overheard. Again, you will have to assess for yourself the arguments about how to respond to the poem's speaker. I would simply suggest that such an assessment requires that you be able to talk about elegiac poems and about the tone of voice in O'Hara's poem in particular, before you enter the arguments about the poem's author or the political implications of his subject matter.

It may be that poems focused on representations of a speaker's attitudes and feelings, that is, poems that are in ways "about" tone of voice, are more likely than others to raise questions about the relationship between the author and the speaker (and so about the politics of the poem). In any event, a similar set of questions (as well as some new questions) arise when looking at Elizabeth Bishop's "Filling Station," written only six years after O'Hara's poem and equally a poem that depends on a reader's ability to hear the modulations of tone of voice:

Oh, but it is dirty!
— this little filling station,
oil-soaked, oil-permeated
to a disturbing, over-all
black translucency.   5
Be careful with that match!

Father wears a dirty,
oil-soaked monkey suit
that cuts him under the arms,
and several quick and saucy   10
and greasy sons assist him
(it's a family filling station),
all quite thoroughly dirty.

Do they live in the station?
It has a cement porch   15

behind the pumps, and on it
a set of crushed and grease-
impregnated wickerwork;
on the wicker sofa
a dirty dog, quite comfy.   20

Some comic books provide
the only note of color —
of certain color. They lie
upon a big dim doily
draping a taboret   25
(part of the set), beside
a big hirsute begonia.

Why the extraneous plant?
Why the taboret?
Why, oh why, the doily?   30
(Embroidered in daisy stitch
with marguerites, I think,
and heavy with gray crochet.)

Somebody embroidered the doily.
Somebody waters the plant,   35
or oils it, maybe. Somebody
arranges the rows of cans
so that they softly say:
ESSO – SO – SO – SO
to high-strung automobiles.   40
Somebody loves us all.

Like O'Hara's poem, "Filling Station" at first seems full of realistic local detail, capturing our attention with its careful observation of a 1960s American setting – one that does not seem metaphorical – and its representation of a colloquial, speaking voice. Ironically, as I have noted before, the more specific, contemporary details a poem includes, the more likely it is to require footnotes. For example, since Exxon took over Esso, there are no longer Esso filling stations along highways in the United States. You might then need to look up the fact that Esso was a brand of gasoline. Doilies and taborets – low side tables – are not particular to a certain time period. Still, they tell us something about both the speaker and those whom she observes. Specifically, it is a bit pretentious of the speaker to refer to a side table as a "taboret," although a catalogue selling matching "sets" (from which we might guess the filling station's set of wickerwork has come) might do so. More interestingly, in 1965, doilies would have been a mark of class. They were used in lower- or lower-middle-class homes trying to look fancier than they were. I confess that when I first read "Filling Station," I laughed out loud at the line "Why, oh why, the doily?" But thinking more about the way in which the speaking voice distances itself from (and perhaps looks down upon) the family filling station – opening "Oh, but it is dirty!" – has since given me pause and made me wonder about my own perspective on the scene in the poem. I have also come to think my self-awareness is part of the poem's point. Let me spell out why this is so.

The first six lines – perhaps even the first thirteen lines – sound as if we are listening to someone commenting on a specific, not a generic, place: "*this* little filling station." The diminutive "little," as well as the exclamation marks and the idiomatic expression "Oh, but it is dirty!" not to mention the use of the adjective "disturbing," further suggest that the speaker is condescending, and probably out of her usual element (as when she warns "Be careful with that match!"). The first line, in particular, echoes the sort of thing a mother might say to a child: "Oh, but you're dirty." "Oh, but it is dirty!" acknowledges the facts, at the same time that it implies surprise. It is not that the speaker is *actually* surprised that a filling station is dirty. It is more a rhetorical surprise, signaling that dirt *ought* to be surprising, suggesting that the speaker is used to cleaner places. Further, the deictics ("this" and "that"), something like O'Hara's use of the present tense, place us as readers in the setting with the speaker and even invite us to share the speaker's judgments, as in line 13 when she characterizes the people in the scene observed as "all quite thoroughly dirty."

While the words chosen are plain-spoken, they also suggest a speaker more educated than the family – the "Father" and "several quick and saucy / and greasy sons" – at least as the speaker perceives them. Latinate, multi-syllable words ("permeated," "translucency," "impregnated," "hirsute," "extraneous") as well as "quite thoroughly," are not the diction a filling-station attendant would use. In short, there is a marked class difference between the filling-station family and the speaker. At the same time, there is a pattern of sound (rhymes and near rhymes) that seems to have less to do with characterizing the speaker. True, there are four uses each of the words "dirty" and "oil[y]" in the poem – three each in the first thirteen lines alone – which do seem designed to represent for us (and perhaps to draw us into) the speaker's fastidious reaction to the filling station. The poem continues to use similar words such as "black," "dim," and "gray" through line 30. However, the "y" sounds of "dirty" and "oily" (and "greasy") begin to rhyme with increasingly dissonant words: first, "monkey" in line 8, but then also "saucy," "family," "comfy," "doily," "daisy," "somebody," and "softly." The direct rhyme of "oily" and "doily" (with the assonance in "embroidered") is particularly striking.

There seem to be two ways in which one can talk about such patterns of sound. One way is to hear them as marking for us a shift in the speaker's perspective. That is, the speaking voice subtly begins to modulate around line 14, with the question, "Do they live in the station?" We have gone from someone expressing dismay at a lack of hygiene, and describing the men at the filling station as if they were just more oil-soaked foreign objects, to someone who comes to see human and domestic life informing the scene before her, as she notices details such as a sofa, a dog, comic books, a doily, matching pieces of furniture, flowers both real and embroidered. In other words, at first the poem seems to give us a portrait of mid-twentieth-century industrial America, something like the image in Edward Hopper's well-known 1940 painting, entitled "Gas," of a mostly deserted filling station (Mobil, not Esso), which bespeaks loneliness and a lack of human community. Bishop's station is described in the first two stanzas of her poem as distastefully dirty (although the speaker does mention "Father" – a more intimate form of naming than "a" or "the" father – and his sons); yet, like Hopper's landscape, Bishop's at first seems almost a still-life. If it is inhabited, the inhabitants are not quite fleshed out. However, by the third stanza, the eye (or "I") of the poem picks out a room (a porch) and a dog, indeed, a "comfy" scene. Moreover, "comfy" is slang and a word (unlike the diction in stanzas one and two) in keeping with the scene described, as if by asking her question the speaker comes to see life in the scene and even to participate in it. The tone of the fourth stanza then wavers between the early condescension – there is only one "note" of "certain color," the doily is "dim," the begonia hairy – and a more generous or sympathetic perspective, as the speaker recognizes the comic books, the draped table, the matched set of furniture, a recognition that seems to precipitate the cascade of questions in the fifth stanza.

I have been talking about "the speaker," although by the fourth stanza the poem – like "Design" – may be using tone to position my attitude toward the filling station (or the slice of mid-century, working-class American culture portrayed), as much as dramatizing a character's voice. Yet line 32 reminds me there is a speaker – who says "with marguerites, *I think*," suggesting she is unsure of the kind of flowers embroidered on the doily – and, more importantly, reminds me there is a speaker who is not omniscient . . . and not the author. There is also a way in which Bishop's poem (whether intentionally or not) echoes Frost's "Design," because it is a poem *about* design and explicitly raises the question of why all the observed details are there ("What had that flower to do with being white?" and "Why the extraneous plant?"). Frost's sonnet ends suggesting that there is either a malign supernatural designer, or perhaps simply brute happenstance.

"Filling Station" suggests on the contrary that there is "somebody" who has taken care to decorate this place, somebody who has even straightened the cans (which would be cans of oil) "so they softly say: / ESSO – SO – SO – SO." Given the kinds of design to which the narrative of the poem alludes (flowers, embroidery), it seems to me, as to most critics reading this poem, that the most likely designer is the mother of the family. These seem to be feminine touches, and the most conspicuously absent member of the family has been the mother. The poem also loads the dice (so to speak) by the use of verbal design: there is the sibilance heard in "arrange<u>s</u> . . . row<u>s</u> . . . can<u>s</u> / <u>s</u>o . . . <u>s</u>oftly <u>s</u>ay:/ E<u>SS</u>O-<u>S</u>O-<u>S</u>O-<u>S</u>O/ . . . <u>s</u>trung automobile<u>s</u>," the repeated "so" sounds that precede line 39 ("somebody," "so," "softly"), as well as the near rhyme of "rows" and "so" and the anaphoric repetitions of "Why" (in lines 28–30) and of "Somebody" (in lines 34, 35, and 41).

Earlier I noted that the patterned sounds in the poem could be read in at least two ways. It may be that they call our attention to the attempts at aesthetic order (by an unseen mother), showing the speaker's dawning awareness, even her redemption from her first, unconsciously dismissive, remarks. I say "redemption" although the final line of the poem – "Somebody loves us all" – sounds like the kind of motto someone might well embroider, something like "God Bless Our Home" stitched on a sampler. Yet while such language – what the critic Bonnie Costello calls "sampler rhetoric" – is usually used unselfconsciously, this does not mean it does not express genuine feeling. And if we condescend to those who use such language to bring order or meaning to their lives, it may be we are as guilty as the speaker is in the first stanza of not knowing how different ways of using language (even cliché or "sampler rhetoric") can be equally expressive. Admittedly, some critics have read the entire poem as ironic, hearing "Somebody loves us all" as a dismissive gesture suggesting that "only a mother" could love the oily filling station or that there is someone foolish enough to love even this filling station. As I already indicated, I am inclined to see more of a turn at the end, a recognition that in ordinary language (as in the poem's ordinary setting), there is something redemptive . . . not Frost's supernatural designer, but rather a common human desire for the comforts of aesthetic order. The title adds to my sense that the end of the poem is not simply ironic: rather than calling the poem "Gas Station" or "Service Station," Bishop chose "*Filling* Station," and "filling" connotes nourishment. In this sense, too, it seems that the patterns described (the matched furniture, the arrangement of the oil cans) and the patterns of sound (rhyme, assonance, and alliteration) align the desire of the "somebody" – the mother – in the poem with the desire of the poet. If there is irony, then, I would argue that it is as much at Bishop's expense as condescendingly at the filling-station family's expense. That is, the tone may suggest some skepticism about the value of such comforts (of poetry in our world, of trying to beautify a filling station), but there is – on my reading – a leveling effect, as the distance is gradually diminished between the speaker and those she describes (finally not distancing the poet or reader either). In other words, the voice that says "Oh, but it is dirty!" seems to have a different tone – a different attitude toward what is described – than the voice that says "Somebody loves us all." Although I am not certain I would ultimately characterize the speaker as a dramatized character *per se*, the movement of the poem seems to me to enact a guarded movement toward a sense of commonality. You need not agree, but (again) whatever your reading of this poem (or of Frost's or O'Hara's), a sense of tone of voice – even of voice as a poetic theme – will surely inform your interpretation.

Tone and diction (like rhythm or meter) are features of almost all poems, even if they are not always as *thematically* central as I think they are in O'Hara's and Bishop's poems. I have also mentioned here (discussing O'Hara's poem) what I called a "mode," namely elegy, which can describe both a theme (death or loss) and a tone of voice ("elegiac," or mourning). The next chapter will turn to yet another mode: the ode. Some critics have suggested that elegies concern themselves with loss or absence but find consolation or presence at the end (another reason I hear O'Hara's poem as an elegy). Odes can be seen as the opposite of elegies: they are poems that concern themselves with presence or praise, but find loss or absence.

Terms used

colloquial style	neologism
diction	objective genitive
elegy	slang
finite verbs	stative verbs
formal style	style
idioms	subjective genitive
informal style	syntax

Other poems that might be read

Robert Browning, "My Last Duchess" (1842)
Lewis Carroll, "Jabberwocky"(1871)
e. e. cummings, "who's most afraid of death? thou" (1925)

Wallace Stevens, "The World as Meditation" (1952)
Josephine Miles, "Reason" (1953)
A. R. Ammons, "Corsons Inlet" (1965) [in part a response to the Frost poem]
John Berryman, "Sonnet 7" (1967)
Larry Levis, "Earl the Chicken Farmer" (1971)
Philip Larkin, "This Be the Verse" (1971)
Heather McHugh, "Language Lesson, 1976" (1976)
Alice Fulton, "Second-Sight" (1983)
Thylias Moss, "One-Eyed Mother Selling Mangoes" (1991)
Lois-Ann Yamanaka, "Kala: Sitting on Our Bikes by the Catholic Church" (1993)
Vern Rutsala, "Billie Holiday" (2004)

Useful further reading

Marie Borroff, *Language and the Poet: Verbal Artistry in Frost, Stevens, and Moore* (Chicago: University of Chicago Press, 1979).

Bonnie Costello, *Elizabeth Bishop: Questions of Mastery* (Cambridge, Mass.: Harvard University Press, 1991).

David Crystal, *A Dictionary of Linguistics and Phonetics* (Malden, Mass.: Blackwell, 2003).

Randall Jarrell, *Poetry and the Age* (New York: Knopf, 1953).

Cary Nelson, ed., "Modern American Poetry," <http://www.english.uiuc.edu/maps/poets/> (30 August 2006).

Peter Sacks, *The English Elegy: Studies in the Genre from Spenser to Yeats* (Baltimore: Johns Hopkins University Press, 1985).

Chapter 6

Modes, Odes, and Odic Gestures

in William Collins's "Ode on the Poetical
Character" (1746), William Wordsworth's "Ode"
(1802–4), and Josephine Miles's "Purchase of
a Blue, Green, or Orange Ode" (1941)

The previous chapter defined odes as poems concerned with presence that come to find absence. This definition, while useful, draws on certain theoretical presuppositions about how to characterize **modes** of poetry. Modal terms usually describe orientations and do not necessarily entail set forms, styles, or even themes; modes are thus closer to tones of voice than to forms like the sonnet. Still, odes have been characterized by some as public utterances written using variable line lengths, heightened diction, and ingenious rhyme schemes (a more formal definition). Yet others have offered a history of odes. This last endeavor may be the most difficult, since the history of odes is a bit like the game called "gossip" or "telephone," where one person whispers a word or phrase to the next, who hears it differently; thus the original gets changed, becoming unrecognizable as it passes from person to person.

Almost everyone who writes about English (and later American) odes has to confront the fact that the ode has an odd history. To cite Stuart Curran (on whose book, listed at the end of this chapter, I am drawing), "the history of the ode is that it has little history." There were Greek and Latin odes, some of which came in set forms and most of which were poems of praise, which is to say encomiums, praising everything from drinking and love to athletic prowess. Perhaps the best-known classical odes were by Pindar, who wrote (in the fifth century BCE) on public occasions, often praising victorious athletes, and whose odes are formally complicated (not to mention syntactically difficult). Pindar's odes – thought to draw their form from the movement on stage of choruses in classical Greek drama – have three parts: a **strophe**, sometimes called a **turn** in English; an **antistrophe** or **counter-turn** (using the same formal pattern, but often conceptually moving in a different direction, in counterpoint to the strophe); and an **epode**, also known as a **stand**, using a different form from the strophe and antistrophe. On the analogy with the movements of a chorus on stage, the movement of a **Pindaric ode** can be visualized as the chorus going first to the right, then to the left, and finally standing still. Conceptually, one might think of a Pindaric ode as a dialectic, with a thesis, an antithesis, and then a synthesis (although there is disagreement about whether the epode meaningfully synthesizes the contradictory movements of the odic strophe and antistrophe).

The other well-known classical precedent for odes was set by Horace in the first century BCE. **Horatian odes** tend to be more reflective or personal in tone than the public praise found in Pindaric odes; formally Horatian odes are **homostrophic**, which is to say they are composed of regular, more or less identically formed stanzas. By the time the English ode became popular, though, it seems that "a Horatian voice was invested in a Pindaric form" (to again quote Curran). There were seventeenth-century odes in English that more carefully followed classical models, but there were also by the end of that century misunderstandings of Pindar's Greek (often known only through Latin translation) in circulation. I'm not going to rehearse which English poets knew Greek and which did not. It suffices to say that by the eighteenth century, what is now called the **irregular**, **English**, **great**, or **pseudo-Pindaric ode** had become quite the rage; the form, however, often had little to do with what Pindar wrote (either thematically or formally).

The eighteenth century was a period which tried to categorize and spell out the features of literary genres, specifying among other things what topics, diction, and forms might be appropriate for each subgenre. In this climate, the irregular ode served as what has been called the free verse of the eighteenth century. I like best the characterization of one of my former professors. Talking about the classifications used by eighteenth-century literary scholars, my teacher called the ode "the what-not drawer" of the period. That is, just as the most organized households still have at least one drawer into which everything that has no other place gets tossed, so too what seemed indecorous or unprecedented (or just plain excessive) appeared in eighteenth-century English odes.

As I mentioned when discussing Charlotte Smith's sonnet "To Dependence," eighteenth-century Britain also showed an increasing interest in what we would now call psychology. In line with this (although a full account of the history is far beyond my purpose here), the irregular ode became also the vehicle for what the period called the **sublime**, which was related to extreme states of mind and to the language of the Hebrew Bible or to prophetic and visionary voices (although in ways the sublime might be seen as the what-not drawer of eighteenth-century psychology, given that there was at first no single agreed-upon definition of it). A sublime poet-speaker and what came to be the signature of odic style – incomplete sentences, exclamation marks, heightened and often confusing diction, and contradictory claims – were then often aligned. By the early eighteenth century, we even find people making fun of poets who tried to sound sublime. Certainly, the style of some mid-eighteenth-century odes in English can seem strained. But the poems are still interesting, not least because of how the very excessiveness of their language shows the ode as a vehicle for anxiety about poetic vocation. This is not surprising, given both the ode's association with the sublime (and the claim to sublimity might well be a difficult one to sustain) and the fact that poetry's public role was increasingly unclear (so that what was heard by eighteenth-century poets as the authority of earlier poetry seemed a difficult act to follow). Again, I will not detail the full history of poetics here, but it does help to know something about how writers thought of (or worried about) their vocation.

It helps, too, to read a concrete example of what I am talking about when I mention mid-eighteenth-century English odes. So before I talk more about odes in general, I want to look at an ode, William Collins's 1746 "Ode on the Poetical Character." I won't here offer a line-by-line reading of the poem (although one could); I am more interested in looking broadly at the voice, concerns, and movements in the poem:

1
As once, if not with light regard
I read aright that gifted bard,
(Him whose school above the rest
His loveliest Elfin Queen has blessed)
One, only one, unrivaled fair   5
Might hope the magic girdle wear,
At solemn tourney hung on high,
The wish of each love-darting eye;
Lo! to each other nymph in turn applied,
    As if, in air unseen, some hovering hand,   10

Some chaste and angel-friend to virgin-fame,
    With whispered spell had burst the starting band,
It left unblest her loathed, dishonoured side;
    Happier hopeless fair, if never
    Her baffled hand with vain endeavour   15
Had touched that fatal zone to her denied!
Young Fancy thus, to me divinest name,
    To whom, prepared and bathed in heaven,
    The cest of amplest power is given,
    To few the godlike gift assigns   20
    To gird their blest prophetic loins,
And gaze her visions wild, and feel unmixed her flame!

2
The band, as fairy legends say,
Was wove on that creating day
When He, who called with thought to birth   25
Yon tented sky, this laughing earth,
And dressed with springs and forests tall,
And poured the main engirting all,
Long by the loved Enthusiast wooed,
Himself in some diviner mood,   30
Retiring, sat with her alone,
And placed her on his sapphire throne,
The whiles, the vaulted shrine around,
Seraphic wires were heard to sound,
Now sublimest triumph swelling,   35
Now on love and mercy dwelling;
And she, from out the veiling cloud,
Breathed her magic notes aloud:
And thou, thou rich-haired youth of morn,
And all thy subject life was born!   40
The dangerous Passions kept aloof,
Far from the sainted growing woof;
But near it sat ecstatic Wonder,
Listening the deep applauding thunder;
And Truth, in sunny vest arrayed,   45
By whose the tarsel's eyes were made;
All the shadowy tribes of Mind
In braided dance their murmurs joined,
And all the bright uncounted powers,
Who feed on heaven's ambrosial flowers.   50
Where is the bard, whose soul can now
Its high presuming hopes avow?

Where he who thinks, with rapture blind,
This hallowed work for him designed?

3
High on some cliff, to Heaven up-piled,   55
Of rude access, of prospect wild,
Where, tangled round the jealous steep,
Strange shades o'erbrow the valleys deep,
And holy genii guard the rock,
Its glooms embrown, its springs unlock,   60
While on its rich ambitious head,
An Eden, like his own, lies spread;
I view that oak, the fancied glades among,
By which as Milton lay, his evening ear,
From many a cloud that dropped ethereal dew,   65
Nigh sphered in heaven its native strains could hear;
On which that ancient trump he reached was hung;
        Thither oft his glory greeting,
        From Waller's myrtle shades retreating,
With many a vow from Hope's aspiring tongue,   70
My trembling feet his guiding steps pursue;
        In vain – such bliss to one alone
        Of all the sons of soul was known,
        And Heaven and Fancy, kindred powers,
        Have now o'erturned the inspiring bowers,   75
Or curtained close such scene from every future view.

If you find yourself confused by what you have just read, you are not
alone. Confusion was often the response of Collins's contemporaries, as
well. You can, however, get your bearings if you start with the fact that the
first and last sections each have twenty-two lines, largely in rhymed couplets using iambic tetrameter, pentameter, and hexameter, although the
rhyme scheme is varied by the ninth line of each matching section. The
middle section of the poem, however, has a different number of lines and
is entirely in rhymed couplets. What we have, in short, is a strophe (section
I), an epode (section II), and an antistrophe (section III). That this is not
the order in which Pindar's odes characteristically proceeded already suggests that the poem is reinventing Pindar. I might note too that, although
the epode or stand may serve as a momentary point of equilibrium, the
poem ends with the antistrophe or counter-turn, so even the structure tells
you that it does not move to some final resolution.

Also, each section – especially the strophe and epode – begins by defer-
ring to some other authority. That is, the epode gives us a creation myth,

but it is not presented as the speaker's; it is offered as what "fairy legends say," as folklore. The strophe opens with even less self-assurance: "As once, if not with light regard / I read aright." I'll return to the antistrophe in a moment, but let me first say more about the beginning of the poem. The "gifted bard" in line 2 is Edmund Spenser: the "Elfin Queen" is a reference to his long poem *The Faerie Queene*, and lines 5–16 retell a story taken from *The Faerie Queene*, that of Amoret, whose "vertue of chast love, / And wivehood true" entitled her to wear a magic girdle named "Cestus" (in Spenser, the girdle seems both to mark and at the same time to bestow virtue). Actually, Collins has not got the story quite right, but it is still recognizable (and its source – Spenser – would have been known to Collins's early readers if only because he provided footnotes for them). In other words, you do not have to know Spenser's work (or even that lines 1 and 2 adapt phrases from Spenser) to read this ode; Collins's primary point is that – not what – he is drawing from an earlier poet. In the second line of the poem, the speaker may even imply he has not read Spenser's poem "aright."

The grammar of Collins's first lines is not entirely clear. The opening couplet most basically suggests that what follows is something the speaker read (and with admiration; that is, not "with light regard") in Spenser. Still, there is something self-deprecating in the tone; the speaker does not specifically say he has studied Spenser. He says, far more tentatively, that what follows is something he "*once*" read, as if casually. Then, of course, he qualifies this: "if not with light regard." We might expect him to say "*but* not with light regard." Using "if" makes the same point; however, "if" sounds less self-assured. Moreover, notice the contradictory tone. Strophes and antistrophes may sketch the broad back-and-forth (or dialectical) movement of odes, but Collins's very first lines already seem infected by such a movement: he implies he read only once and then quickly protests that his one reading took Spenser seriously. Literally, he says he once read "aright," but the intervening clause ("if not with light regard") – as well as the suggestion this is only something he read once, in the past – does not reassure us that the speaker knows that about which he speaks. And this seems part of the point, setting the tone as a whole. After all, Collins could far more authoritatively have begun by saying he read Spenser seriously, or even that he has what he will describe on good authority. Instead, the first couplet focuses us on the speaker's lack of authority: he defers to Spenser, whom he "once . . . read"; and he himself at least tacitly raises the possibility that he may not have read properly.

It is also worth noting that the parenthetical aside in the second couplet not only identifies Spenser (if in a roundabout way); it also suggests that

Spenser's famous poem has been "blessed" by a school of Spenserian poets, by poetic followers or heirs, and the idea of being blessed as a state only held by one person – or poem – at a time is echoed in the stories that follow. Ultimately, the strophe rehearses three different stories about being "blessed" (the word is used in lines 4, 13, and 21). There is the story about Spenser's long poem being "blessed" (which seems to mean it is praised or famous). Then there is the story supposedly from Spenser (about nymphs competing for a belt, also called a "band" or "zone" or "cest"), which draws on a part of *The Faerie Queene* that is about chastity (in Book IV, Canto V). Collins retells the story as if it were centrally about competition and ambition, with the caveat that trying and failing is worse than not trying. These themes *are* also in Spenser, although Collins concentrates in a way Spenser does not on the feelings of the publicly "unblest" and so dishonored nymphs who are shown to be unworthy of the belt. (In Spenser, the fable seems more about how to tell who has or does not have virtue, and less about the shame of pretending to virtue one does not have, although the distinction between appearing worthy and actually being worthy is indeed Spenserian.) Finally, there is Collins's own story about Fancy (begun in line 17), which he says is like Spenser's story of the competition for the magic girdle, showing us what it is about Spenser's story that appeals to him. When he starts his story (writing "Young Fancy *thus* . . .") he basically says, "in the same way that nymphs vie for a magic girdle in Spenser's poem, so I know a story of people vying for Fancy's 'cest of amplest power,' although few will be 'blest' with that power." In short, the power of fancy (another word for imagination in the period) rather than moral virtue is Collins's theme.

I know it is difficult to parse the sentences that tell us these three structurally parallel stories (not to mention that you, like Collins's first readers, may need to turn to the notes to figure out the reference to Spenser). One question is why? That is, why are we given a compulsive retelling of three analogous stories, and why is the voice (and the syntax) of the poem so convoluted? At least part of the answer to the second question lies in Collins's characterization of imaginative power, outlined in lines 20–2, namely that it is aligned with prophecy, wild visions, and fiery imagination (or fancy), which for him are the earmarks of strong poetry. So the "wildness" of his voice seems his bid for imaginative power. To say this may seem a bit of a leap, but the poem's title makes clear that it is about "the poetical character" and the last fable – Collins's own fable – in the strophe is about imagination and its (or in Collins's allegory "her") power. By analogy (or as Collins might say, "thus"), it seems the earlier stories are there because they are also stories about or allegories of imaginative power.

I suspect that Spenser serves Collins as a kind or type of poetic power for several reasons. First, he has gone down in literary history for writing a long, impressive poem, *The Faerie Queene*. Indeed, in Collins's day, we find some of the first literary histories of English poetry, which do make it sound as if the muse honored one poet per generation: Chaucer, Spenser, Shakespeare, and then Milton. (Ironically, if you look back at Milton's "Il Penseroso," you can see that he already had a sense of this list of literary luminaries, even if in 1631 he had not yet made it onto the list.) Second, Spenser, in Collins's ode, is seen as a poet of power because Collins reads (or misreads) Spenser's story about virtue (specifically chastity) as a parable or allegory about poetic ability. I take it this is not simply a misreading of Spenserian allegory (although it is that) but also a sign of how Collins read and was impressed by Spenser. In other words, what Collins takes from Spenser's poem is not so much the thematic content of *The Faerie Queene* as a sense of Spenser's standing as a poet and his impact on readers (and his followers or "school"), which Collins then takes (or mistakes) as the point of Spenser's story of the girdle.

In this light, it makes sense that Collins would write about the dishonor of failed ambition. That is, if you write poetry, you may have ambitions. If you make public what you have written and everyone finds it dull (or worse), you might cover yourself by saying it was just a draft or something you just threw together. On the other hand, if you write something and tell everyone (as you make it public) that it is the best thing written in your generation, and your readers *then* find it unimpressive, that is embarrassing. This seems to be another reason Collins dwells on the story of a competition for something like poetic laurels. He has hope of becoming the next great poet, but to say so (or show these ambitions in his poem) may embarrass (if not "dishonor") him. I have already mentioned that the "wildness" of the voice (the syntax, the difficult references, and more formally the varying line lengths) show Collins's bid to write major (or sublime or fiery) poetry, although it is also the case that he does not explicitly claim to be one of "the few" gifted poets (line 20 says the gift is only assigned to a few). Indeed, Collins covers himself: he says explicitly that his topic is from Spenser and does not then claim it as a sign of his own attempt at imaginative power.

While I am not going to go through the epode in as much detail, I think you can see that it too is difficult to follow, written in a voice of excitement (with long, grammatically complex sentences), even as the voice claims only to report what "legends say." Collins then describes the creation of the world and the simultaneous creation of poetry as well as offering an allegorical description of the weaving of Fancy's belt. (Harking back to the root meaning of the word "one inspired by God," the "Enthusiast" is probably Fancy; the "youth of morn" probably Apollo, the god of poetry, although most of the myth is Collins's invention). You might want to look more closely for yourself at the somewhat transgressive images of how the god of poetry is begotten or at the grand claims made for the belt or cest of poetry: we are told it is woven of ecstasy and wonder, passion (but not dangerous passion), truth, mind, and power, among other things.

What interests me most, here, is what we are told in the last four lines of the epode, where an authorial voice (not that of "fairy legend") returns:

> Where is the bard, whose soul can now
> Its high presuming hopes avow?
> Where he who thinks, with rapture blind,
> This hallowed work for him designed?

The "hallowed work" seems to be both the belt ("presuming hopes" recalls the presumptuous nymphs trying for the magic girdle in the strophe) and the work of poetry. The concluding questions, however, are more puzzling: are they rhetorical, implying (humbly) that Collins's era has no "bards" worthy of the name? Or are they again *Collins's* bid to be named the poet of his age (implying *he* is the bard)? Or, given the image of "rapture blind," and given that Milton was blind by the time he wrote his major work, *Paradise Lost*, do the questions proleptically signal Milton's appearance in the antistrophe (although line 51 does say "now" and Milton died almost three-quarters of a century before Collins wrote "Ode on the Poetical Character")? As at the end of the strophe (where Collins does not come right out and say he wants to be one of "the few" to whom Fancy gives poetic power), the ambiguity seems deliberate, perhaps a sign of Collins's anxiety about his poetic abilities.

The antistrophe, on the other hand, opens differently from the strophe and epode. For one, it does not at first defer to earlier writers or writings, so that for the first nine or ten lines of the final section of Collins's ode you might think – indeed, you are encouraged to think – that he is giving us and claiming his own original vision. The "ambitious head" in line 61 is literally that of a cliff, but it also calls to mind the earlier hints of Collins's own ambition. At the same time, the landscape "to Heaven up-piled" is reminiscent of both classical and biblical stories of overreaching, stories like those of the Titans or of the tower of Babel. Indeed, it seems Collins is piling up clauses ("High on some cliff . . . Of rude access . . . Where . . . While . . .") so that for seven lines we have no idea what the subject of his sentence is. When we finally are told, it seems for a moment quite the right subject for a poet who wants to be original; Eden is a powerful trope of origins, of being first. Yet this impression of an original vision lasts for less than half a line. What Collins's visionary speaker sees is not Eden, but an Eden "like [someone else's] own." The "I" (which reappears for the first time since line 2 of the poem) has a vision (saying in line 63 "I view" not "I read" or "I have heard"). But what he views, it seems, has already been written by Milton.

Put another way, Collins's vision is of how his vision is not after all original, signaling that he is not one who can gird his "blest prophetic loins, / And gaze [Fancy's] visions wild, and feel *unmixed* her flame" (lines 21–2). His vision is already mixed with Milton's, at second remove. He has a vision of Milton having a vision, of Milton being given poetic inspiration directly from heaven. Literally, lines 64–6 describe Milton lying by an Edenic oak while the "native strains" (or singing, as in "Il Penseroso's "prophetic strain") of heaven are heard. Collins then describes Milton reaching up to a trumpet – a long-standing symbol of epic or high poetry – hung on the oak and playing the music of the spheres. When Milton is imagined as lying by the oak while heavenly music drips into his "evening ear," the implication is that for Milton vision was a gift, not a matter of work. Edmund Waller (1605–87) – whose shade, or apparition, Collins says he will avoid – wrote smaller, song-like love poems (for which the "myrtle" of line 69 stands); Collins's point is that he wants more sublime "glory," like that of Miltonic poetry.

Part of the reason the desire to be blessed (in the strophe) seemed to me to be about writing is that I knew the pattern of competing for first place in literature runs throughout the whole ode. It is most obviously repeated at the end of the poem in lines 72–3, where Collins writes that "such bliss *to one alone* / Of all the sons of soul was known." (Note the strong alliteration aligns "blessed" and "bliss," too.) Similarly, the antistrophe finally explicitly states Collins's aspirations but also repeats the sense found at the end of the strophe and the epode that such aspirations are no longer tenable. Eden, or the original landscape of "inspiring bowers," is overturned, an image of the fall and expulsion from Eden recast as (or as an allegory of) the modern state of no longer being able to write anything as powerfully original as the earlier poetry Collins admires. In short, poetic originality is no longer available, and the first coy implications that Collins hoped to be one of the few, or the newest major poet, are disclaimed at almost the same time he finally makes explicit that he has such ambitions. Once again, the back-and-forth movement of the ode is clear: Collins, in essence, says he hopes; he sees his hopes are fruitless; he aspires; he cannot aspire. The conceptual syntax of the English ode is laid bare in "Ode on the Poetical Character," saying (over and over) "Yes, but no."

I think you can see, first, that something has happened to Pindar's praises of the winners of athletic competitions: the ambition enacted and described in Collins's ode is far more psychological or internalized; the subject of the ode, poetry itself. I think, too, you can see why it is useful to talk about odes as poems that set out to praise or find presence (the "yes") but come to find absence (the "no"). Collins may try, with "many a vow from Hope's aspiring tongue," for originality, but he ends saying he has failed or will fail. Or does he? Some have suggested that Collins's final image of what is "curtained close . . . from every future view" is an image not so much of seeing curtains close in front of him, but of him closing the curtains behind himself. This is not an implausible claim. If Spenser and Milton created original literary worlds, Collins may be one of the first English poets to make poetic anxiety palpable. If Collins does not convince himself that he has the power of earlier poets to make the subject of his poems present or to see as if for the first time that about which he writes, he does offer a powerful presentation of anxiety (of what Harold Bloom would call his sense of belatedness). One might say he succeeds at failure; insofar as his poem is about the absence of what is conceived of as poetic power, it succeeds at making this absence present.

Discussing the "presence of absence" may seem to have led us into the realm of abstractions, although I gave you Collins's ode because I think it embodies and so helps with an understanding of more theoretical accounts of odic gestures. For example, you may have noticed I began talking about "the speaker" in Collins's poem but gradually shifted, identifying the voice of the poem simply as Collins's voice. While my interpretation still refers to Collins-in-his-poem (or as a speaker, not as the person with a life outside of poetry), my language points toward a sense of hearing the poet – and the poet's sense of what Paul Fry calls "ontological and vocational doubt" – which is common in odes. Indeed, let me sketch a bit more fully Fry's approach to odes, which he analyzes in terms of characteristic rhetorical, psychological (and ultimately psychoanalytic) gestures as opposed to the more historically located account of English odes I earlier drew from Stuart Curran's work. The critical approaches offered here are about the same poems; they agree on many of the features of odes, although they disagree about whether modes of poetry reveal or shape poets' attitudes, and they disagree about whether such attitudes are universal or specific to certain periods and cultures.

It is probably clear that my own tendency is to read poems as historically and culturally specific. Still, while this is not the approach taken in Fry's book on the poet's "calling" (a calling, of course, is a vocation), and while my discussion might dismay Fry (since I will not dwell on his ultimately psychoanalytic approach), I find much of his discussion useful. For Fry, odes concern something he thinks all poets fret about: namely, presence, or the ability of poetry to perform a kind of verbal magic, wanting "not merely to participate in the presence of voice but to *be* the voice." Beginning (as Curran also does) with the historical relationship between hymns and odes, Fry is suggesting that in the same way God is said to create by fiat – when God said, "Let there be light," there was light – so too poets want to call some presence into being with their poems. While for Fry this would be true of all poets, for him it is the ode that most nakedly exposes this desire or calling. Actually, Fry puns on the word "calling"; as he puts it, odic invocation is "a purposeful calling in rather than a calling out."

Of course, as I said in the chapter on night pieces (which may be a subset of odes), if one calls something, it will not necessarily come. Indeed, to "call in" is to admit that what is called is not there. In this sense, calling and desire are related: if you desire something, by definition you do not have it; similarly, if there were no distance between caller and called, there would be no need to call. Another reason Fry says that odes are models of all poetry is that things and spirits simply *are* always absent from words; certainly, unless the writer has used a pot of glue, he or she will not be able to make any thing present in poems. When we read, we read words, not things. Basically, this is the absence some critics would say haunts all poems, the combined desire and absence that odes in their voiced desire for presence unmask. As Fry again puts it, the voice in the ode "writes itself hoarse," knowing it will ultimately fail, but either refusing that knowledge or, as Fry would have it, ultimately overcoming the fear of failure by guaranteeing it. Finally, Fry notes that these odic gestures manifest in the use of two figures of speech and one figure of thought. His point is that the combination of these figures results from the complex and contradictory gestures of odes – that they call in (using invocation) and that they proleptically know they do not and cannot have what they call for. Along with invocation and prolepsis, odes use what Fry calls dialectic (or irony). This is what I have called the "yes, but no (but yes, but no)" or back-and-forth structure of the ode. Fry, I would add, concludes noting that the contradictory gestures of his three figures (invocation, prolepsis, and dialectic) are a Freudian emblem of compulsion neurosis, where one keeps saying "in other words," trying to keep what one knows at bay. And for Freud (and Fry) this ultimately concerns sex and death.

I already confessed that my own inclinations are not to found my readings of poems in psychoanalysis. At the same time, it does strike me that Fry is correct in saying odes (like Collins's) compulsively, over and over, try to make themselves see or speak in a way they know from the start they cannot. If you think about it, without the back-and-forth (or "yes, but no" or dialectic) odes would be very short. Collins's "Ode on the Poetical Character" would be a poem that stated from the start the impossibility of its ambition to present a powerfully original voice. It might go: "I want poetic power. I don't have it." (Fry might say the deeper narrative is more like: "I don't really want to be taken over by some power, and I won't be.") In either case, the ode prolongs the time between the (qualified) invocation or "yes," and the final (if foreseen) failure or "no." On this account, most odes are long poems because part of their project is to resist moving too quickly from desire to failure. In other words (and it seems to me entirely appropriate that trying to characterize odes results in odic formulations like "in other words"), the ode – at least the English or pseudo-Pindaric ode, which Fry calls the ode of presentation – usually tells a story more like: "I want poetic power; I don't have it; I might have it; I (or someone else) once had it; I want it; I don't have it. But I want it . . ." Yes, but no . . . but yes, but . . .

A few paragraphs cannot do justice to Fry's book (nor, earlier, did I do justice to Curran's historical account of odes). Still, I wanted to offer you a vocabulary (and to be clear that critical vocabularies arise from theories, often entailing presuppositions) for the vacillation of the voice in the ode. I am also trying to show that you can borrow from the insights of other critics without necessarily accepting all that they propose – as long as you are clear about what you are doing. For example, I draw on Fry's rhetorical (and to a lesser extent his psychological) analysis, while not using his psychoanalytic framework. This is not to say you need to follow my example; you might find Fry's use of Freudian psychology compelling. Or you might wish to evolve your own theory of irregular or presentational odes. This is not something you would do without reading more odes, of course, and far more odes than I can give you here. Still, I want to introduce you to at least two more odes, one from the nineteenth century and one from the twentieth.

The ode to which I turn next is by William Wordsworth. For convenience, I have numbered the poem's sections (although when Wordsworth published the whole in 1807 he did not include numbers). I might also tell you that most critics identify sections 1–4 as a strophe, sections 5–9 as the antistrophe, and section 10–11 as the epode, although I will question whether the epode does not precede the antistrophe. However you finally decide the poem works, as you read it you should notice how the characteristic "back-and-forth" or vacillating motion of the strophe and antistrophe (as in Collins's ode) is everywhere, within as well as between sections of the poem. That said, it does make sense to see sections 1–4 as the first movement (the strophe), since Wordsworth wrote those sections in 1802, and then stopped writing. Sections 5–11 were not completed until 1804. Moreover, as printed in 1807, the poem was called, simply, "Ode." It was not until 1815 that Wordsworth changed the title to "Ode: Intimations of Immortality from Recollections of Early Childhood" and added a headnote or **epigraph**, taken from one of his own poems, which read: "The Child is father of the Man; / And I could wish my days to be / Bound each to each by natural piety." Although it is not what most anthologies ask you to do, I want to read the poem as it was published in 1807. Neither version of the poem can strictly be called "the real poem," and there is debate among editors about the principles on which one would decide which versions of poems to use: The first? The first published? The last printed in an author's lifetime or under an author's supervision? Here, I think it suffices to admit that it would be silly to pretend Wordsworth did not finally add the references to childhood and to piety (in the title and epigraph). It is nonetheless also the case that in 1807 Wordsworth published the following (minus the section numbers) under the title "Ode":

1
There was a time when meadow, grove, and stream,
The earth, and every common sight,
      To me did seem
    Apparell'd in celestial light,
The glory and the freshness of a dream.   5
It is not now as it hath been of yore; —
    Turn wheresoe'er I may,
      By night or day,
The things which I have seen I now can see no more.

2
    The Rainbow comes and goes,   10
    And lovely is the Rose;
    The Moon doth with delight
Look round her when the heavens are bare;
    Waters on a starry night
    Are beautiful and fair;   15
The sunshine is a glorious birth;
    But yet I know, where'er I go,
That there hath pass'd away a glory from the earth.

3
Now, while the Birds thus sing a joyous song,
    And while the young Lambs bound   20
      As to the tabor's sound,

To me alone there came a thought of grief:
A timely utterance gave that thought relief,
      And I again am strong.
The Cataracts blow their trumpets from the steep,   25
No more shall grief of mine the season wrong;
I hear the Echoes through the mountains throng,
The Winds come to me from the fields of sleep,
        And all the earth is gay,
              Land and sea   30
      Give themselves up to jollity,
           And with the heart of May
    Doth every beast keep holiday,
          Thou Child of Joy,
Shout round me, let me hear thy shouts, thou happy Shepherd Boy!   35

4
Ye blessed Creatures, I have heard the call
      Ye to each other make; I see
The heavens laugh with you in your jubilee;
      My heart is at your festival,
          My head hath it's coronal,   40
The fullness of your bliss, I feel – I feel it all.
      O evil day! if I were sullen
      While the Earth herself is adorning,
         This sweet May morning,
      And the Children are pulling,   45
        On every side,
    In a thousand valleys far and wide,
    Fresh flowers; while the sun shines warm,
And the Babe leaps up on his mother's arm: —
      I hear, I hear, with joy I hear!   50
     —But there's a Tree, of many, one,
A single Field which I have look'd upon,
Both of them speak of something that is gone:
      The Pansy at my feet
      Doth the same tale repeat: 55
Whither is fled the visionary gleam?
Where is it now, the glory and the dream?

5
Our birth is but a sleep and a forgetting:
The Soul that rises with us, our life's Star,
      Hath had elsewhere it's setting,   60
        And cometh from afar:
      Not in entire forgetfulness,
      And not in utter nakedness,

But trailing clouds of glory do we come
        From God, who is our home: 65
Heaven lies about us in our infancy!
Shades of the prison-house begin to close
        Upon the growing Boy,
But He beholds the light, and whence it flows,
        He sees it in his joy;   70
The Youth, who daily farther from the East
        Must travel, still is Nature's Priest,
            And by the vision splendid
            Is on his way attended;
At length the Man perceives it die away,   75
And fade into the light of common day.

6
Earth fills her lap with pleasures of her own;
Yearnings she hath in her own natural kind,
And, even with something of a Mother's mind,
        And no unworthy aim,   80
        The homely Nurse doth all she can
To make her Foster-child, her Inmate Man,
        Forget the glories he hath known,
And that imperial palace whence he came.

7
Behold the Child among his new-born blisses,   85
A four year's Darling of a pigmy size!
See, where mid work of his own hand he lies,
Fretted by sallies of his Mother's kisses,
With light upon him from his Father's eyes!
See, at his feet, some little plan or chart,   90
Some fragment from his dream of human life,
Shap'd by himself with newly-learned art;
        A wedding or a festival,
        A mourning or a funeral;
            And this hath now his heart,   95
        And unto this he frames his song:
            Then will he fit his tongue
To dialogues of business, love, or strife;
        But it will not be long
        Ere this be thrown aside,   100
        And with new joy and pride
The little Actor cons another part,
Filling from time to time his "humorous stage"

With all the Persons, down to palsied Age,
That Life brings with her in her Equipage;   105
    As if his whole vocation
    Were endless imitation.

8
Thou, whose exterior semblance doth belie
    Thy Soul's immensity;
Thou best Philosopher, who yet dost keep   110
Thy heritage, thou Eye among the blind,
That, deaf and silent, read'st the eternal deep,
Haunted for ever by the eternal mind, —
    Mighty Prophet! Seer blest!
    On whom those truths do rest,   115
Which we are toiling all our lives to find;
Thou, over whom thy Immortality
Broods like the Day, a Master o'er a Slave,
A Presence which is not to be put by;
    To whom the grave   120
Is but a lonely bed without the sense or sight
    Of day or the warm light,
A place of thought where we in waiting lie;
Thou little Child, yet glorious in the might
Of untam'd pleasures, on thy Being's height,   125
Why with such earnest pains dost thou provoke
The Years to bring the inevitable yoke,
Thus blindly with thy blessedness at strife?
Full soon thy Soul shall have her earthly freight,
And custom lie upon thee with a weight,   130
Heavy as frost, and deep almost as life!

9
    O joy! that in our embers
    Is something that doth live,
    That nature yet remembers
    What was so fugitive!   135
The thought of our past years in me doth breed
Perpetual benedictions: not indeed
For that which is most worthy to be blest;
Delight and liberty, the simple creed
Of Childhood, whether fluttering or at rest,   140
With new-born hope for ever in his breast: —
    Not for these I raise
    The song of thanks and praise;
    But for those obstinate questionings

Of sense and outward things,   145
    Fallings from us, vanishings;
    Blank misgivings of a Creature
Moving about in worlds not realiz'd,
High instincts, before which our mortal Nature
Did tremble like a guilty Thing surpriz'd: 150
    But for those first affections,
    Those shadowy recollections,
        Which, be they what they may,
Are yet the fountain light of all our day,
Are yet a master light of all our seeing;   155
    Uphold us, cherish us, and make
Our noisy years seem moments in the being
Of the eternal Silence: truths that wake,
        To perish never;
Which neither listlessness, nor mad endeavour,   160
        Nor Man nor Boy,
Nor all that is at enmity with joy,
Can utterly abolish or destroy!
    Hence, in a season of calm weather,
        Though inland far we be,   165
Our Souls have sight of that immortal sea
          Which brought us hither,
        Can in a moment travel thither,
And see the Children sport upon the shore,
And hear the mighty waters rolling evermore.   170

10
Then, sing ye Birds, sing, sing a joyous song!
        And let the young Lambs bound
        As to the tabor's sound!
    We in thought will join your throng,
        Ye that pipe and ye that play,   175
        Ye that through your hearts to day
        Feel the gladness of the May!
What though the radiance which was once so bright
Be now for ever taken from my sight,
        Though nothing can bring back the hour   180
Of splendour in the grass, of glory in the flower;
        We will grieve not, rather find
        Strength in what remains behind,
        In the primal sympathy
        Which having been must ever be,   185
        In the soothing thoughts that spring
        Out of human suffering,

> In the faith that looks through death,
> In years that bring the philosophic mind.
>
> 11
> And oh ye Fountains, Meadows, Hills, and Groves,   190
> Think not of not any severing of our loves!
> Yet in my heart of hearts I feel your might;
> I only have relinquish'd one delight
> To live beneath your more habitual sway.
> I love the Brooks which down their channels fret,   195
> Even more than when I tripp'd lightly as they;
> The innocent brightness of a new-born Day
>   Is lovely yet;
> The Clouds that gather round the setting sun
> Do take a sober colouring from an eye   200
> That hath kept watch o'er man's mortality;
> Another race hath been, and other palms are won.
> Thanks to the human heart by which we live,
> Thanks to its tenderness, its joys, and fears,
> To me the meanest flower that blows can give   205
> Thoughts that do often lie too deep for tears.

Although Wordsworth's style is less confusing than Collins's, the number of sudden shifts of tone as well as the liberal use of exclamation points may remind you of Collins's ode. The tone is, not surprisingly, odic; the voice excitedly seems to be calling for something (or in Fry's terms, attempting to call something in). *What* the ode invokes, however, is another question. The beginning and end of the strophe (sections 1–4, the sections written in 1802) speak of a lost "glory" (lines 5 and 18) and a lost "dream" (lines 5 and 57), but what glory or a dream of what? If you were reading a later version of the poem (or read it with preconceived ideas about Wordsworth's beliefs), you might decide it is lamenting the loss of unselfconscious joy in the physical world or of childlike perception. Others, knowing Wordsworth's biography, have proposed that it is about a loss of youthful idealism. Wordsworth was in France during the French Revolution; he was nineteen years old when it began, and in the eleventh book of his long autobiographical poem *The Prelude*, about the events of 1789, he uses images similar to those found in "Ode," writing "Bliss was it in that dawn to be alive / But to be young was very heaven." By 1802, however, hopes that the revolution would change the world for the better were not so easily sustained, and it may be Wordsworth's felt loss of political hopes that informs the ode. Yet, while other writings by a poet may help you see possible contexts for, or even be intertexts for, a particular poem, they are not the last word. The "Ode," in fact, could more generally mourn the loss of poetic vision, not specifically the vision of youthful political idealism or of childhood innocence.

At very least, that people have interpreted the motivation (one might say the pre-text) for the poem in so many ways suggests the poem itself invokes a felt sense of loss more strongly than it attends to *what* precisely is lost. In fact, from the first line of the poem, you can hear a sense not only of loss but of doubt about the nature of what is lost (a form of prolepsis, according to Fry). That is, Wordsworth writes of "common" sights (line 2) that "did seem / Apparell'd in celestial light" (lines 3–4). On the one hand, the first five lines give us an image of a luminous world, almost a dreamscape, as if the poem is trying to recreate the way the world might look to someone full of hope, or to a child, or to someone in love: fresh and as if supernaturally charged. On the other hand, the poem begins in the past tense; "there *was* a time," and uses the word "seem," suggesting that what the speaker used to see (or think he saw) may have been an illusion (the world only *seemed* to him to be glorious). The image of a landscape "apparell'd in celestial light" is similarly guarded: apparel is outer-wear, after all. When Wordsworth writes, "The things which I have seen I now can see no more," then, it is unclear whether something that used to exist in the world has disappeared or whether the world is unchanged but the speaker sees differently, perhaps more clear-sightedly than "of yore." The archaic usage ("of yore"), like the fairytale opening ("there was a time"), may suggest the latter, although the images and diction do not let us *or* the speaker decide definitively whether the loss described entails a shift of perception or a shift in the world.

In the second section of the strophe, then, the speaker shifts his position, sounding at first determined to look at the world more realistically (there's no celestial light; the heavens are "bare"). You might note too that rainbows, roses, and moons are all transient, not lasting, which adds poignancy to the speaker's attempt to find them sufficient, or to settle for the "glorious birth" of mere sunshine (set against the now lost "glory" of line 5). By the second section, as well, you can hear the dialectic of the odic voice in full swing, as the poet proclaims earth was glorious, but no longer is; that he used to see, but no longer does; that things are still lovely, "But yet" (line 17) something really is missing. Moreover, the third section continues this back-and-forth movement: if the speaker has just concluded something (line 18 suggests it is something that "really" used to be in the world) "hath passed away," section 3 returns to the present ("now") and insists, no, everything else (birds, lambs, land, sea, cataracts [waterfalls], children, shepherds) seems still to live in something like "the freshness of a dream," in the spring, the season of birth and new beginnings. Vowing not to "wrong" the season, the speaker appears to have reverted to his earlier sense that it is his perspective, not the world, that has gone awry. The real drama of the strophe is, I think, this back-and-forth motion, tracing something like an inner argument: "yes, it was real; no it was not; yes, it was; but I can no longer see it." Typically for an ode, the poem is not inviting us to add up what is said in order to figure out whether the world or the speaker has changed; it is enacting the speaker's vacillation or doubt. The somewhat mysterious "timely utterance" mentioned in line 23 may be the sound of the outer world breaking in on the brooding thoughts of the speaker (perhaps the shout of the shepherd, although this is not identified until line 35) or perhaps the dreamy "echoes" and "winds . . . from the fields of sleep" (in lines 27–8) or maybe the speaker's own ability to give voice in the invocative (but vacillating) poem we are reading.

Section 4, then, sounds as if it is reaching a conclusion, revisiting the images of and perhaps about to resolve the dilemma set in section 1. While the ode began with the loss of celestial light, by line 36 we are told that "creatures" are again "blessed" and (in line 41) full of "bliss" (like Collins's chosen few, perhaps) and that "the heavens laugh with" them (in line 38). The celestial, in short, seems to have returned. If what was lost was the speaker's vision in section 1, section 4 seems to recuperate vision: "I see," the speaker says in line 37. Moreover, unlike the predictable rhythms of the failed attempt to recover freshness of sight in section 2, section 4 is full of variations in rhythm, repeated words, and exclamations: "I feel — I feel" (line 41); "I hear, I hear, . . . I hear!" (line 50). You might compare the straightforward iambic trimeter of lines 10 and 11 with the more expansive and yet less predictable iambic pentameter of:

```
w    s [elision] s    w   w  w   w  s  ww
The heavens     laugh with you in your jubilee;
o    B  ô       B    o  B̄  ὔ    B o B̄
```

Of course, in chapter 4 we saw that rhythmically complicated lines – places in the poem where the speaking voice and the underlying metrical contract are not easily aligned – can suggest perturbation or (as in Donne's poem) an inability to "get with the program." In Wordsworth's ode, the rhythms and style of the language in lines 36–50 are presented in what, thematically, sounds like a recovered ability to delight in – or with – the world. However, it may be that even before we read the telling "But" (the turn in line 51), we already hear an uneasiness in the speaker's voice. The repeated insistence that he can feel and hear also makes it sound as if the speaker protests too much; to say "I feel" three times in one line suggests more a willful, desperate insistence than genuine conviction. Nonetheless, line 51's transition is on the face of it an abrupt turn-about.

As you might expect, much critical ink has been spilled on the question of how to identify the tree, the field, and the pansy of lines 51–4. Each is conspicuously called singular (not part of a common or shared jubilee). It has been noted that two of the iconic images of the French Revolution were the liberty tree and the Champs Elysée, the latter meaning literally the Elysian Fields, classically the fields of the blessed, an Edenic setting (although also in Paris an avenue ending in the Place de la Concorde, where the guillotine was set up). If you think back to Collins's (Miltonic) Eden, it too was characterized by a tree (an oak) and a field (the glade). As in the earlier sections of the poem, it is not clear whether Wordsworth's final images in the strophe – a field, a tree – are of original (or innocent) vision or of his earlier political idealism. Moreover, the pansy does not obviously work in any of these registers. It may be that it is singular in having less resonance than the tree and field, although it may equally be significant that the pansy is a common flower (like "every common sight") or that in French it is called a "pensée," meaning "thought." (Ophelia in Shakespeare's *Hamlet* also says: "And there is pansies, that's for thoughts.") In any case, the pansy *does* reflect the very thoughts the speaker has been trying to suppress.

The end of section 4 could in some ways be the end of Wordsworth's poem. Ironically (but not surprisingly in an ode), it seems the first fifty-seven lines of the poem are about the way the world no longer seems full of meaning, as if "Apparell'd in celestial light," for the speaker. The irony is that by lines 55–7 the world actually *is* (again) full of meaning: it is just not the meaning the speaker says he wants. Still, the pansy is talking (it "Doth the same tale repeat," the same, that is, as the story the tree and field tell). And the story is a story of loss: "Whither is fled the visionary gleam? / Where is it now, the glory and the dream?" Admittedly, the story does not bring back the glory or the dream. Yet the world (tree, field, pansy) is presented as full of meaning. By the heartfelt (and, I think, moving) cry heard in those two questions, then, we could say Wordsworth makes a success of failure, much as Collins did. On this reading, the apparent estrangement from the world lamented in the first lines is overcome, insofar as the world is infused with meaning and echoes (or is a projection of) the speaker's thoughts. Yet this resolution obviously did not satisfy Wordsworth, even though he left those questions hanging – not completing the poem – for two years.

I will not discuss the various historical and autobiographical events that might have inspired the completion of "Ode" (including Coleridge's response to the strophe, in his poem "Dejection: An Ode"). Nor will I treat the next movement of the poem, in sections 5–9, anywhere near as carefully as I have the strophe. If this were a book on how to read Wordsworth's poetry, I would dwell on specific passages more. However, insofar as I am here discussing odes, or Wordsworth's "Ode" *as* an ode, it makes more sense simply to point out that the poem continues the dialectic. It is not just that odes are generally long poems. It is that vacillation ("yes but no but yes") or dialectic is what odes perform. Thus, section 5 begins with a more authoritative tone, as if Wordsworth had found an answer to his questions of where the light, glory, and dream went. Thematically, the answer he offers in the next sections of the poem is (to put it starkly) something like "that's life." That is, the speaker tries a new story, about the necessity of maturation as that which moves everyone away from some original vision. Presumably it might blunt one's sense of loss to realize that loss is "natural" or that there is commonality in loss (as much as in joy). Nonetheless, it seems to me that what we are told, starting in section 5, is, even if comforting, self-consciously a fiction. It is not that Wordsworth converted to a belief in reincarnation (which is what the story told ultimately suggests); it is that the ode – being an ode – continues to try on ways of saying "yes," of having something to say, ways that keep collapsing.

Indeed, if you began reading "Ode" with a sense of Wordsworth as a poet of nature, you were probably surprised to find nature characterized as a nurse (not "mother nature"), then a foster-mother, then something very like a jailer (of "Inmate Man" caught in the "prison-house" of the world). The odic vacillation persists as the speaker creates a myth – a common story – of the naturalness of the loss of "celestial light," then protests (not without ambivalence, to judge by the images of prison) that there are "pleasures" to replace what is lost. Finally – most obviously when retold in section 7 as the story not of mankind but of an individual – the myth seems, as I say, to collapse. Certainly, to say of a child (apparently closer to celestial light than the adult man in the "cover story" or myth that is entertained), that the child accepts loss "as if his whole vocation / Were endless imitation" (lines 106–7) is not so consoling. If the story of how everyone moves away from innocence or idealism or freshness of vision is initially comforting (because it is about shared experience), being consigned to repeat a common story no longer sounds so attractive by section 7. There is a similar, but even more abrupt collapse, followed by a surprisingly sudden recovery, between sections 8 and 9, the first invoking the child's early vision (the child is called a "Philosopher" and an "Eye among the blind" in lines 110 and 111) and then chastizing the child for wanting to mature. So much for finding comfort in a common story; the tone modulates as the speaker describes growing up as finding that "custom [will] lie upon thee with a weight, / Heavy as frost, and deep almost as life!" (lines 130–1). If "that's life" seemed to blunt the sense of loss earlier, by the end of section 8 life is nothing like springtime ("heavy as frost") and its depths sound more like those of the grave than those of philosophical thought. Yet (the odic "but" is tacit in the turn), section 9 suddenly announces "O joy!"

While what section 9 says is that the recollection or memories of earlier (if now lost) vision can still be celebrated, the central drama of the poem is, again (or still), the drama of the speaker's vacillation. As I said more abstractly at the beginning of this chapter, the ode may be a poem that sets out to find presence, but finds absence or failure. On Fry's account of odes of presentation or Curran's account of Romantic odes, such poems ultimately make a success of failure. I argued, of course, that Wordsworth's "Ode" seems actually to accomplish this successful failure by the end of section 4. I am not thereby suggesting he could or should have radically edited his poem. The last two sections – which in their return to the strophe's images and rhymes sound like an antistrophe – may leave the speaker where he already was in section 4, but the process we witness (or even in which we participate) between sections 4 and 10 is the point. If psychologists now talk of "working through" grief or a "process of mourning" enacted in elegies (also often long, vacillating poems, sometimes seen as the mirror opposite of odes), then perhaps odes might be seen as a process of coming to terms with the necessarily frustrated desire for presence in poems.

Turning to the details of sections 10 and 11 more specifically, you may already have noticed that the singing birds, bounding lambs, and sounding tabor of section 3 are recalled or, more precisely, called back (since the voice of section 10 is not describing but invoking). Section 3 tells us the speaker alone feels grief "while the Birds . . . sing"; section 10 tells the birds to sing, and announces there will be no thoughts of grief. Note, too, that the ending of the poem moves to something like common prayer. The lone "I" of sections 3 and 4 is replaced (for the most part) with the first-person plural, "we," in sections 10 and 11, suggesting the alienation from the world described and enacted in the strophe is overcome (or compensated for), perhaps by a shared sense of loss. This, again, makes a success of failure. Thus, while the world is no longer seen as glowing, those who do take joy in it are joined (if now only "in *thought*," line 174), and the sense of abandonment is countered by a sense of common suffering (lines 187–9), even acceptance ("the philosophic mind" of line 189). Section 11, then, seems to continue to articulate this apparent resolution of the problem (line 190 begins with "And") while returning to line 1's images of "meadows, grove, and stream" (the stream becomes "fountains," a more Edenic image, in line 190). The first-person "I" does return (and for a moment seems poised to add another "no" or enact again the inability to sustain a satisfactory resolution – as in line 192's "*Yet* in *my* heart . . ."). Similarly, the repetition of "sing" (three times in line 171) may sound strained. And the images are of the end of a day (the sun is "setting" in line 199), unlike the image of daybreak (in line 16). Nonetheless, at least through the last two lines, you could hear the tone as one of acceptance (even of giving thanks).

What, then, is the tone or import of the very end of the poem? It is worth noticing that the ordinary pansy of the strophe is recalled in the line about the "meanest flower that blows." "Blows" most obviously means "flowers" or "blooms," although of course it also brings to mind the less attractive sense of "a blow" as an act of violence, something like "the blows of fortune"; "meanest" almost certainly has the dictionary definition of "ordinary" (as in "that's no mean feat"), but of course it too has less celebratory connotations. And what *are* thoughts that lie too deep for tears? "Tears" rhymes with "fears," but is this counterpoint or continuation? The rhythm of the final lines is not quite lulling, either. To be precise, the final four lines may all be fairly regular iambic pentameter lines (albeit with an initial trochaic inversion in all but line 205). That is, the rhythmic pattern of the final line may with one small deviation repeat the pattern of lines 203–4:

```
s           w  s    s  w  s    w    s    w  s
Thoughts that do  often lie too deep for tears,
B           ꝺ·   B o B  o  B    o  B
```

Yet the sense of the words and the rhythm that has been set up are not easily reconciled. Normally, as an auxiliary verb used for emphasis, "do" would be emphasized or stressed. To stress "do," however, would make the final line extremely awkward metrically, even unmetrical, so the stress on "do" probably is demoted. At the same time, why use an auxiliary verb to add emphasis, if one is forced to ignore that emphasis? I am suggesting that your tongue cannot comfortably maintain at the same time both the rhythm and the sense of the ode's last line. Similarly, something lying "too deep for tears" may bring to mind the "eternal deep" of line 112 (that transcendent realm with which the child-philosopher is said to be in touch in section 8) and the "philosophic mind" claimed at the end of section 10. Yet there are more disturbing echoes, as well; the last time the words "lie" and "deep" appeared in the poem (with a qualifying adverb, although the adverb was "almost" rather than "often") was in lines 130–1: "And custom lie upon thee with a weight, / Heavy as frost, and deep almost as life!"

If we hear these more disturbing echoes and rhythms, where does this leave us, or where does the poem leave its speaker? Some would say that the double readings I have just sketched (wherein the resonances of the images and the rhythm do not unequivocally imply the speaker has resolved his problem) simply encapsulate the vacillation heard throughout the poem. That is, for a moment we may accept the resolution almost allowed by the rhythm; we may feel for a moment that the pansy's "tale," and the earlier, ominous description of the depth of life, have been subsumed in the final image of the deep (i.e. more philosophical) thoughts to which an ordinary flower might give rise. And yet (the odic "and yet"), the back-and-forth movement set up by the poem may be so strongly ingrained that we are left waiting for the apparent resolution (the "yes") to collapse yet again when we consider that depth is an image that has not been all positive in the poem and that, in any case, the metrically awkward inclusion of the verb "do" ("they do lie too deep, they do") is a bit too much like the earlier repetition of "I feel, I feel" to allow a firm sense of resolution.

When I was new to the profession of teaching, I gave a party to which (in my own act of youthful idealism, perhaps) I invited both practicing poets I knew and colleagues – literary critics – with whom I worked. One rather well-known poet and one of my younger colleagues got into a discussion of Wordsworth's "Ode," the poet insisting that the "Ode" was a sign of Wordsworth giving up on his youthful ideals. Both of my guests read the vanished "visionary gleam" as the effect of political idealism, but the poet understood the end of the poem as giving up on those ideals, as solving the problem by an unsavory act of self-repression. The critic, on the other hand, heard the end as moving precisely because it seemed to him self-consciously to express anguished desire, not any satisfying conclusion. They actually came to blows over this (and ruined my party). I tell the story here because it seems to me indicative of two facts about this ode. First, the desire and sense of failure or loss enacted in the ode are taken seriously and personally by many readers, who invest themselves or are caught up in the odic drama. Second, thoughtful and passionate readers can disagree (to put it mildly), hearing the end as resolution or as anything but resolution, as "yes" and "no," with the poet who heard "yes" being dismayed by it while the critic who heard "no" was moved by it. The different ways of hearing the end may have to do with how my friends heard the gestures of odes: one more invested in the invocation of presence; the other more attuned to the dialectic and deferred but proleptically anticipated failure.

I am not going to take sides (although I will issue warnings against settling arguments about poems with fisticuffs). What I want to do is to conclude this chapter by looking at a final poem, which may or may not itself be an ode and which I think highlights related questions. The poem is by Josephine Miles, an American poet who taught at Berkeley where she wrote not only poetry but criticism, among other things essays on the language of odes and of the sublime. Odes may (as in Collins's and Wordsworth's poems) always be self-referential; Miles's 1941 poem is explicitly so: a poem about odes, perhaps an ode to odes. Admittedly, the poem is not strictly speaking called an ode. With a reference to debates in the 1940s about the effects of consumer culture, its title is "Purchase of a Blue, Green, or Orange Ode":

Jake's store past Pindaric mountain
Over the wash is the only place in a day's ride
To get odes at except close to Mesa City side.

He has one glass a dusty one there
Full of blue green and orange odes sticky but o k,   5
And many come by on that account that way.

Scramble down off the hot flats, swallow a lot of universal wind,
Hear that lone freight pushing around sandy acre,
And they need for the slow swipes one green jawbreaker.

A slug of sweet, a globe of a barber's pole,   10
A suck of human victory out of a crowd,
Sugared, colored, out of a jar, an ode.

"Purchase of a Blue, Green, or Orange Ode" is far shorter than the earlier odes discussed here, and although it uses tercets (rhyming *abb*, *cdd*, *eff*, *ghh*), it seems not to have the triadic structure of a strophe, antistrophe, and epode. It does refer to the Pindaric (or pseudo-Pindaric, English) ode when it identifies the place to find odes as "past Pindaric mountain." Aside from the name of the mountain, however, the diction and the proper names in the first tercet are spoken by a colloquial (and regional) American voice. A "wash" is the dry bed of a stream in the western United States; "Mesa City" actually is a town (in 1941, a very small town) in Arizona. The diction is folksy, not that of an educated speaker (and so almost certainly not offered as Miles's voice). That is, the English is not "proper," as when the speaker gives instructions about where "to get odes *at*" or characterizes odes as "sticky but o k" or – even less elegantly – repeats words, talking of "*one* glass, a dusty *one*" or noting that "many come by on *that* account *that* way." The speaking voice is, then, deliberately that of an ordinary person from small-town or rural, western (even south-western) America, the sort of setting that in 1941 might indeed still have contained general stores known by the name of the owner (in this poem, Jake) that carried inexpensive, so-called penny candy in bulk.

Miles is also obviously using a conceit: odes are metaphorically like penny candy, which is to say scarce (but not rare or expensive). Like Jake's store, odes are characterized in the conceit as old-fashioned, not part of mass culture. The dustiness of the jar and the stickiness of the "odes" imply they have not exactly been flying off the shelves. Nonetheless we are told that "many" go out of their way – the directions suggest Jake's store is not that easy to get to – for odes. The further implication is that odic desire has not disappeared (in 1941) and is as present in rural America as in poetry anthologies. It's worth thinking a bit more about what it means to associate odes metaphorically with cheap candies longed for by ordinary individuals. Candy provides pleasure, perhaps even comfort, but is not nourishment *per se*, which is to say candy is an end in itself, not something one eats for some other purpose (say, because it's good for you). The kind of hard candies (like the "jawbreaker" mentioned in line 9) described also provide solitary pleasure or comfort: they cannot really be shared. Given the description of dust, of the wash or dry stream bed, of a town in the arid south-west (not to mention the wind, sand, and "hot flats" of the third stanza), one might also consider that hard candies wet the throat in dry climates – just as odes, typically long-winded, keep a voice sounding, even if their speakers typically fear not being able to give voice to or call in the numinous *je ne sais quoi* (French for "I don't know what") they desire. (Think of Collins's wanting "visions wild" or "rapture" or an original scene, or of Wordsworth's "visionary gleam" and "glory.")

You can say, then, that Miles's poem recasts the odic desire for some singular, vivid presence and, indeed, for giving voice to some presence, in terms of what for her was contemporary and provincial American culture. If Collins and Wordsworth imply their desire is for something higher, Miles's colloquial speaker suggests that odic desire is not at all abstruse (or academic); it is just like the desire for old-fashioned candy, a desire which involves the process of turning something over in your mouth. True, like odes, the aptly named "jawbreaker" is difficult to get your mouth around; the word is even difficult to say, especially when rhymed with "acre." Yet again, in Miles's poem the difficulty is not manifest in elevated syntax or diction. Her elevation is imaged as more physical (a mountain, a mesa), as is the difficulty – jawbreakers have to be held in the mouth; you cannot chew them up and swallow them on the spot; they take time, even "slow swipes."

I have been referring to Miles's "speaker," but in the third stanza, although the western setting remains, it is not clear that we still have a single speaker, especially when the ode-seekers are referred to as "they" in line 9. There is, in fact, no subject at all to what first seem to be sentences that continue giving directions on how to come by an ode: "Scramble down . . . swallow a lot of universal wind, / Hear that lone freight." By line 9, however, we seem retrospectively to have been listening to sentence fragments describing how some "they" – presumably the ones who will go to Jake's – come to need candy. (Moreover, they seem to need candy to help them make the journey to get candy, an analog of the odic emphasis on process in earlier odes.) The "universal wind" and "lone freight" are especially interesting word choices here, in that they remain unelevated, but no longer sound like what a local – or a professor at Berkeley – might actually say. My guess is that the diction and the image of a "lone freight," in particular, comes from country music (for Miles in 1941, most likely the blues-inflected songs of Jimmie Rodgers [1897–1932]). That is, the poem has taken on the language of song (achieving a kind of lyricism), but it is still insistently populist; country and western music did play on 1941 radio stations, but it, like its audience and like the colloquial speech in the first two stanzas, was not highbrow, by any means.

The question is why Miles has so changed a mode usually associated with heightened diction, elevated invocations, and long "back-and-forth" interior monologues in which we are invited to hear the speaker as the poet and to hear the dialectic as vocational anxiety. My students have on occasion suggested that Miles's poem is making fun of odes by comparing them to less-than-elevated forms of candy and music. I would listen to an argument saying that this is the effect of Miles's poem. It is, after all, not entitled "Ode," but refers to the purchase of an ode, as if odes were not genuine in the sense of being hand-made. Yet a purchase also can be a secure hold or grasp. So the title does not wholly clarify whether the poem is taking odic desire down a peg (it can be bought and consumed like candy) or whether the poem is democratizing what might first seem an elite form, suggesting that odic desire is something within everyone's grasp. The poem may even call forth that on which odes have "a purchase" (their sense of unfilled longing made present even as what's longed for is not present). The democratization of odes, I would add, may in itself be a quixotic project (how can one "democratically" be one of the chosen few?), but it would be more in keeping with what Miles does in her other poems. However, to say this is, as usual, not to settle the issue.

The last stanza, in fact, seems to me (like the end of Collins's poem or the end of Wordsworth's poem) not to let us settle the question of whether this poem dismisses the possibility of writing modern, democratic odes, or whether it too makes a success of what might first seem like a failure to achieve the ode's high lyricism. "A slug of sweet" compares tasting odes to drinking a shot or "taking a slug" of whiskey. In the realm of high culture, this may seem to deflate the ambitions of earlier odes. Yet again, within the cultural myths of working-class America's country music songs, the hero nursing his or her failures while drinking at a bar (and singing about it) *was* (and for that matter still is) odically making failure luminous or lyrical. To dismiss this as "unhealthy" or "low class" may be to participate in the very form of elitism the poem counters. I would add that I'm not entirely sure how to understand the appearance of a barber's pole globe, although such poles, themselves colored like hard candies, do have globes, which both advertise barber shops and, even by 1941, would be a bit old-fashioned, part of an earlier era which (like Collins or Wordsworth) one might feel is lost. In any event, the final lines seem to sustain *our* vacillation. The "suck" of a human victory out of a crowd might well sound like a parody of odic ambitions (sucking on a hard candy is a diminished image of individuation-as-victory). Similarly, we are reminded that hard candies are only colored sugar-water and the ones in the poem are "out of a jar." Yet again: even in an era of chain stores and pre-packaged food, one can take a single hard candy *out* of a jar and one can find sweetness. Moreover, the half rhyme of "crowd" and "ode" further distinguishes the ode claimed; the words "an ode" do conclude the poem on what could well be heard as a triumphant note.

My final question is: In what sense has Miles invoked odes? If she celebrates the desire for what odes used to desire, but finds it is untenable, would this make her poem an ode to odes? Can this be an ode even if the distance between wanting an ode and getting, after all, only "a suck of a human victory" – between yes and no, between success and failure – is severely curtailed, the "back-and-forth" (itself literalized as a journey to a store) taking only twelve lines? Ironically, if Miles's poem is not a parody but presents (and is about) the desire for genuine, original presence, it may still deflate our sense of odic desire, and so highlight the dilemma of "speaking poetry" (or of internalizing the movements and feelings of earlier kinds of poetry) in a world where such speech may seem precious or overwrought. It is (maybe appropriately) difficult to bring a discussion of odes to a close, although I will end with these questions raised by Miles's ode to – or poem about – odes. I would, however, encourage you not only to read more odes, but to read through collections of poems written between 1950 and 2000, considering how many poems not specifically identified as odes are at the very least odic.

Terms used

antistrophe	irregular ode
counter-turn	modes
English ode	Pindaric ode
epigraph	pseudo-Pindaric ode
epode	stand
great ode	strophe
homostrophic	the sublime
Horatian ode	turn

Other poems that might be read

John Dryden, "A Song for St. Cecilia's Day" (1687)
Thomas Gray, "The Progress of Poesy, A Pindaric Ode" (1754)
Samuel Taylor Coleridge, "Dejection: An Ode" (1802)
Percy Bysshe Shelley, "Hymn to Intellectual Beauty" (1817)
John Keats, "Ode on a Grecian Urn" (1819)
John Keats, "Ode to a Nightingale" (1819)
Percy Bysshe Shelley, "Ode to the West Wind" (1820)
Allen Tate, "Ode to the Confederate Dead" (1928)
Denise Levertov, "O Taste and See" (1964)
Donald Justice, "Ode to a Dressmaker's Dummy" (1967)
Robert Hass, "Meditation at Lagunitas" (1979)
Allen Ginsberg, "Plutonian Ode" (1982)
Robert Morgan, "Odometer" (1990)

Useful further reading

Stuart Curran, "The Hymn and the Ode," *Poetic Form and British Romanticism* (New York and Oxford: Oxford University Press, 1986): 56–84.

Paul H. Fry, *The Poet's Calling in the English Ode* (New Haven: Yale University Press, 1980).

William Wordsworth, *Poems, in Two Volumes, and Other Poems, 1800–1807*, ed. Jared Curtis (Ithaca, NY: Cornell University Press, 1983).

Chapter 7

What Is Pastoral?

in Christopher Marlowe's "The Passionate
Shepherd to his Love" (1599); Sir Walter Raleigh's
"The Nymph's Reply to the Shepherd" (1600);
Andrew Marvell's "The Mower Against Gardens"
(1681); William Wordsworth's "The World Is Too
Much With Us" (1807); Denise Levertov's
"O Taste and See" (1964); and two poems by
C. S. Giscombe: "(the future)" and
"(1962 at the edge of town)" (1994)

In this chapter I want to discuss another modal term, namely **pastoral**. We use the word "pastoral" in everyday speech to talk about simple rural or **bucolic** landscapes, which is relevant when speaking of literary pastoral but not adequate to the complexities of what first seems a simple mode. We now talk about novels, plays, and other forms as pastoral or as containing pastoral moments, although most literary critics or handbooks of literary terms describing the pastoral will begin by sending you back to poetry – first to the *Idylls* of Theocritus, a Sicilian poet of the third century BCE, and then to Virgil's poetry in the *Eclogues* (bucolic poems written in the first century BCE) – for classical sources. Although these classical poets did influence writers of pastoral in English, pastoral is not a term found in ancient treatises on poetry, and was then, as now, associated with no specific formal structure. Some critics use the terms bucolic, pastoral, and **idyll** interchangeably, while others distinguish pastorals from idylls (the later being less elegiac, more celebratory) and from **eclogues** (eclogues being more dramatic, often a dialogue between characters). You can get a sense of the range of theories and definitions of the pastoral by looking at the books listed at the end of this chapter. Here, I want a bit more loosely to use the word to pick out a series of gestures usually associated with the pastoral that sometimes intersect or get mixed with other kinds of poetry, to try to show you what people think is at stake when they define or contest different definitions of pastoral.

The word pastoral comes from the Latin *pastor*, meaning "shepherd," and it is clear that some association with simple, usually country, living informs many pastorals. The critic Leo Marx has proclaimed, "No shepherd, no pastoral." But even those who agree – and not everyone does – argue over how and why shepherds are represented in pastorals. Pastorals arose out of urban and urbane life, and some say that from its inception the pastoral was a way of looking back with sentimental nostalgia or through rose-colored glasses at over-idealized country living. Obviously, critics with this view tend not to admire pastoral but to see it as a form of self-deception or escapism. Others have read pastoral as self-conscious from the start, a kind of deliberate artifice that never for a moment thought of its landscapes or shepherds as real. On this view, pastoral portraits of shepherds or of a better simpler life are seen as criticisms of the complexities of modern, urban life (even in ancient Greece), or – alternatively – as celebrating our ability to imagine a better life. Poems that describe cultivating or working, even in idealized ways, are called **georgics**, another related mode that sometimes gets mixed with pastoral.

The interpretation of pastorals as self-conscious about their artificiality – as not naïvely nostalgic – is supported by many poems of the English Renaissance in which pastoral literary landscapes are Edenic. That is, the world represented is **prelapsarian**, an unfallen world known to be unavailable to fallen humans. In more secular ages, the dream of a better but clearly unattainable life may be presented more to value a psychological state (or process). But let me first give you a sense of Renaissance pastoral, starting with a pair of poems. The first is Christopher Marlowe's "The Passionate Shepherd to his Love," written in 1599; the second is Sir Walter Raleigh's "The Nymph's Reply to the Shepherd," written within a year of and as an obvious response to Marlowe's poem. As you read, you might notice how Raleigh's form (iambic tetrameter quatrains), images, and argument echo Marlowe's poem. Here then is "The Passionate Shepherd to his Love":

> Come live with me and be my love,
> And we will all the pleasures prove
> That valleys, groves, hills, and fields,
> Woods or steepy mountain yields

And we will sit upon the rocks,
Seeing the shepherds feed their flocks
By shallow rivers, to whose falls
Melodious birds sing madrigals.

And I will make thee beds of roses,
And a thousand fragrant posies,
A cap of flowers, and a kirtle,
Embroid'red all with leaves of myrtle,

A gown made of the finest wool
Which from our pretty lambs we pull,
Fair-lined slippers for the cold,
With buckles of the purest gold,

A belt of straw and ivy-buds,
With coral clasps and amber studs,
And if these pleasures may thee move,
Come live with me and be my love.

The shepherd swains shall dance and sing
For thy delight each May morning.
If these delights thy mind may move,
Then live with me, and be my love.

Here is Raleigh's poem:

If all the world and love were young,
And truth in every shepherd's tongue,
These pretty pleasures might me move
To live with thee and be thy love.

Time drives the flocks from field to fold
When rivers rage and rocks grow cold,
And Philomel becometh dumb;
The rest complains of cares to come.

The flowers do fade, and wanton fields
To wayward winter reckoning yields;
A honey tongue, a heart of gall,
Is fancy's spring, but sorrow's fall.

Thy gowns, thy shoes, thy bed of roses,
Thy cap, thy kirtle, and thy posies,
Soon break, soon wither, soon forgotten,
In folly ripe, in reason rotten.

Thy belt of straw and ivy buds,
Thy coral clasps and amber studs,
All these in me no means can move,
To come to thee and be thy love.

But could youth last and love still breed,
Had joys no date, nor age no need,
Then these delights my mind might move,
To live with thee and be thy love.

At first reading, Marlowe's poem – perhaps each of the above poems – might well seem a simple, naïve gesture, needing no explication or analysis. You might, as a modern reader, have to look up a few words – "to prove" meant "to test" or "to try" at the turn of the sixteenth century; a "kirtle" was a "skirt or dress"; and "swain" first meant "an attendant or servant, often a knight's servant," but came to mean "a rustic or actual shepherd," or "a literary word for a lover." Aside from these possibly unfamiliar words, though, the poem *is* simple (which is probably why it has so often stuck in readers' minds, from Milton's echo of the poem in "Il Penseroso" to modern parodies). Yet, however simple the poem is, it is not naïve, which is to say that Marlowe is well aware his speaker (not Marlowe, but a "passionate shepherd") offers his lover a fantasy – *as* fantasy. I printed the poems together because I think Raleigh's response helps underline what Marlowe already knew, namely the unreal status of his shepherd's life. Marlowe knew real sheep are far dirtier that the shepherd's, and no one who has sheared a sheep would mistake for realism the poem's description of making gowns from "the finest wool" pulled from "pretty lambs" (where the alliteration and rhythmic regularity make the process sound effortless). Moreover, birds don't sing madrigals; real roses have thorns (and so do not make for comfortable bedding). The idyllic landscape represented in the poem – where rivers are never dangerously deep and nature exists only to accommodate the lovers – is not, I am suggesting, a sign that Marlowe is misinformed about the natural world. His world is clearly imagined, not realistic.

On one hand, this means the shepherd's invitation is synecdochic; it stands for the mental act and exuberance of which it is an instance. Consider a more contemporary analog: when the hero in a romantic comedy says to the heroine, "I promise you the moon," he doesn't expect to be taken literally. Indeed, who would want a literal moon? Where would you put it? The gesture is pastoral; it calls attention to the act of imagining a better life, but not a life anyone is expected to take as realistic. And it is this act of imagining (not what is imagined) that connects the poem to the actual world. As Marlowe's shepherd says in the penultimate line, he expects his "delights [his loved one's] *mind* to move"; the poem offers her (and us) *his mind* in motion. On the other hand, what the shepherd imagines is not quite like an Eden. True, there are a number of items mentioned that are lasting (even cultural symbols of things everlasting): coral, amber, myrtle, and ivy (the last two, evergreens). A world out of time is thus evoked. Yet while – given that this is a Renaissance poem – a Christian view of original innocence in Eden or of heaven may well come to mind, it seems clear that the passion attributed to the shepherd is secular (as is the shepherd); the voice issuing the invitation to "live with me and be my love" is thinking not of higher eternal bliss but of an earthly love affair, imagining not Eden but a more sensual lovers' paradise. At the same time, the shepherd's appeal is not the more usual injunction to "seize the day" because time passes (the theme of carpe diem mentioned in chapter 3) but at least tacitly to ignore reality entirely.

Still, even as Marlowe's shepherd imaginatively sketches a world without want or danger or sadness, his vision includes reminders that (apparently even in imagination) it will not always be spring. And in a Christian culture – which Marlowe's most certainly was, even if Marlowe was not known for his piety – reminders of the end of life presumably would put a damper on the inclination to sin. If carpe diem poems emphasize that time is passing so the present must be enjoyed, they also typically and strategically avoid reference to final, moral judgments. By contrast, as I have argued, Marlowe's pastoral for the most part gives us images of a world of pleasure outside of time, where things don't perish. And yet, to mention "straw" (a common emblem of what doesn't last), or seasonality (cold or May), or roses (common emblems of the ephemerality of beauty, as in Wordsworth's "Ode") seems a miscalculation on the shepherd's part. Such reminders of time passing disrupt the otherwise seductive world described. For the *author* of the shepherd, though, this is anything but a miscalculation; it suggests Marlowe tipping his hand, knowing perfectly well the kind of answer Raleigh could write before it was written.

Raleigh's answer does more than remind readers that shepherds lie (although he does suggest the exaggerated landscape and imaginative exuberance are misleading). He also underlines how time passes, with the imagined female response being not to seize the day but to recognize that aging – and death – mean you should *not* seize the day, because tomorrow you might have to face the consequences. The shepherd's pastoral imaginings are systematically challenged in Raleigh's poem, which says sheep won't stay in fields and rivers are not always shallow; Philomel – as in the night pieces read in chapter 2 – offers a more melancholy image of bird song than Marlowe's madrigals; and we are reminded that sitting on rocks is not so pleasant in winter. You might notice how the mention of "cold" calls Marlowe's shepherd on his slip of the tongue – that is, his reference to seasonal change – in stanza four of "The Passionate Shepherd." Tellingly, Raleigh writes of the shepherd's imagined world as the product of a "honey tongue, a heart of gall," which are "fancy's spring, but sorrow's fall," punning on the arrival of autumn *and* the fall of man from Eden. Lines 11 and 12 of Raleigh's poem, then, acknowledge that Marlowe's speaker is offering an invented world ("fancy's spring" suggests both that the spring is merely imagined and that Marlowe's speaker is celebrating the freshness of the imagination, not of nature). But in Raleigh's poem imagined worlds are seen as morally dangerous (being seduced by them would be both sorrow and a fall).

You might think – given the way Marlowe's poem is aware of its artificiality – that Raleigh's answer is a bit flat-footed, taking "The Passionate Shepherd" too literally. There are, however, two further twists to Raleigh's reply. First, his speaker – again, like Marlowe's – actually seems aware of the other side of the story: the last stanza says that if Marlowe's world were lasting, not just a moment's imagination of lasting love, then of course the nymph would accept the invitation. More interestingly, Raleigh's speaker is identified in the title as a nymph. A nymph is a mythological creature, usually a kind of nature-spirit, and (according to myth) most nymphs are immortal. So there is humor in Raleigh's reply. The poem is not presented as a woman's voice saying that men are fickle, and women suffer the consequences, being abandoned when old (or once fallen). This nymph implies that it is the *shepherd* who will grow old, and need to be cared for, while she is the one for whom "age [may have] no need." You could almost say that by making his speaker a nymph, Raleigh has the realm of imagination (of which the nymph is an inhabitant) talk back to the one imagining it; at least he populates and brings the imagined world to life.

Neither Marlowe nor Raleigh can thus be accused of nostalgia for some implausibly represented rural or simple past. They both play with what can be imagined, knowing their speakers and the worlds represented are artifices. Playfulness itself, like the playfulness in the Renaissance sonnets read in chapter 3, is the point (and for both Raleigh and Marlowe the play is seductive, despite their different value judgments about seduction). Mental wit or play could then be said to be part of these Renaissance pastorals, presumably offering a respite from the grittier realities of Renaissance London and court life, in which the authors (unlike their shepherds and nymphs) lived, and in which Raleigh was ultimately executed for treason, Marlowe killed in a bar-room brawl. This might be escapism, but not necessarily escapism as denial or bad faith; it is more like the turn to the mountain nymph (a pastoral figure), presented as a turn to inner resources, found at the end of Charlotte Smith's "To Dependence."

The self-consciousness of early English pastorals was apparently as evident to early readers as it is to us. Writing a bit over eighty years later,

Andrew Marvell builds on the gestures of pastorals like Marlowe's and Raleigh's for his dramatic monologue, "The Mower Against Gardens":

> Luxurious Man, to bring his vice in use,
>   Did after him the world seduce;
> And from the field the flowers and plants allure,
>   Where Nature was most plain and pure.
> He first inclosed within the garden's square   5
>   A dead and standing pool of air,
> And a more luscious earth for them did knead,
>   Which stupefied them while it fed.
> The pink grew then as double as his mind;
>   The nutriment did change the kind.   10
> With strange perfumes he did the roses taint;
>   And flowers themselves were taught to paint.
> The tulip white did for complexion seek,
>   And learned to interline its cheek;
> Its onion root they then so high did hold,   15
>   That one was for a meadow sold:
> Another world was searched through oceans new,
>   To find the Marvel of Peru;
> And yet these rarities might be allowed
>   To man, that sovereign thing and proud,   20
> Had he not dealt between the bark and tree,
>   Forbidden mixtures there to see.
> No plant now knew the stock from which it came;
>   He grafts upon the wild the tame,
> That the uncertain and adulterate fruit   25
>   Might put the palate in dispute.
> His green seraglio has its eunuchs too,
>   Lest any tyrant him outdo;
> And in the cherry he does Nature vex,
>   To procreate without a sex.   30
> 'Tis all enforced, the fountain and the grot,
>   While the sweet fields do lie forgot,
> Where willing Nature does to all dispense
>   A wild and fragrant innocence;
> And fauns and fairies do the meadows till   35
>   More by their presence than their skill.
> Their statues polished by some ancient hand,
>   May to adorn the gardens stand;
> But, howsoe'er the figures do excel,
>   The Gods themselves with us do dwell.   40

You might note, to start, that if Marvell's sense of imagining some other better world is reminiscent of the gestures found in the earlier poems, his diction is nonetheless more ornate than that of Marlowe or Raleigh, as is the use of couplets, in paired pentameter and tetrameter lines. The line lengths may vary, but the variation is so regular (pentameter followed by tetrameter, each linked by rhyme, and with all but four of the couplets end-stopped) that the overall impression is of a highly polished artifact. Although the speaker opens with a moralizing tone – the very first word, "luxurious," means "lecherous" or "voluptuous" – characterizing humans as full of and fostering vice, by seducing the world, he does not sound like the nymph or the shepherd, nor like the voice of nature "plain and pure," the nature he celebrates.

Still, insofar as Marvell's poem is "against gardens," and less explicitly (not to mention more ambiguously) against artifice, at least thematically it sets itself against earlier pastorals, with their unreal and seductive images of idyllic settings. Moreover, unlike the first two pastorals discussed here, the first eighteen lines of "The Mower Against Gardens" include several references to contemporary events. That is, Marvell is not simply referring to past pastorals. By line 5 of what sounds like an allegory or parable, Marlowe's speaker notes that "Man" "enclosed" space in a garden. First, of course, this is a reversal of the expulsion from Eden; instead of being expelled from the garden of Eden, fallen man lures nature *into* gardens, which sound less than pleasant with dead air, fertilizer (that is, "more luscious earth"), and stupefied flowers and plants. Second, however, "enclosing" land – known as "enclosure" – was a hot topic in seventeenth-century England. Indeed, British writers from the sixteenth through the nineteenth century are full of complaints about wealthy landowners fencing in what had previously been common land in order to graze sheep and profit from the lucrative wool trade. The practice was seen as driving agricultural workers off the land and depriving people of sustenance. It is not that Marvell is writing political allegory *per se*. However, like the tulip craze (causing speculation in and inflated prices for tulip bulbs), and the similar runaway enthusiasm for flowers imported from the New World (like the "Marvel of Peru," an actual species), the glancing reference to enclosure ensured that Marvell's early readers would link the parable-like story being told with late-seventeenth-century realities. Most baldly put, the poem identifies the fallen world against which the speaker rails with the world in which Marlowe and his readers lived.

You might conclude that Marvell's world is thus not pastoral, since it does not focus on some imagined other life. Yet there are two realms juxtaposed within the poem (not unlike the juxtapositions in Marlowe's and

Raleigh's poems, both individually and as Raleigh's poem responds to Marlowe's). In "The Mower Against Gardens" we have gathering references to, on one side, the corrupt and apparently greedy, even "unnatural," world of civilization and, on the other side, nature "plain and pure," "sweet fields," or wildness. We are told disapprovingly that humans "graft upon the wild the tame" and hybridize what was natural, selling grafted fruit or tulips or transplanted Peruvian flowers for high prices, as opposed to Nature's free gift of "wild and fragrant innocence." The language used for civilized life is a language of decadence and, indeed, of sexual deviance as Marvell – a participant in the Puritan uprising of the mid- to late seventeenth century – might have understood it. The sexual imagery, in fact, begins in the first couplet, where man is described as lustful ("luxurious") and seductive, and continues in the description of flowers as if they are fallen women (seduced and turned into prostitutes or brazen hussies using "strange perfumes" and "paint" or cosmetics) or the image of harems ("seraglios") and eunuchs.

As the argument of the poem continues in lines 19–30, the speaker notes that the practices disapprovingly described in the first nine couplets "might be allowed" (although the tone of lines 1–18 suggests they really should not be), if man's pride had not begun grafting "forbidden mixtures." In the context of a discussion of vice, inverted gardens, and "adulterate" fruit – that is, counterfeit, but with also the connotation of having sex outside of proper bounds – the reference to "forbidden mixtures" obviously brings to mind forbidden fruit, the fruit of the tree of knowledge forbidden in the garden of Eden. At the same time – coupled with the verb "enforced" in line 31 – the description of the garden as a "seraglio" (such stereotypical images of eastern tyrants were set pieces of political insult in England in the period), suggests that political as well as moral, social, and sexual disorder reign in the dystopic fallen world, identified with the historical world, the poem describes.

Only at the end of the poem does Marvell's speaker turn his attention back to the world of "Nature . . . plain and pure" first mentioned in line 4. By line 33, nature is further characterized as "willing," which surely suggests an act of moral choice or will, yet also – after the image of the harem – almost suggests something like free love is being set against harems and the earlier images of flowers as prostitutes. There are no shepherds, strictly speaking, but we do get an image of an idyllic world set against the world of civilization, art, or artifice. In short, we have pastoral. Indeed, Marvell's other world, like Marlowe's and Raleigh's, is explicitly imagined, not least because it is cultivated by fauns and fairies. There is work involved (the fauns and fairies "till" the meadows), but it is a clear fantasy of work: they do not need "skill." Just being there ("their presence") makes the meadows productive, apparently. This gesture is worth considering further, especially since it seems at first to make Marvell's "nature," like his polished poetic style, unnatural . . . as much an artifice as the artificiality of civilization the poem denounces.

In considering the end of Marvell's poem, it helps to know that there were a number of theological and literary debates in the period about the relative value of art and nature, distantly related to our debates over nature as opposed to nurture, although informed as well by assumptions about original sin (that is, about man's nature). There were also debates about labor, or work, as either man's punishment for original sin, or a salutary part of human experience, a form of stewardship and a way of avoiding idleness. Milton's *Paradise Lost*, for example, does not see work *per se* as punishment for man's original sin, but imagines Adam and Eve happily working before the fall. On first reading, Marvell's poem takes one side in these debates: artifice is vice; nature is good. Work and artifice are also related, both part, it seems, of the fallen world. Even art is thus unnatural, a counterfeiting of nature. For example, by line 39 Marvell's garden is where we find figures or man-made statues of fauns and fairies (not the "real" fauns or fairies). When the poem talks about these creatures cultivating the fields outside gardens by their mere presence, then, it suggests that a real or living spirit is found only outside civilization, outside human work, work which can produce only unnatural facsimiles of nature – or its spirits – in gardens and garden statues.

Actually, I have slightly overstated my case. Through line 30 of "The Mower Against Gardens" we do get a sense of pastoral used as criticism of the modern – and, for Marvell, fallen – world, which is treated caustically as a world of greed, including prostitution, acts of enclosure, "unnatural" breeding and so unnatural creations. Yet the tone changes in the last five couplets. Instead of a diatribe against painted flowers, adulterate fruit, and sexless cherries, we hear about sweet fields, willing Nature, and innocence. Logically, it seems that art would be part of the civilized world, an unnatural creation. Yet in the poem itself, statues of fauns and fairies are not treated the same way grafted (or "unnatural") cherries are; the statues are said to "adorn the gardens" and to "excel," even if they are explicitly less excellent than the actual presences – the "Gods" – of which they are figures. And there is an even sharper shift of tone and emphasis in the final line: "The Gods themselves with us do dwell." The question arises: why or to what effect does the poem's tone shift at the end? There is also the preliminary, if smaller, grammatical question of to whom the first-person plural, "us," refers.

To start with the last question first, "us" is usually an inclusive pronoun. That is, we as readers may first be inclined to feel we are invited to include ourselves in the realm where gods "dwell." On closer reading, however, this is not clearly the case. The speaker is a mower – although unlike fauns and fairies, mowers did exist in the late seventeenth century; scythes would have been used to make hay or clear meadows. What is interesting about Marvell's speaker is that he includes himself as part of the poem's wilder (and less humanly populated) world. The mower, then, presumably cultivates an imaginary and, indeed, still Edenic nature. However, he doesn't "till" or plant – he mows, which is to say he cuts down natural growth. If we are in a world of mythical or allegorical creatures (fauns, fairies, and so on), then at least for a moment the figure of a male with a scythe surely brings the grim reaper to mind.

Where then does this leave us as readers? The mower seems part of an imagined world, not our world. But he is, if not quite the grim reaper, a reaper nonetheless. Are we to conclude there is mortality even in the pastoral, much like the reminders of the passing seasons in Marlowe's and Raleigh's poems? The answer is probably yes. In fact, the trope is common; Arcadia – or rural Greece – was the setting of Virgil's early pastorals, in the *Eclogues,* and by Marvell's day a conventional pastoral setting. The Latin phrase "**Et in Arcadia ego**" circulated in Renaissance painting (so Marlowe would surely have known of it). The phrase is usually translated as "I too [or I also] am in Arcadia," and it is taken as spoken by death. It serves as what is called a **memento mori**, a reminder of death. In short, the idea that pastoral worlds (appearing in pastoral poems as imagined constructs) are not timeless is not new. And this idea seems to inform "The Mower Against Gardens," in which a spokesperson for some other world (like Raleigh's nymph) inveighs against the deadness, greed, and corruption of the historical world, but also tacitly acknowledges that imaginations of escape are just that, imaginings, and so as such are always already part of the real world of time and death.

You might have noticed that I have been distinguishing between pastoral worlds or landscapes (which often are images of simpler, even Edenic places) and pastoral poems that represent such worlds or landscapes (and which are typically aware their images are invented and even focus on the act of invention as what matters). In fact, I began discussing "The Mower Against Gardens" by noting that the voice of the poem – the mower's voice – is not a simple voice; the diction and the poetic form are clearly from the world of art and civilization the poem apparently criticizes. Here, too, it seems the imagined world of fauns, fairies – and mowers – is self-consciously presented as artifice. I've already suggested that poetic figures or images of fauns are very like statues of fauns: they are figures, not presences. You might think of Marvell's gesture in spatial terms: the poem describes a garden as a square of dead air, which by the end seems an artificial simulacrum of paradise set against the more natural wild fields of the mower. Yet this "other space" of meadow and field and indwelling gods is itself inscribed in a poem. And the poem on the page is, literally, an artifice, a square of printed words. In other words, I am suggesting Marvell knew full well that his poem is like a garden, in which we have figures (not statues but figures of speech) that only represent something "outside" the world of art, whether horticultural or poetic. The irony is that no work of art can get outside itself. If the image of the gardens with statues of fauns and fairies alludes to the artificiality of earlier pastoral poems, which by Marvell's day had become set pieces, Marvell's mower gestures toward a new "outside" or pastoral space. Yet Marvell is aware he is simply creating new figures, which are still figures, not living presences. In this sense, pastoral poems have some relationship to odes, which also call for a presence that cannot be found in poems (or in any form of re-presentation, since, if you think about the word, *re*presentation is not presentation). Marvell's poem is not, however, odic. His mower is a self-consciously fictive presence; there seems to be no invocation, in part because pastorals like Marvell's or Marlowe's or Raleigh's recognize and accept the unreal status of the worlds they imagine. There is a dialectic or irony in these poems, but it is not the "yes but no" or back-and-forth motion of the ode.

This is not to say that the odic and the pastoral cannot combine in interesting ways or that the features of pastorals were set once and for all in the early modern period. By the nineteenth century, poets reconstruct the Arcadian or Edenic pastoral world. Shepherds disappear, for the most part, although not surprisingly in the face of the industrial revolution some writers use pastoral to criticize not only city life but industrialization's encroachment on rural life, so that their poems are sometimes closer to an odic calling for unalienated work or even to georgic, reimagining the workplace for industrial laborers. This latter incarnation of pastoral is why the critic William Empson, writing in the 1930s, called all proletarian literature "pastoral," although other critics would make a distinction between pastoral and georgic imaginations of work. At times, too, one finds modern poets offering images of an idyllic (and, often, markedly imagined) good life in the city, sometimes called **urban pastoral**. Moreover, ecocriticism has at times associated pastoral with **green poetry**, which as you might expect often views self-consciously imaginary landscapes like Marlowe's or Marvell's with suspicion. With such changes being rung on earlier pastorals, some critics claim that pastorals simply disappeared at some point in the nineteenth century. And yet the gestures of pastoral do seem to persist, even if they have changed over time, and the term still seems useful, if only to remind us that not all imaginations of an unreal "elsewhere" are naïvely escapist.

I want, then, to consider what happens to this mode as we move toward the modern era, first by looking at two more poems: one from 1807 by a poet whose work you have already read in earlier chapters, namely Wordsworth, and one from 1964 by the American poet Denise Levertov. It is not that pastorals always come in pairs or involve what Marvell calls a "double . . . mind," although self-consciousness about artifice or representation may indeed involve a kind of consciousness doubled on itself, a form of pastoral irony. Still, as with the pairing of Marlowe's and Raleigh's poems, I think pairing Wordsworth's "The World Is Too Much With Us" and Levertov's "O Taste and See" helps underline features of each poem that might be less easily noticed when reading the poems individually. I would say, further, that Levertov's poem is not just a response to but a useful interpretation of Wordsworth's.

Here then are the two poems, beginning with Wordsworth's.

> The world is too much with us; late and soon,
> Getting and spending, we lay waste our powers:
> Little we see in nature that is ours;
> We have given our hearts away, a sordid boon!
> This Sea that bares her bosom to the moon;
> The winds that will be howling at all hours,
> And are up-gathered now like sleeping flowers;
> For this, for everything, we are out of tune;
> It moves us not. – Great God! I'd rather be
> A Pagan suckled in a creed outworn;
> So might I, standing on this pleasant lea,
> Have glimpses that would make me less forlorn;
> Have sight of Proteus rising from the sea;
> Or hear old Triton blow his wreathed horn.

And here is "O Taste and See":

> The world is
> not with us enough.
> **O taste and see**

the subway Bible poster said,
meaning **The Lord**, meaning
if anything all that lives
to the imagination's tongue,

grief, mercy, language,
tangerine, weather, to
breathe them, bite,
savor, chew, swallow, transform

into our flesh our
deaths, crossing the street, plum, quince,
living in the orchard and being

hungry, and plucking
the fruit.

Although Wordsworth's title refers to "the" world, the first quatrain of his poem, in a gesture recognizable from earlier pastorals, juxtaposes two worlds: that of "getting and spending" (which by now is an idiom so common many users probably no longer realize it comes from Wordsworth) and that of "nature." The poem seems to be pastoral at least insofar as, like "The Mower Against Gardens," it juxtaposes two worlds in order to criticize the workaday world, that in which making or spending money takes precedence. In this context, I would assume that "late and soon" marks a sense of being on a schedule – looking back and forward – rather than living in the present. Moreover, the first quatrain uses a series of economic images, images of getting, spending, wasting, owning, and giving. We are told that getting and spending are, from a different perspective, a "waste" (of "powers"); owning material things (or "getting") seems to lead to seeing little as "ours" (presumably a less material kind of possession); and while "we" (who live in the modern world) get things, we give away our hearts. "Boon," if you look up the word, means "benefit" or "gift," with the apparent suggestion that the hearts we have lost are degraded.

A few other things may strike you right away about "The World Is Too Much With Us." First, "the world" that is too much with us is by line 3 clearly marked as not the world of nature, but closer to the world we have in mind when we talk of "worldliness" or "worldly concerns"; the economy which the poem values (that of the power of seeing in a certain way, that of owning our part in or of nature, that of hearts) is not a moneyed or consumer economy. When Wordsworth describes what lies outside of the materialistic world, he does not imagine another realm so much as a world perceived in a new (or, actually, for Wordsworth, an older) way. In other words, the very act of imagining seems to have become the pastoral world.

You might even say that for Wordsworth seeing imaginatively is what has to be imagined.

Also, the poem is a Petrarchan sonnet. As such, one would expect the second quatrain (the end of the octave, with its *abbaabba* rhyme scheme) to develop the theme found in the first quatrain. While this may be precisely what the second quatrain ultimately does, it does not do so by extending the economic images found in the first four lines. The sea, moon, winds, and flowers are, among other things, natural images. Moreover, nature is personified – seen imaginatively. I would add that the sea baring "her bosom to the moon" is not, I think, doing a striptease so much as offering maternal nourishment: the images of "howling," "up-gathered," and "sleeping" winds suggest a mother and child (with the later image of being "suckled" further emphasizing that the sea's bosom is more maternal than erotic). Given the reference to not seeing in nature what "is ours," it might be that the second quatrain is the speaker's attempt to recapture a more humanized nature (or more naturalized humanity). Once again, he is trying to image seeing imaginatively when he looks at the seascape before him, sees calmness, and reads that serenity, metaphorically, as a kind of nurturing family scene. Note, too, that the deictic "this" ("this sea") in line 5 invites us to participate, as if the scene pointed to is present both to the speaker and to us.

When "this" is repeated in line 8 (closing the second quatrain), however, it refers back to the whole vision of nature infused with maternal care described in lines 5–7, so it is the imagining of the landscape, not a feature in the landscape, to which the pronoun refers. And the final effect of line 8 is to close down or disclaim the vision or act of envisioning: "For *this* . . . we are out of tune" suggests both a lullaby (another maternal image, but one that is not so comforting because out of tune), and even more clearly what I might call a failed pastoral. That is, the speaker cannot sustain the vision of nature – presumably a vision that includes feeling (or hearts), seeing less coldly, more holistically, than one does in the world of getting and spending. The gesture is almost odic (in that, as in Wordsworth's "Ode," it collapses – or says "no" to – the alternate vision – the "yes" – it invokes). Line 8, too, begins what might be called a wide turn (the turn more traditionally found in line 9 of sonnets). The first quatrain laments the loss of "heart" and seeing, not unlike the feeling and seeing felt to be lost in the earlier "Ode." The second quatrain, odically, attempts to see the natural world feelingly. Yet after sustaining this vision – which retrospectively looks like a conceit, even a strained conceit – for three lines, Wordsworth's speaker shows his distance from it: "for this [that is, seeing in this way] . . . we are out of tune."

The turn begun in line 8 continues, as one might expect, in line 9. First, the switch from "this" to the more objectified "it" enacts the kind of emotional distance at issue. That is, when Wordsworth says "this," the inference is that he has or had something – "this" – in front of him. When he says "it," there is no such inference. So, when the voice of the poem cries "*It moves us not*," the very pronoun underlines the speaker's distance from – and how little he is moved by – such visions. From one perspective, you could say that, unlike Marlowe, Raleigh, or Marvell, Wordsworth does not accept the distance entailed by self-consciousness and artifice; his poem laments that distance when he writes "It moves us not." Yet the interjection that follows – "Great God!" – suddenly suggests the speaker *is* moved, even if he is moved by how little moved he is. He is, one might say, making a success of failure. And the stuttering voice in line 9 (the three caesurae, the exclamation point, and the dash) underlines the rising emotion.

In fact, the entire sestet seems characteristically odic. For example, there is, at the end of line 9, a tantalizing moment where the language suggests a kind of presence (not being too late or too soon), when we read "— Great God! I'd rather *be*" (and "being" or presence hangs in our ears over the line break). Yet line 10 tells us the god and the kind of "being" called for are impossibilities. Thematically, the line simply says the speaker wishes he had been brought up in a world where nature could be seen as inspirited (perhaps by figures like Marvell's fauns and fairies or Raleigh's nymph). However, unlike Marvell or Raleigh, who accept, and even play with, the artificiality of their pagan demigods, Wordsworth seems to cry out for actual belief. And yet (this is the odic "yes but no"), he introduces such belief as "Pagan," as "a creed outworn," which forecloses any belief almost before it can be entertained. At the same time, line 9 includes an interjection that sounds like the apostrophes to Zeus in classical literature; it's not "good God," or "my God," but "Great God!" as if Wordsworth could call forth older gods by the strength of his desire. And yet, he can't: "outworn" reaches forward to the rhyme word "forlorn," and lines 11–12 move from the first-person plural "we" to the more isolated first-person singular ("I" and "me"). The sense of community with or in the natural world suggested by seeing what is "ours" in nature and by the use of the first-person plural is set against the alienation, if I can call it that, of the isolated first-person singular.

Wordsworth does place himself in a country setting, a "pleasant lea," or field, presumably overlooking the ocean. But the lea is just a place to stand: it is not, then, pastoral or a pastoral world *per se*. It seems rather, as I have said above, that a way of perceiving the world, with imagination and feeling (or "glimpses" of presences), is Wordsworth's pastoral, in which case you could say that the sonnet is an ode to pastoral, although, of course, the earlier pastoral poets read here never actually thought their otherworldly glimpses were present. In the final analysis, I would add, I am not certain that Wordsworth thinks so either. The last two lines of the poem could be read as simply listing the kinds of pagan nature deities Wordsworth cannot believe in: Proteus and Triton, both sea gods (not the mothering sea of the second quatrain, but gods that were, in the fiction of Wordsworth's sonnet, real to earlier cultures). Still, it is interesting how Wordsworth tells us about what he "might" under other conditions see (presumably in the pattern of the waves), namely Proteus, *or* hear (also in the waves), namely Triton. Proteus was a god known as a shape-shifter, and Wordsworth's non-exclusive "or" not only offers us shape (or at least image) shifting, but also ends the poem with considerable imaginative and linguistic energy. The end of the poem is also full of sound. Not only are the melancholy associations of "outworn" and "forlorn" shifted with the final rhyme – Triton's "horn" – but the assonance of the "e" sounds in "me," "Proteus," "sea," and "wreathed" also forms a rich verbal texture. So we *are* seeing and hearing something, if not Proteus and Triton. What that "something" is can be debated, of course, although it may be the poem can claim to make present sheer desire for presence, the odic presence of absence. If you read the poem just as an ode, it is not necessarily pastoral. If, however, you read it as aware of the sleight of hand at the end, where the sound of Triton's horn is replaced by the poem's sounds, it may be pastoral in a new guise, wherein the act of imagination central to earlier pastorals becomes more thematically central. It may even be an ode to pastoral thus redefined.

While some of what I have said about Wordsworth's poem draws on my understanding of other poems (like "A Night Piece" and "Ode") that he wrote around the same time, it also is informed by the fact that before reading "The World Is Too Much With Us" I had already read Levertov's poem. And Levertov's response may not have a quarrel with Wordsworth's poem, although when first encountered her free verse in irregular stanzas certainly looks like a more modern poem and her setting – a subway (or metro) and then a city street – is not only more modern, it seems at first most unpastoral. Indeed, the first two lines of "O Taste and See" seem explicitly to contradict Wordsworth. Levertov says, no, it's not that the world is too much with us but that "The world is / not with us enough." She also defines "the world" in her poem as an urban world that looks a bit like the world of getting and spending Wordsworth found mind-numbing. More specifically, Levertov's first stanza, following her apparent reversal of the title of Wordsworth's sonnet, seems to tell us that the proper response to not feeling or seeing is not to wish we were pagans or to retreat to the country, but to immerse ourselves in whatever world surrounds us. The use of boldface – which we come later to see mimics the typography of a poster in the subway – first seems to command us to taste and see the world around us.

By the first line of the second stanza, we know the language of line 3 is taken from a poster (which helps us understand that "The Lord," in line 5, is also language found in the subway). But line 5 as a whole operates for a moment (before we head into line 6) like the turn in Wordsworth's sonnet. That is, we can almost hear someone calling out for meaning – "meaning . . . **Lord**, meaning" – much as Wordsworth exclaims "Great God! I'd rather be." It seems fair to say that both poets are seeking a way of seeing the world as infused with meaning. The end of Levertov's second stanza says as much, translating what those who posted the religious exhortation in the subway presumably meant by "the Lord" into "meaning / if anything all that lives," which is a spiritual claim, but not quite orthodox in its sense of immanence or spiritual presence. Living (as in "all that lives") is then further connected to "the imagination's tongue" in line 7, which suggests that divinity resides in imaginative seeing – or tasting – which makes the world sensually present. In an essay called "Some Notes on Organic Form," published the year after "O Taste and See" appeared, Levertov speaks of her poetic interest in contemplation as follows: to contemplate, she says, is "not simply to observe, to regard, but to do these things in the presence of a god." Interestingly, this seems very like what Wordsworth's poem wants, which is why I suggested that the two poets are not that far apart.

Wordsworth's poem may be more odic; it voices frustrated desire. Levertov's poem seems less vexed (to use Marvell's word, a word also used by contemporary literary critics). From one perspective, Levertov's poem is a performance of its own tasting and seeing. That is, not only does Levertov suggest that a feeling of presence is available anywhere, including when reading subway posters, but in the last three stanzas of her poem, in which the syntax of the sentence (and after line 2, the poem is all one sentence) becomes difficult to parse, the voice seems to be excitedly tasting words as much as flavors or feelings or the environment. In short: the speaker seems to be experiencing the world in just the way she has read (or misread) the subway poster to say she should. Her very act of rereading the poster is a way of tasting and seeing. This is not necessarily odic, in that there's little sense the poem is straining to invoke what it already proleptically knows is a "creed outworn." It does, I would add, mean that "O Taste and See," although a sixteen-line poem, has something of the structure of a sonnet;

the first two stanzas place us (and the speaker) in an urban world, setting both the outer scene and the intellectual problem: how to see the world, to make even the "unnatural" world "ours" (which, of course, is consistent with Wordsworth's desire, although Levertov's is an urban pastoral). The tone shifts, then, after line 7, and the end of the poem works much like a sonnet's sestet might – and, on one reading, much as Wordsworth's poem works, addressing the problem set in the way the voice seems to delight in the words it "tastes."

The words Levertov gives us, however, are not just sounds (although the end of her poem in particular is full of sounds). If you read almost any version of Psalm 34, the language of the whole poem echoes the psalm's language, as in verses 1, 8, and 10: "I will bless the Lord at all times; his praise shall continually be in my mouth"; "O taste and see that the Lord is good"; and "The young lions suffer want and hunger, but those who seek the Lord lack no good thing." Moreover, Levertov draws on an image of transubstantiation when she describes savoring, biting, and chewing something like a communion wafer to "transform / into our flesh our / deaths." Finally, she places us in an Edenic setting by line 14 with that "orchard" (not to mention the fruit). Admittedly, religious language seems to be imaginatively transformed in the poem, and not just in the rereading of the poster. While the poem is clearly concerned with spiritual presence (as is Levertov in her other writings), it seems "O Taste and See" identifies spirituality with the imagination. Further, transubstantiation usually transforms the material into the spiritual, not death into flesh. I think I understand what it means to transform "grief, mercy, language, / tangerine [and] weather" into "our flesh," namely that we make the things of our world (inner and outer) fully, sensually, part of ourselves, digesting them, if you will. But to make death part of ourselves in the same way is not quite so easily understood. Perhaps, if we take the act of perception Levertov both describes and enacts as her version of Arcadia – now a process of imagination, not an imagined place – then lines 12–13 may be Levertov's version of "Et in Arcadia ego"; like Marvell's mower, she is underlining the sense of living in a world of time. Indeed, looking back at the nouns in lines 8 and 9, many (moods, weather) offer a similar sense of what is ephemeral. And this might help to explain the slight oddity of the very last two lines in Levertov's poem.

I say "oddity," because the tone of the last two lines puzzles me. On one reading, we seem to be returned, with and by the speaker, to an imagined Eden: "living in the orchard and being" (the line break here letting us dwell in the present for a moment). We are not just "being," though; by line 15, we are "being / hungry." It could be that desire is part of Levertov's Eden, even part of what can be celebrated. Indeed, if the hunger is for spiritual or sensual presence, it is a hunger quickly assuaged by "plucking / the fruit." But what fruit? That of the imagination? The implication would be, I suppose, that the process of imagining *is* Eden (reminiscent of Wordsworth's focus on the act of imagining) and in itself fulfilling, which would make this poem a recasting of earlier pastorals. Yet, on a second reading of "O Taste and See," plucking fruit in Eden is a potent image (especially when offered by a woman writer). Is this then defiance? I confess that after the sensuality and excitement of the language in lines 8–14, I don't quite hear defiance in those last two lines. Nor do they seem ominous, that is, they do not seem to caution that a desire for knowledge might have unfortunate results.

Insofar as the poem's attempt *is* to invite us to imagine a new kind of Eden, not as imagined artifice but as something made sensually present in the very act of imagining it, then it may after all be pastoral (because it imagines imagining as Edenic and because it contrasts the world to which we pay no attention with the contemplated world made vivid in the poem). Yet I find myself wondering if the last line of Levertov's poem does not hint that an expulsion from the orchard will come next. So, perhaps there is something odic after all in "O Taste and See." Actually, what I have said about both Wordsworth's and Levertov's poems leaves up in the air whether you should read either of these poems as self-conscious or as somewhat more single-gestured, if increasingly more internalized, pastorals. These are questions you will have to decide for yourself – they are open questions – although I hope you can see how a consideration of the pastoral and of the ode might inform interpretations of both poems.

To avoid suggesting that all modern pastorals or reconsiderations of pastoral are similar, I want to end this discussion with two short poems by a contemporary writer, C. S. Giscombe, both taken from a 1994 volume of poetry called *Here*. The poems can be read individually (each was published as an individual poem before the book appeared). Still, reading poems in the context of the books in which they appeared can be useful. *Here*, for example, makes a few things about the poems I have extracted from it clearer: it refers throughout to the poet's visit to the southern United States to attend his grandfather's funeral in 1962; and it tells us that the poet, Giscombe, grew up in the midwestern United States, is taken with rural settings, and is African American. The first poem from *Here* that I want to give you, entitled "(the future)" – the parentheses are Giscombe's – is only five lines long:

Looking at my bad attitude toward the pastoral
& only seeing myself on one of those red dirt roads
I'd seen from the air, caught unlucky
w/ night more palpable every minute, that
for the future

And here is the second poem, entitled "(1962 at the edge of town)":

No West Indians that I could see at my grandfather's funeral

"Long lost relatives always eat a lot," sd my mother (meaning
just as well) on the ride to the graveyard at the furthest Negro edge
of Birmingham proper

— the city got lush in places then gave way   5
so descriptive shoulders of hills came into view over which
ranged pine trees & on a ridge, through those,

some white people went by on a train
(so near I could see them from where we stood under the canvas,
their pale arms & faces at the window, clearly),   10

the pastoral looming up close as well,

"the mosaic of brightest southern colors" – it was that

for decades my grandfather was doctor too

to people out past the edge of town & took payment for that
in hams, in baskets of greens & fruit: 15

but all *value* is assigned, is brought in:

still, being the density & mirror both
was what I found confusing —

the fickle layers to endure, the worth standing in

Before talking about the voice and tone in the first poem, I might point
out that Giscombe's use of typography – especially of dashes, parentheses,
and stenographic conventions such as the ampersand ("&") or the use of
"w/" for "with" and "sd" for "said – like his refusal of standard punctuation
or syntax, stand out, but do not stand alone. Before this point, I have not
given you examples of twentieth-century experimental or avant-garde
poetry. But such poetry was being written in France, England, and the
United States. In America, in particular, practitioners such as Charles
Olson, himself looking back to the modernist poetry of Ezra Pound, used
what is sometimes called **open field composition**, marked among other
things by a lack of stanzaic structure (the lines are often not even aligned

at the left margin) and the use of short-hand conventions such as "sd" and "w/" or "&." Poet to poet, the reasons given for such untraditional uses of language can vary, although most often the use of stenographic conventions suggests these poems are, as it were, taking notes on movements of the mind as they occur, notes from thought-in-motion. At the very least, the way such poems look tells you they are not, and are not intended to be, traditional. So Giscombe's "(the future)" does not set us, as readers, in the same position – or require from us the same questions – as the pastorals to which the first line refers.

To be invited to reposition ourselves is not surprising. Giscombe himself is from the start in a different position from most writers of pastoral. It is not simply that he has (as he says) "a bad attitude toward the pastoral" – which opens the poem with a sense of humor rather than a bad attitude – but that to an African American bucolic landscapes would look different. For one thing, the "natural" (at least in its association with the uncivilized or simple or primitive) is what racist stereotypes have associated with Africans and African Americans. In something like the way actual shepherds probably do not stage their imaginations of another world in sheepfolds, African America might well think twice about imagining itself as simpler or more natural: that imagination is already someone else's and not attractive. Relatedly, the rural areas of the southern United States do not usually elicit nostalgia *or* imaginative exuberance if one is African American; in African American history it is a setting more often associated with slavery or with post-Reconstruction poverty, lynchings, and disenfranchisement than with anything Edenic. I would add that "red dirt roads," while they are also found in other places, are characteristic of the rural south in America, and "red dirt" is often used as a synecdoche for rural poverty (since red dirt marks relatively unproductive agricultural land).

All of the above seems relevant to "(the future)." It is a highly self-conscious poem, a poem that, as its appearance on the page suggests, presents the speaker's thought-in-motion. Indeed, to say "the speaker" suggests a dramatic staging of thought that implies more distance between speaker and author than I think we hear in the poem, which foregrounds the presence of thought. Although clearly any writing is in some ways a form of dramatization (because it is not thought but notes on thought), it seems to make more sense simply to call the voice (or mind) of the poem Giscombe's. That is, from the start, the poem is so much not *about* having a bad attitude (or asking us to adopt the same attitude) as it is a poem of someone tracing how they feel and think. The title of the book in which these poems appeared – *Here* – further suggests the work is not only about places but also about what is made present in the poems, "here," on the page. (There is also a pun on "hear," in that the poem's diction and usage are drawn from a range of regional, ethnic, literary, and other registers of speech.)

As "(the future)" unfolds, then, we follow Giscombe looking at his atti-tude, seeing instead only an image of himself on rural southern roads, as if in a picture. By the third line, we are told he has only seen these roads "from the air" (presumably from the airplane taken back to Alabama for his grandfather's funeral), so this is not memory but a kind of rebellion of the imagination, offering images that are not what the poet expected (or so "& *only* seeing myself on one of those red dirt roads," implies). There are at least three doublings of consciousness here: Giscombe looks at his attitude toward the pastoral, but he sees only a picture of himself in a rural setting; and the picture is imagined. In some ways, he captures the distant, soft-focus of pastoral worlds as imagined worlds when the picture that comes to mind is like the world seen from an airplane. In other ways, however, his imagining of what we (and he) would expect to be a pastoral setting is unique; it is rural, but it is neither exuberant nor welcome. So perhaps he does have a bad attitude toward the pastoral.

Certainly, the end of line 3, through line 4, sounds a more ominous note. If popular culture and American history often portray the rural south as picturesque, for an African American to imagine himself in that landscape might indeed be unsettling. Specifically, to be "caught unlucky / w/ night more palpable every minute" is Giscombe's imagination of what it feels like to be "caught" outside in such a landscape – even in imagination. Being "caught" by nightfall is an idiomatic way of saying one is out later than one expected to be, but it also implies one might be trapped in poverty or even caught in the sense of being preyed upon by a pursuer. To say that one is caught as night becomes "more palpable every minute" both suggests the vividness with which the scene is being imagined and – since "palpable" means tangible or "capable of being touched" – gives a sense of physical threat. The last clause in the poem – which ends without punctuation – is a bit more puzzling, but seems to show us the poet's mind skirting the image of physical threat, putting it off to consider another time. It may even verge on confronting its own version of "Et in Arcadia ego," although the land-scape is clearly not Arcadian. By implication, more traditional pastoral is inescapably tainted by the real history of rural black America. Further, the poem tells us that imaginations are not autonomous; history and culture mark even the scenes we imagine (Levertov notwithstanding).

"(1962, at the edge of town)" seems to deepen this meditation on what it means to imagine one's self elsewhere, especially in a natural landscape.

The poem begins narratively: it tells us the Giscombe family may originally be West Indian; it humorously sets Giscombe's mother (more concerned with whether there is enough food at his grandfather's funeral) against his apparent concern with his family's roots – perhaps suggesting his disinclination to trace his heritage back to "Birmingham proper," a phrase that includes both the city limits of Birmingham, Alabama and the "proper" – which is to say white, "civilized" – members of Birmingham society (which in 1962 did place non-white citizens socially and physically "at the edge of town"). Yet as the poem and the thought, here including memory, unfold, we are shown an affectionately observed landscape (with "shoulders of hills" and "pine trees"). And there is an interesting reversal. We are placed by the perspective of the narrative with the poet, en route to and then at the burial and graveyard, at the rural "Negro edge" of town (and in 1962 the family would have said "Negro," not "African American," suggesting the language as well as the scene is remembered). The landscape includes the faces of people looking at the burial from a train. The poem is, again, clearly aware of racial perspectives. What to "white people . . . on a train" might look picturesque – or even pastoral – is where we stand with the poet, in the countryside, looking at the people looking at him. (I did note that these poems are highly self-conscious; you could even say the poem looks at the poet looking at people looking at him.) Line 11, moreover, aligns the poet's view of the white people ("so near") with "the pastoral looming up close as well." So the white train passengers and the pastoral approach together. The question is: who is pastoral to whom? The white people's view of the burial makes the funeral pastoral. The poet's view of the white people on the train in one way challenges their view of the pastoral. This has some similarities to Raleigh's nymph talking back, although the speaker here is not at all imaginary and in ways is trying to take himself out of other people's pastorals. And yet the poet too seems affected by the way the scene is framed, among other things by memories of his grandfather in that rural scene, as something like pastoral.

By lines 11–15 of the poem there are, then, three kinds of pastoral considered. There is the pastoral that is dismissed. There is also advertising language, presumably from the local Chambers of Commerce promoting and pastoralizing the natural beauty of the region with slogans like "the mosaic of brightest southern colors"; and there is the poet's at least momentary nostalgia for what sounds like the simple country life in which his grandfather, a doctor, cared for people on the margins, getting paid not in money but "in hams, in baskets of greens & fruit." This last image is of a community and a kind of plenitude outside the world of getting and spending. It sounds pastoral. Yet the poem claims this version of pastoral, at least for a moment. Consider, for example, the way the word "that" functions at the end of line 12. "That" may be a pronoun, used to dismiss the slogan about "southern colors" (and tacitly suggesting that color in the south is more vexed than advertising would allow). In other words, after we are told the pastoral loomed, line 12 might be understood as saying, yes, the pastoral was *that* kind of picturesque local color made marketable by advertising. Yet "that" may function as a conjunction, meaning "also" or "namely," and since line 11 ends with "as well" and line 13 with "too" (both adding information), we are invited to hear the end of line 12 as following suit. In fact, the word finally seems to serve as a hinge: we (and perhaps Giscombe) first expect "that" to refer back to the slogan – *that* is what the pastoral was, and we don't like it – but we find it also leads forward to another pastoral, the one Giscombe sketches as his imagination of his grandfather's life. Of course, the word "but," which then begins line 16, immediately qualifies this new pastoral: "but all *value* is assigned, is brought in." The line suggests Giscombe is calling himself on his construction of a good life (not the stereotypical life of the rural southern African American nor of tourism, but still a construction and possibly even one "brought in" from poems like Marlowe's).

If this is right, then the end of this poem underlines the complexity of pastoral gestures. I am not entirely sure what it might mean to be both "the density & mirror," but I do think we can use what the rest of this poem and "(the future)" tell us to say some things about this image. Being a mirror suggests serving as a surface in which others see – or by means of which they compose – themselves. In the context of "(1962 at the edge of town)," this could suggest the ways in which African American "naturalness" was used historically to inscribe white "civilization" (making African Americans, as it were, the props in someone else's pastoral). Yet it also may suggest the ways in which the poet makes himself an image in his own imaginations. He is the mirror not only because used by others but because of his own self-consciousness. Similarly, to be "the density" would indicate one is a material presence, both in the somewhat negative sense of being a body in a scene and in the more positive sense of being real, not a simulacrum or image. The "fickle layers" then could suggest the double thinking of both mirror and density, while the final phrase, "the worth standing in" (typically for a poem that expresses ambivalence about the pastoral), can also be double read. I think the question is left open as to whether "worth" is a preposition or a noun. Does "worth standing in" suggest that it *is* worthwhile to stand in the middle of this confusion? Or does it suggest that the idea of something's worth, its culturally assigned value, only substitutes – or stands in – for the thing itself?

I heard the poet, C. S. Giscombe, give a talk on "Poetry and the Oblique" in Philadelphia, Pennsylvania, in late December of 2004. He was asked after the talk whether he considered himself more an African American poet or more an experimental poet, to which he responded, "You can be black and still have ambivalence, which *is* imagination." Ambivalence is not quite the term I'd have used to describe attitudes toward artifice found in earlier pastorals. Still, Giscombe's poem seems to me a new incarnation of pastoral self-consciousness, suggesting that reports of the death of pastoral as a mode have been greatly exaggerated, even given a modern – with Giscombe, one might say postmodern – skepticism about the nature and sources of the imagination's power. This increasing skepticism about imagination's power is illustrated also in the three poems I will consider in the next chapter.

Terms used

bucolic	memento mori
eclogue	open field composition
"Et in Arcadia ego"	pastoral
georgic	prelapsarian
green poetry	urban pastoral
idyll	

Other poems that might be read

Edmund Spenser, Eclogue 10 ["October"] from *The Shepheardes Calendar* (1579)
Sir Philip Sidney, "Ye Goatherd Gods" from *Arcadia* (1593)
Thomas Campion, "I Care Not for These Ladies" (1601)
Ben Jonson, "To Penshurst" (1616)
John Milton, "Lycidas" (1645)
Robert Herrick, "The Argument of his Book" (1648)
Andrew Marvell, "The Garden" (published posthumously in 1681)
William Butler Yeats, "The Lake Isle of Innisfree" (1892)
Paul Laurence Dunbar, "Sympathy" (1899)
William Carlos Williams, "Pastoral" (1916)
Alan Ginsberg, "A Supermarket in California" (1956)
Kathleen Halme, "A Dialogue between the Shepherdesses and Mowers" (1998)

Useful further reading

Paul Alpers, *What Is Pastoral?* (Chicago: University of Chicago Press, 1996).

Lawrence Buell, *The Environmental Imagination: Thoreau, Nature Writing, and the Formation of American Culture* (Cambridge, Mass.: Harvard University Press, 1995).

William Empson, *Some Versions of Pastoral* (London: Chatto & Windus, 1935).

Henry Louis Gates, Jr., *The Signifying Monkey: A Theory of African-American Literary Criticism* (Oxford and New York: Oxford University Press, 1988).

Terry Gifford, *Pastoral* (London and New York: Routledge, 1999).

Leo Marx, "Pastoralism in America," in Sacvan Bercovitch and Myra Jehlens, eds., *Ideology and Classic American Literature* (Cambridge: Cambridge University Press, 1986).

Annabel Paterson, *Pastoral and Ideology: Virgil to Valery* (Berkeley: University of California Press, 1987).

Mark Wallace and Steven Marks, eds., *Telling It Slant: Avant-Garde Poetics of the 1990s* (Tuscaloosa: University of Alabama Press, 2002).

Chapter 8

Traditions, Legacies, and Individual Talents

in William Wordsworth's "The Solitary Reaper"
(1807), Wallace Stevens's "The Idea of Order at
Key West" (1935), and John Ashbery's "Le Livre
Est Sur La Table" (1956)

In this chapter I want to offer you a model of how you might read three featured poems, while also raising the question of how to discuss the relationship between poems that are – as these are – self-consciously related by theme, allusion, and reference. In a sense, I am revisiting the second chapter's discussion of intertextuality, but I have here chosen texts that do not share a single mode or form, even though, like the poems featured in chapter 2, they are poems from different eras and countries. On the face of it, what the following three poems have in common is that they each feature a similar scene; they are poems that present women, usually singing, by real or metaphorical seas. These shared characters and settings would be trivial (not all poems that feature women or even women and oceans are interestingly related), except for the fact that each later poem can be read as returning to Wordsworth's "The Solitary Reaper" in order to think about the power of lyricism or about song-like, expressive poetry. Let me then begin, then, with "The Solitary Reaper":

Behold her, single in the field,
Yon solitary Highland Lass!
Reaping and singing by herself;
Stop here, or gently pass!

Alone she cuts and binds the grain,   5
And sings a melancholy strain;
O listen! for the Vale profound
Is overflowing with the sound.

No Nightingale did ever chaunt
More welcome notes to weary bands   10
Of travellers in some shady haunt,
Among Arabian sands;
A voice so thrilling ne'er was heard
In springtime from the Cuckoo-bird,
Breaking the silence of the seas   15
Among the farthest Hebrides.

Will no one tell me what she sings?—
Perhaps the plaintive numbers flow
For old, unhappy, far-off things,
And battles long ago;   20
Or is it some more humble lay,
Familiar matter of today?
Some natural sorrow, loss, or pain,
That has been, and may be again?

Whate'er the theme, the Maiden sang   25
As if her song could have no ending;
I saw her singing at her work,
And o'er the sickle bending—
I listened, motionless and still;
And, as I mounted up the hill,   30
The music in my heart I bore,
Long after it was heard no more.

You have now read a number of Wordsworth's poems and so, I hope, recognize the odic gestures – for example, in "Will no one tell me what she sings?" The poem may also be pastoral, although Wordsworth's reaper is nothing like Marvell's; she is not a grim reaper in any way, nor is she mythological. Still, the speaker views and idealizes a rural world from which he is exiled, self-conscious that he imagines some features of it, namely the content of the woman's song. I would add that it is implied the speaker cannot understand the reaper's song because she is a "Highland Lass," that is, from Scotland, where in 1807 a Scots agricultural worker would be singing in Erse, not English. In other words, there is a language barrier. As critics from Wordsworth's day to the present have also noticed, there are other ways in which the reaper is not like the speaker or the author: she is female and an agricultural laborer, as well as a Scot.

In the very earliest reviews of this poem, some critics from England and America found it "silly" or "trivial" because it waxes lyrical about someone who would have been seen as unimportant: a woman, a peasant-like worker. These days, people are more inclined to criticize the poem because they think it speaks for or "colonizes" someone who cannot assume the same kind of social or political position as the speaker – a poet who speaks English – can. You might think of this criticism as like that which would be elicited if one of the passengers on the train in C. S. Giscombe's poem were to write a poem celebrating the innocence of the "Negro funeral" they had passed. It is not that Wordsworth's poem is immune to such criticism. For instance, the speaker seems to be projecting his own feelings of isolation (and perhaps also his feelings about the vocation of – or work done by – poetry or song) on the reaper. Notice how the poem almost compulsively emphasizes solitude: the title calls the woman "solitary," and the first three line reiterate that she is "single," "solitary," and (in case we missed the point) "by herself." She seems also to cultivate more than a field; like Marvell's fauns and fairies she seems just by singing to make the "Vale profound" overflow. We may imagine that the valley in which she works is of lower altitude than the surrounding mountains, but of course "profound" suggests metaphysical as much as physical depths. It is as if her song were a form of spiritual irrigation, and this power of song is what Wordsworth may wish for his own lyrics.

In Wordsworth's defense, there are a few other features of the poem worth noting. Yes, it does seem at first that we are offered a portrait or still-life of a picturesque reaper. Yet if you look closely, the poem never claims to understand the woman, nor to imagine her life for her. In fact, the first stanza warns against intruding on her: "Stop here, or gently pass!" and "O listen!" address us (as well as suggesting the speaker's warning to himself). The comparisons in stanza two are all negative (her voice is not like a nightingale's or cuckoo's). And stanza three is obviously pure speculation about what the reaper sings, not making any claims to know; indeed, the last stanza opens "Whate'er the theme," confirming the speaker's self-consciousness about his ignorance. Moreover, the form of Wordsworth's poem is drawn from the **ballad**. And ballads were (and still often are) popular forms, that is, forms from those who are not among the elite. Traditional ballads tell common stories, including stories of "battles long ago," or "sorrow, loss, and pain," or "unhappy, far-off things." Originally (and often still) sung, folk ballads usually use four-line stanzas – sometimes with added refrains – often in alternating iambic tetrameter and iambic trimeter, rhyming *abcb*. Wordsworth has adapted the folk form: his first and last stanzas rhyme *abcbddee*, a form that adds two rhymed couplets to the four lines that more closely resemble folk-ballads; the middle two stanzas are the same, except that the third line of each of these stanzas rhymes with the first. The third line of all four stanzas moves from tetrameter to trimeter, although lines 26 and 28, in the last stanza, have extra unaccented syllables, technically called **end anacrusis**. Varying numbers of unaccented syllables also appear in folk ballad lines, although not just at the end of the lines. My point is that the form and rhythms of "The Solitary Reaper," like the simplicity of diction, mark it as a tribute to or an echo of just the kind of song a Highland reaper might actually sing.

Wordsworth's use of the ballad form also makes some sense of the second stanza, which contrasts the reaper's common or folk song favorably with more exotic songs: those of (presumably literary) nightingales or the *Arabian Nights'* tales of exotic places. The images in the second stanza are still of course about the sound (not the sense, which the speaker cannot follow) of the reaper's singing. Metaphorically, in the same way an oasis – which would indicate not only shade but water in a desert – is welcome to travelers, so too the reaper's song is welcome. Or rather, the reaper's song is more welcome. The metaphor, you might notice, continues the liquid image of the song ("overflowing" and more welcome than signs of an oasis); the mention of the nightingale (a bird of poetry I trust is now familiar to you) underlines that the song is a "melancholy strain," with "strain" once again meaning "song." Presumably we are to imagine that the melancholy tone of the reaper's song is indicated by its rhythms or perhaps the use of a minor key, since the speaker does not speak her language. The last four lines of stanza two tell us the song, melancholy or no, is not just welcome but "thrilling." Like "Behold" (the first word), this suggests a certain awe. The metaphor of the cuckoo bird implies not only that the cuckoo's song is thrilling because it heralds the arrival of spring in a harsh climate, but also that the birdsong relieves the feeling of isolation; the Hebrides are an archipelago of islands, relatively few of which are populated, off the west coast of Scotland. They are known as isolated, windy, and wilderness-like. In one sense, they are the opposite of the desert; in another, however, they too figure a place where signs of life would be welcome. Admittedly, there is the question of how a cuckoo's song breaks "the silence of the seas." You would think that the seas breaking on island shores would not exactly be silent. My guess is that the image contrasts organized sound – birdsong – with the constant, background noise of the ocean, which would come to seem like white noise. The song is "thrilling" in part because it stands out against its background. By implication, folk song and metered verse similarly capture our attention or refresh our sense of the world.

As I mentioned, although it celebrates the singing of common people, "The Solitary Reaper" tells us little about its title character; you cannot even say Wordsworth ventriloquizes the reaper, really, since he never pretends to put any words in her mouth or to speak for her. We know only that she works and sings. Beyond that, we are told how her song affected the *speaker*: it sounds melancholy; it's welcome and thrilling; it seems "as if" (but only as if) it will never end, which may be an image of its apparently transcendent quality or a reference to the way folk songs are passed on through generations; ballads are among the oldest forms of popular literature. In either case, without the speaker's response and his speculations about what the woman might be singing – which are marked as mere speculation by the string of open-ended questions that form the third stanza – we would have a much shorter poem. The questions more modern, political readings of the poem pose are: Is Wordsworth then appropriating a working woman's image to make his own song? Or, to the contrary, when he leaves bearing her music in his heart, is he including himself – and inviting us to include ourselves – in a chain of songs passed on from person to person? Whose song does he (or do we) hear? I'd add we know that historically Wordsworth took the image of the moving, singing reaper from someone else, from Thomas Wilkinson's description of *Tours to the British Mountains*, which is to say the poem is not autobiographical; if *Wordsworth* was moved, it was by the account of Wilkinson being moved by a song in Erse. In this sense, at least, it seems the poem may most generally be about being confronted by a scene or sound you can neither ignore nor understand and may further be quite self-conscious about how a laboring singer, like her song, can resist understanding but still haunt or touch a listener. If so – although the poem is still about the viewer's mind as much as about what is seen – it is not so because it is pastoral. The reaper is represented not as imagined, but as material, as much density as mirror (if I may use Giscombe's images). That is, the poem may deliberately pose the problem of how poetry can represent others or of how we can give voice to what we know is outside our experience.

In suggesting that what first looked like a still-life of a picturesque Scottish laborer may be a poem that confronts the question of how with delicacy to represent other not-so-imagined people and their worlds, I may be going out on a limb. Still, Wordsworth's era debated questions about the poor, about laborers (and women), in the popular press and discussed what it meant to use people as poster-children. (Although this is our vocabulary, the ethical question posed was around in Wordsworth's day). So my speculations about the poem are not obviously anachronistic, even if they are speculations. I confess, however, that I am reading Wordsworth through at least two lenses about which he could not have known. The first is the approach of more modern politically-minded critics. (Most critics in Wordsworth's own day worried about the portrait not because it condescended to or pastoralized the reaper but because, being poetry and not journalism, it found a reaper a worthy poetic subject in the first place.) Second, I know some of my understanding of Wordsworth's poem relies on my reading of a poem by a later poet, Wallace Stevens, also about a woman singing. It then may be that I am reading Wordsworth somewhat anachronistically after all.

The Stevens poem I have in mind is the 1935 "The Idea of Order at Key West." As you read the poem you might note that the seas in the Hebrides or the images of song as liquid are echoed in an image of a literal ocean in Stevens's poem, and that the following is an ode, with strongly marked and contradictory ("yes but no") movements:

> She sang beyond the genius of the sea.
> The water never formed to mind or voice,
> Like a body wholly body, fluttering
> Its empty sleeves; and yet its mimic motion
> Made constant cry, caused constantly a cry,   5
> That was not ours although we understood,
> Inhuman, of the veritable ocean.
>
> The sea was not a mask. No more was she.
> The song and water were not medleyed sound
> Even if what she sang was what she heard,   10
> Since what she sang was uttered word by word.
> It may be that in all her phrases stirred
> The grinding water and the gasping wind;
> But it was she and not the sea we heard.
>
> For she was the maker of the song she sang.   15
> The ever-hooded, tragic-gestured sea
> Was merely a place by which she walked to sing.
> Whose spirit is this? we said, because we knew
> It was the spirit that we sought and knew
> That we should ask this often as she sang.   20
>
> If it was only the dark voice of the sea
> That rose, or even colored by many waves;
> If it was only the outer voice of sky
> And cloud, of the sunken coral water-walled,
> However clear, it would have been deep air,   25
> The heaving speech of air, a summer sound

Repeated in a summer without end
And sound alone. But it was more than that,
More even than her voice, and ours, among
The meaningless plungings of water and the wind,   30
Theatrical distances, bronze shadows heaped
On high horizons, mountainous atmospheres
Of sky and sea.
                    It was her voice that made
The sky acutest at its vanishing.   35
She measured to the hour its solitude.
She was the single artificer of the world
In which she sang. And when she sang, the sea,
Whatever self it had, became the self
That was her song, for she was the maker. Then we,   40
As we beheld her striding there alone,
Knew that there never was a world for her
Except the one she sang and, singing, made.

Ramon Fernandez, tell me, if you know,
Why, when the singing ended and we turned   45
Toward the town, tell why the glassy lights,
The lights in the fishing boats at anchor there,
As night descended, tilting in the air,
Mastered the night and portioned out the sea,
Fixing emblazoned zones and fiery poles,   50
Arranging, deepening, enchanting night.

Oh! Blessed rage for order, pale Ramon,
The maker's rage to order words of the sea,
Words of the fragrant portals, dimly-starred,
And of ourselves and of our origins,   55
In ghostlier demarcations, keener sounds.

Stevens's poem talks about "mimic motion," and one could see the ebb and fall of his speaker's belief that song can capture the actual world ("the veritable ocean," of line 7) as mimicking the movement of waves. Moreover, his use of blank verse (stressed and unstressed syllables following one another in stately regularity) may do the same. Note, too, the number of 'c' and 's' sounds throughout the poem. Lines 4–6, for example, are not atypical in containing sixteen such sounds:

Its empty sleeves; and yet its mimic motion
Made constant cry, caused constantly a cry,
That was not ours although we understood.

There are also the end rhymes in lines 10–12 and 14. Talk about a world "overflowing" with sound. For Stevens, I would guess, the texture of his language illustrates what the poem means when it says it may be that the sound of the water "in all her phrases stirred" (line 12). Of course, we are hearing the sounds of words, not of ocean. And this is explicitly Stevens's point: "But it was she and not the sea we heard" (line 14), he writes, returning to the same point in lines 37–43. I take it, too, that the first line of the poem says much the same thing: "She sang beyond the genius of the sea" may imply that her singing was better than the sea's but most likely – drawing on the meaning of "genius" as "the attendant spirit of a place" – it suggests that the singer's ocean-side song may mimic (or represent), but is not giving voice to the spirit or substance of, the actual ocean.

Indeed, the first seven lines of Stevens's poem take issue with Wordsworth's "The World Is Too Much With Us." Wordsworth wants to look at the ocean and see Proteus (or hear Triton). For Stevens, the "water never formed to mind or voice," presumably not even for pagans with creeds outworn, which is to say that for Stevens the pagan gods were always fictional. And yet if Stevens is, as we might say, post-pagan, he cannot imagine the world wholly without mythologies; the very fact that I have to speak of him *imagining* the world makes the same point: to think of the world, in this case, the ocean, is already to imagine it. In another poem, called "Another Weeping Woman," Stevens says that the imagination is "the one reality / In this imagined world," again suggesting that everything we know, we know because we see through our imaginations. Yet his constant return to the subject of what he elsewhere calls reality and imagination suggests also a hunger for the real, which he odically hopes song or poetry might invoke. If in earlier odes there was a three-part movement (strophe, antistrophe, and epode), in Stevens's poem, as in Miles's, the movement is not staged so decorously. Just look, for instance, at lines 3 and 4, describing the brute fact (without mind or voice) of the ocean as "like a body wholly body, fluttering / Its empty sleeves." To say the ocean is all and only body is to describe a world outside the human imagination, but it is also already a figure of speech, specifically a simile. The speaker underlines this fact when he images the ocean waves as arms waving or arms in sleeves. Yet, before we get to the word "sleeves," the word that clinches for us the image of the personified waves, we are told the garment in which Stevens's imagination has clothed the waves is "empty": the body has departed. While this may be in part an image of how waves form and collapse, it is also odic. That is (to trace the "yes, but no" in lines 3–7), the speaker uses a simile to describe the ocean as a body; he sees that to do this is to personify the ocean, that is, to imagine or dress it up or see in it "what is ours"; as he does this, he recognizes that the "real" ocean's essence or sound (again notice the echo of or argument with Wordsworth) is "not ours." And yet (the odic "yet") it cries, and, even if the cry is inhuman, Stevens's speaker insists we still understand it.

You might find my last two sentences, just above, are confusing. They are, I'd say, at least as confusing as – and less sonorous than – the odic voice in the poem. This is a quandary that odes, and especially Stevens's, often present to readers or critics. One way to cope with this is to step back from an attempt to paraphrase line by line, and to note the overall effect of the voice's odic motion, which is that of odic invocation and an impossible desire to make something present in song or poetry. It is useful, too, to consider the difference between Wordsworth's odic gestures and Stevens's. You might say that Wordsworth lamented the lack of spirits or gods in the world, knowing such presences were for his day and age "outworn." Stevens seems rather to want the world in itself – physically present, "wholly body" – but by the time he has named what he wants, in language or thought, it is not itself, but mere dress, "ever-hooded" (line 16). Both poets speak of some absence, but what is absent is not the same thing.

I have been describing Stevens's poem in terms of "The World Is Too Much With Us," but it is even more closely related to "The Solitary Reaper." Wordsworth asks: "Will no one tell me what she sings?" Stevens speculates on the contents of the song from *his* singing woman for the first forty-three lines of his poem. That is, we are told her song does not give us the ocean: "it was she and not the sea we heard" (line 14). At the same time, "she" and "sea" rhyme; moreover, we have been told there "may be" (line 12) something of the ocean in her song. Then, again, we are told the sea was just "a place by which she walked." Indeed, there is a potentially infinite regress suggested in the poem. The woman tries to invoke the world, specifically the sea. The speaker tries to invoke the woman invoking the sea. And we as readers are trying to invoke the speaker's invocation of the woman's invocation of the sea.

Although there is no single message to be extracted from "The Idea of Order" (a definitive answer about what the woman sings would cut short the speaker's singing), lines 18–20 nonetheless seem to pose the *question* that drives the speaker throughout the poem: "Whose spirit is this? we said, because we knew / It was the spirit that we sought and knew / That we should ask this often as she sang." After disclaiming the ability to capture the spirit of a place ("the genius of the sea"), the speaker still insists that music (or lyricism) evokes a sense of some kind of spirit. Notice, too, how lines 18 and 19 end saying "we knew" (and "we sought and knew") at each line break, so that the speaker seems to claim knowledge, even though finally he only claims knowledge of what he does not know. The act of questioning, however, is clearly emphasized. The one thing the speaker knows is that "we should ask this often" (line 20). The questions asked are deliberately left unanswered, but we as readers can rehearse the questions: What has the woman to do with the ocean, the speaker to do with the woman, or the reader with the speaker? It seems, finally, that lines 18–20 call attention to the way unanswered questions keep the imagination in motion. As I said earlier, it may be that I read Wordsworth through Stevens, but I found Wordsworth's poem may have done something similar, given the way the speaker's speculations and unanswered questions form the body of "The Solitary Reaper." When Stevens asks whose spirit he hears, one answer is: Wordsworth's. Indeed, you might note that line 41 of "The Idea of Order at Key West" clearly echoes the first word ("Behold") and the insistence on solitude found in "The Solitary Reaper." Stevens writes: "As we *beheld* her striding there *alone* . . ." (Lines 36 and 37 also echo Wordsworth's repeated insistence on his singer's solitary state.) Stevens further contrasts the way his singer's voice – which "measured" (line 36) the sky – with what he calls the "meaningless plungings of water and the wind" (line 30). In other words, in the same way Wordsworth contrasts the cuckoo's song with the background noise of the sea, so too Stevens sets measured sound (or humanly organized sound, including metered poems or songs) against "meaningless" sound. Both poets, then, claim (and perhaps demonstrate) that there is something haunting about the sounds of poetry, what we might call the lyric quality of poems.

Ultimately, the end of "The Idea of Order at Key West," like the end of "The Solitary Reaper" on one possible interpretation, suggests how the effect of song is passed on to readers or listeners. But it does something else, as well. Through line 44, the "we" of Stevens's poem seems to mean all humans or at least the writer and his readers. Yet in line 44, we suddenly realize there is a dramatized scene: the speaker is talking to someone, Ramon Fernandez, in a specific place: Key West. And suddenly the questions are not just about what the woman has to do with the ocean, but about why the woman's singing by the ocean seems indeed to have ordered the world or made it stand out: the fishing boat lights "*Mastered* the night and *portioned* out the sea, / *Fixing* . . . *zones* . . . / *Arranging*" (all words indicating ways of imposing order). Moreover, if earlier the poem's speaker seemed not to want any definitive answer (and answers are ways of ordering), here it seems that at least the passion for order (the "rage for order" and the "rage to order") is apostrophized: "O! Blessed rage for order." Admittedly, the desire or passion for something is not the same as the thing itself; indeed, this may be another way of configuring odic desire.

Still, the phrase in line 53 – "The maker's rage to order *words of the sea*" – is worth considering. What kind of "of" is Stevens using here? As in Frost's "Design," which I discussed in chapter 5, the "of" may be either the objective or the subjective genitive, indicating either words about the sea or the sea's words. The ambiguity tantalizingly suggests that there may be something – the sea's words – outside the speaker's desire invoked after all.

If Wordsworth seemed to want to see and hear some spirit infusing the physical world, Stevens most obviously invokes human orders (or ordering): it is the *human* spirit, the process of the imagination, perhaps, that is invoked when the poem's speaker calls out for the rage to order. And the numinous image in the penultimate verse paragraph is of the way human markers – fishing-boat lights – trace patterns or impose order on the otherwise blank slates of ocean or night. You could say that what is at stake for Stevens in maintaining ambiguity is that his indecision keeps him calling, imagining, and writing poetry, even if he proleptically knows that all orders are imagined and so provisional. It may even be that Stevens's idea of poetry (or "idea of order") involves a kind of solipsism, which is the idea that he lives in his own mind and does not believe there is necessarily anything outside of his own mind – that, to use his own words, "there never was a world for [him] / Except the one [he] sang and, singing, made" (lines 41–2). In short, if the conclusion drawn from the woman's inability to capture something outside herself is that she "makes up" the world about which she seems to sing, then, logically, Stevens makes *her* up (and, I suppose, we make up Stevens). None of us calls forth anything solid, although we keep calling "as if" we could. At first, then, it seems that, unlike Wordsworth, Stevens does not believe for a moment he can conjure the intimate relationship between an outside world and language that Wordsworth's solitary reaper seemed to him to have; indeed, Stevens may not finally want to settle anything, wanting instead to keep speculation alive. On the other hand, Wordsworth may already have been skeptical about what he could know or represent. Moreover, the end of Stevens's poem – with that ambiguous use of the word "of" – gently hints that perhaps some world, the sea's words, *is* after all what he wants. In other words, if reading Stevens may alert us to the skepticism already there in Wordsworth's poem, knowing Wordsworth's poems may help us to hear the Wordsworthian yearning in Stevens's voice. The poems cast light on each other.

It is not, however, just the words "of the sea" for which Stevens calls. There are also words "of . . . portals," "of ourselves and of our origins" (lines 53–4). I'm not certain what the portals are ("portals" sounds first like a nautical term, but unlike "port," "portals" are doorways or thresholds). It sounds as if Stevens's portals are a passageway between the human and some other world, if only the world outside of his mind. Further, by adding selves and origins to the things he wants "to order" – things of which he wants to make sense or to which he wants to give voice – Stevens suggests that even the inner self, or the self which is imagining, is not that easily pinned down. No wonder the poem ends talking of "ghostlier demarcations, keener sounds." That is, the presence for which Stevens calls seems more attenuated than that for which Wordsworth calls. The music of poetry or song spoke of something (he wasn't sure what) to Wordsworth; Stevens is not certain the sounds he hears or makes do speak of anything outside *or* inside the self (although he keeps the possibility open). In this light, "keener" is an interesting word for him to have chosen: it means "sharper" or "more acute" (as if the sound of calling or desire gets clearer while *what* the lyric calls for recedes). But there is also an echo of the word "keening," which is a lamenting or wailing for what is lost. Moreover, the last line of Stevens's poem is full of repeated sounds: the modulations of the 'o' sounds in "ghost," "demarcations," and "sounds"; the whispering "s" sounds; the alliteration of "n" and "d" sounds; the sharp "c" and "k" sounds; and the internal slant rhymes in "ghostl*ier*" and "k*eener*" as well as in "*d*emarcations, *k*eener." Whether this aural texture is an end in itself – offering us comforting human sounds that replace the sounds of local deities like Triton – or whether we are to hear the sound of someone lamenting a lost "creed outworn" is, typically and effectively, left open, not least I suspect so that *we* will extend the speculations that comprise and are central to the poem.

I could stop a discussion of the conversation between Wordsworth and Stevens here, noting that we know Stevens at the time he was writing "The Idea of Order at Key West" was reading at least book reviews about Wordsworth's poetry (and about the fact that Wordsworth's poems were always about his own mind, not the world) as well as a review of William Empson's book about pastoral, mentioned in the previous chapter. So, simply from the perspective of literary history and intellectual history, it is not surprising that Stevens might revisit Wordsworth's poem and use it to think about the power of poetry's sounds (as odic or pastoral and perhaps subject to charges of being mere sonorous solipsism). Stevens's idea of poetry's musical qualities may be more skeptical than Wordsworth's in that he seems less convinced there is some metaphysical presence or numen toward which lyricism leads him or us, but he clearly has not given up a commitment to the power of sounds in poems. To say this would, I think, be true, and might be just the place to turn to an even more skeptical poet, writing in 1950s America, namely John Ashbery. But I want first to raise a few questions about the kind of reading I have offered of Stevens's poem.

In an essay published in 1920 called "Tradition and the Individual Talent," T. S. Eliot denies that past poetry – the tradition – is a series of dead monuments. Instead, he talks about an historical sense of the presence, not the pastness, of the past, noting too that when one new work is added to the tradition, it changes everything that has come before it (perhaps because we then read past poems in a new light). Eliot also says the history of the arts is not a record of progressive improvement (the way scientific history may be). He cites someone talking about how dead writers seem remote because we know more than they did, to which Eliot replies: "Precisely, and they are that which we know." I am not interested in using everything Eliot says in that essay (among other things, he has a sense I do not share that there is one single tradition being forged or even perhaps discovered). However, the ways I have been reading poetic conversations across time are consonant with Eliot's sense that we read earlier poems in light of later (as I read Wordsworth in light of Stevens) as well as with his tacit suggestion that we may pay more attention to poems that later poets have revisited – because they form interesting intertexts or resonant verbal tissues or echoes we find meaningful.

Without disclaiming what I have already said about Stevens's poem, I want to point out that poems and poets (even those who are skeptical about our knowledge of the real world) live also in real worlds. I mentioned Frost's "Design," above, for example. I don't think it is accidental that, like Stevens's poem, Frost's poem thinks about order or design in the world. The two poems were published within a year of one another (1935 and 1936). Ideas of order and the question of whether order or meaning was real or imagined had contemporary relevance in mid-1930s America: the Depression made questions about whether art or imagined orders mattered (and why) pressing for those whose lives were spent making art. Further, the rise of fascism in Europe raised equally urgent questions about imposing ideas of order on the world.

I have already mentioned that Stevens was reading about Wordsworth's lyricism as potentially solipsistic, an issue that again, in 1935, in Depression-era America, raised the question of the uses of lyric poetry, about whether poetry helped people more clearly in need of material help. It strikes me that, unlike Wordsworth, Stevens may add a second person, namely Ramon Fernandez, to his poem to avoid the sense that his idea of order was only in his (or his speaker's) mind, to evade the charge of solipsism. But Stevens was also reading the work of someone named Ramon Fernandez. When asked, Stevens said he had just made up a name. But poets don't always reveal (and, perhaps, sometimes do not remember) what has triggered their poems. Despite Stevens's comment about making up a name, I think it is relevant that Ramon Fernandez published a rather well-known 1934 essay called "I Came Near Being a Fascist," in which Fernandez repented of his attraction to fascist ideas of political order. It seems, then, that Stevens is contrasting his imagined and provisional orders with the ideas of order others were imposing on the world, saying in effect that if you know order is just imagined, you can reimagine it. Specifically, Stevens's poem may suggest that Fernandez is correct in saying that fascist orders are first imagined, they arise from theories, and so are subject to challenge.

There is, finally, another way in which current events inform (but do not appear in) Stevens's poem. I draw this fact from reading James Longenbach's book (which is listed at the end of this chapter). It does seem at first that Stevens's poem dreamily imagines someone watching a Wordsworth-like singer in an exotic setting in order to illustrate his imaginative process. There may, as I just said, be political implications to this insistence on the power of imagining orders. Still, Key West – on the southern tip of Florida in the United States – is a tropical place Stevens visited on vacations and so might be thought of as an escape. Yet in 1934, on a visit to Key West just before he wrote his poem, Stevens would have looked out over the harbor and seen not only fishing boats, but twenty-nine US battleships being sent by President Roosevelt to Cuban waters to make the American presence visible following an army takeover in Cuba led by Fulgencio Batista. The battleships and the army suggest not-so-imagined ways of imposing order, and even if the orders thus imposed still originate in someone's imagination, they may seem to trump poetic imagining. Put another way: Stevens celebrates imaginative activity, but he may have been well aware of how the world might put such celebrations to the test. "Master[ing] the night and portion[ing] out the sea" takes on more sinister connotations if it is battleships rather than fishing boats that master and portion out the ocean.

I do not think the above reading replaces my earlier reading of Stevens's poem as a response to Wordsworth. However, if Stevens is skeptically testing whether there is some transcendent or numinous spirit invoked by poetry (and, even if there is, whether such invocations affect the world), historical pressures made such skepticism more than purely intellectual or philosophical. Do poetic orders challenge or help us think about political or military orders? In theory, they do, but the case is not so easily made in hard times. In other words, I am suggesting that poets speak poetry, and may indeed think about the world through other poems, but that poetry is at the same time a way of speaking from and to political, social, and historically real worlds. I have mentioned the dates and cultures that produced all the poems read in this book for this reason – not to suggest that poetry illustrates history but to sketch some ways in which poems are both part of and a response to historical worlds. Poets "speak poetry," but they do so also in conversation with the world in which they live.

Having said this, I want to turn to a poem written roughly twenty years later than Stevens's – in 1956, postwar America. John Ashbery's "Le Livre Est Sur La Table" seems at first reading far from having contact with anything historical, although you might note as you read that birds, a woman, writing (if not singing), and the sea – Wordsworth's and Stevens's tropes – circulate through this poem's two sections:

I

All beauty, resonance, integrity,
Exist by deprivation or logic
Of strange position. This being so,

We can only imagine a world in which a woman
Walks and wears her hair and knows   5
All that she does not know. Yet we know

What her breasts are. And we give fullness
To the dream. The table supports the book,
The plume leaps in the hand. But what

Dismal scene is this? the old man pouting   10
At a black cloud, the woman gone
Into the house, from which the wailing starts?

II

The young man places a bird-house
Against the blue sea. He walks away
And it remains. Now other   15

Men appear, but they live in boxes.
The sea protects them like a wall.
The gods worship a line-drawing

Of a woman, in the shadow of the sea
Which goes on writing. Are there   20
Collisions, communications on the shore

Or did all secrets vanish when
The woman left? Is the bird mentioned
In the waves' minutes, or did the land advance?

If you are scratching your head wondering what Ashbery's poem is "about," you are not alone. Like Stevens's poem in ways, Ashbery's poem resists any line-by-line paraphrase, although unlike Stevens or Wordsworth Ashbery does not give us a single scene or an implied narrative or even an implied narrator for most of the poem. I do think, however, that knowing "The Solitary Reaper" and "The Idea of Order at Key West" can help you to see that Ashbery, like Wordsworth and Stevens, is concerned with the question of what language can invoke, or perhaps how language works in readers. There's no critical agreement about how Ashbery *answers* these questions, I would add. Nonetheless, I want to look at section I and under-line not so much what it means but how consistently it flirts with (while still resisting) meaning, and then to ask why it does this.

You might notice, first, how strongly enjambed each of the first four tercets are, using not only conjunctions but the language of logical argu-ment: "This being so"; "Yet we know"; "But what." Since the first sentence in lines 1–3 also sounds like a logical proposition, the very grammar of the poem leads us to make, or expect, some connections, as does the decorous stanzaic structure. Yet our expectations are thwarted. What does it mean to say that because "beauty, resonance, integrity / Exist by deprivation or logic / Of strange position," we "can only imagine a world in which a woman / Walks"? Actually, because I have read Stevens and Wordsworth, I immediately do consider that the qualities mentioned in the first line – "beauty, resonance, integrity" – are qualities of certain kinds of lyrical poems. Having thought about odic calling (and the absence of what is called), I am also tempted to agree that beauty and resonance (at least) may exist by deprivation. That is, if the odic poet's desire to conjure presence or to find answers were fulfilled, there would be no more need to speak; the resonance of the poetic voice, its beauty, would cease. I have skipped over "logic / Of strange position" (the line break itself putting "logic" in a strange position syntactically), but – since I read the rest of the sentence as referring to the allure of lyric poetry (as beautiful, hauntingly resonant, forming a whole) – I'm inclined to interpret the logic of strange position as alluding to poems like Wordsworth's and Stevens', which highlight, and indeed mimic, how things (singing women or the lights of fishing boats) stand out or capture our attention when they are defamiliarized, so that they seem significant, perhaps gesturing toward some ineffable, numinous "spirit."

At this point, then, Ashbery's poem seems like what we might call a meta-poem, a poem about how poetry works. The second stanza, in this light, seems a repetition of Stevens's lines about his singing woman: "there never was a world for her / Except the one she sang and, singing, made." If this means that whatever numinous presence song or poetry contains is that of the poet's or singer's words (not of what the words seem to be about), then, logically, there never was a world or a woman for *us*, except the one *we* make when we read. In short, to look ahead to line 18 of Ashbery's poem, on Ashbery's account Wordsworth's reaper and Stevens's singer are just "line-drawings," poetic images or indeed our images of poetic images of women. Any sense of presence is projected: "We can only imagine" that these poetic women are living, physical presences, with interior lives. You might notice the use of line breaks in the second tercet: Ashbery's woman "knows / All that she does not know. Yet we know." Knowing is emphasized, but what is known is teasingly withheld. At the end of line 5, we think we will be told what the woman knows, but line 6 does not fulfill our expectation: she knows only what she does not know. This may suggest that, Socrates-like, the woman knows her own ignorance. Yet it also has the ring of a non sequitur. She knows "all." But that "all" is not known (certainly not to us). Like Stevens's body fluttering its empty sleeves, the woman's knowledge is gone almost before the poem posits its existence. Another way of looking at this is to say that Ashbery's meta-poem is demonstrating how poets are moved to imagine presence – to fill in the blanks – by images of lyrical singers like Wordsworth's reaper or like Stevens's woman.

Some critics would say that Ashbery demystifies poetic figures of singers who have significant knowledge. We may have been moved by these images, but in fact what *we* know, according to Ashbery, is only what the woman's "breasts are. And we give fullness / To the dream." This is almost a bad joke, suggesting a full-bodied woman, although it may also suggest something like the figure of mother nature in the octave of Wordsworth's "The World Is Too Much With Us." I'm tempted to say the poem is talking about the way we fill in blanks, or flesh out (the pun may be Ashbery's) narratives. We know Wordsworth's reaper and Stevens's singer are simply images in poems. However, reading their poems, we sketch in our heads an image – hair, breasts, the physical outline of a woman – and make what is in fact a poet's image (or imagination or dream) seem real . . . even though the reality only exists in *our* minds. On another interpretation, the image of giving fullness suggests exactly the kind of attempt to "put the poem together," to give it integrity, in which I have just engaged. I suppose this would make the poem not just a meta-poem about how or why we are moved by lyrics like Wordsworth's or Stevens's, but a meta-meta-poem, about how readings of poems demonstrate *our* "rage for order" as readers.

I have, somewhat coyly, not yet said much about the title of Ashbery's poem: "Le Livre Est Sur La Table." The French phrase literally means "the book is on the table," although the translation in line 8, which "means" the same thing in one sense, shifts the grammar and so, in another sense, shifts the way we see the relationship between book and table: "The table supports the book." Perhaps this is the logic of strange syntactical position. Ashbery's title, in fact, is a reference to grammar; specifically it would bring to mind language lessons for anyone of Ashbery's generation – he was born in 1927, schooled in the United States, and was living in France by the time the poem was published. Generations of American students learned French prepositions by being made to intone variations of that sentence: "The book is on the table; the book is under the table; the book is next to the table" ("Le livre est sur / sous / à côté de la table"). The possessive was taught with variations of the sentence "Où est la plume de ma tante?" ("Where is my aunt's pen?"), which seems to be echoed in line 9.

At this point, I think you have to make a critical choice. Is Ashbery's logic of strange position almost a joke, like the one in Woody Allen's story about a man, granted a wish by a genie, who asks to be transported into the world of any French book and finds himself not in something like *Madame Bovary* but rather in a French grammar book? That is, does "Le Livre Est Sur La Table" give us a sampler of the tricks of the lyric poet, a sampler designed not to move us but to unmask how language moves us? It would aim, on this account, to demystify how lyric poets move us with tricks of grammar, resonances with earlier poems or poetic gestures, showing that the uncanny effects – the spirit – of lyrics like Wordsworth's and Stevens's poems are rhetorical tricks. I assume there would be a point to such demystification: in a world of "sound bites" as well as of political and commercial propaganda, understanding how empty rhetoric can manipulate us might be an important lesson. Still, it is also possible that Ashbery is suggesting we are still legitimately moved, still haunted by a desire for some spirit, or maybe haunted by a desire for that desire, even in a world deeply skeptical about what language can invoke.

Which reading you find plausible will decide how you read the fourth tercet's sketch of melancholy. Notice the diction: "dismal," "old," "pouting," black cloud," and "wailing." Notice, too, how the enjambment at the end of line 11 suggests the woman has died and is being elegized: she is "gone," and we need to cross the line break before being told she has simply gone into a house. Is the wailing about loss? A child's wailing? We are told the poet has constructed a "dismal scene," and we could take this as a winking acknowledgment that the scene is staged; we can see how the diction, the line breaks, even the smooth iambic pentameter in line 12, might manipu-late us into fleshing out an entire tragic narrative. Or we may take the tone as more seriously tracing a scene of loss. The leaping plume of line 9 raises similar questions. Is it another bit of humor: while intoning mere grammar lessons – Où est la plume de ma tante – we *still* construct imaginary stories, in this case presumably about lost pens. Or, since in English "plumes" are feathers, instruments of flight as well as archaic writing implements, we could take the leaping plume as a figure of inspiration. On this reading, lines 8–9 are not about how we are hoodwinked into imagining language has real reference, but a more celebratory illustration of the fact that we can still imagine worlds, even while doing grammar lessons. On this second reading, the final scene of section one becomes genuinely moving (if still fictional), a demonstration that demystification is not necessarily the end of lyric effects. One can reveal that images of peasant singers or singing women who look at home in the world are pastoral figures and nonetheless suggest the "sea / . . . goes on writing" (lines 19–20), that is, that there continues to be significance we can read in (or into or out of) the world.

My last sentence made two assumptions I would like to make clearer. First, when I say we can read meaning or significance "in (or into or out of) the world," I am suggesting that Ashbery is more skeptical even than Stevens: he is not sure whether the sense of significance registered in lyric poems is illusion, or whether such feelings, illusion or no, are constructed in us or in the world or in some interaction between us and the world. My allusion to lines 19–20, moreover, assumes one can continue to read the second section of "Le Livre Est Sur La Table" as something like an allegory of poetic lyricism's power. Students in my classes have done so convincingly, for example reading the young man with his bird-house as Wordsworth or Stevens: he is the figure of a poet who makes a structure (a poem) to house the source of song (Wordsworth's singing woman is explicitly like a nightingale or cuckoo). If the bird-house is now empty and the songs of later generations of poets merely derivative (or pre-packaged, as the "boxes" might suggest), this does not dismiss earlier lyrics out of hand. Of course, in a poem as self-conscious about how we construct meanings as "Le Livre Est Sur La Table," that we can – indeed, that we are invited to – explicate the poem's meaning in this way does not mean we should. In other words, if we, as experienced readers of poems, are tempted to read meaning into the second section of Ashbery's poem, the poem may be less interested in having us hear what it is saying than in making us notice how we are making meaning, filling in the blanks. Certainly most line-by-line readings of the second section of the poem as allegory seem a bit wooden. And yet the images – of the sea, of "a" woman (not, notice, clearly to be identified as "the" woman in section one), of birds, and of gods – resonantly return us to Wordsworth's images.

Wordsworth insisted some presence with which to interact is needed to move us; otherwise nature has no resonance: it "moves us not." After reading Stevens's poem, we may understand Wordsworth's insistence as marking desire, not assuredness, noting that the poetic voice of "The Solitary Reaper" in all but the first stanza is made possible because of the speaker's "deprivation," because of what he cannot understand, the blanks he must fill in. In the light of Wordsworth's and Stevens's poems, the final section of "Le Livre Est Sur La Table" still at least raises the possibility that Ashbery's poem about resonance is seeking – not mocking – poetic resonance, and that Ashbery, skeptical though he may be about the earlier spirits sought, is still haunted by spirits or by their absence. It is, in any case, easy to hear a continued commitment to the music and spirit of lyricism in the questions that end Ashbery's poem. The last five and a half lines are still typically difficult: "Are there / Collisions, communications on the shore / Or did all secrets vanish when / The woman left? Is the bird mentioned / In the waves' minutes, or did the land advance?" The lines *may* just further demystify Wordsworth's and Stevens's senses of some natural or supernatural spirit; the secret may be that there never were any secrets. Yet the passage always makes me want to answer its rhetorical questions by affirming that something (poetic speech or meaningful sound) remains: yes, there *are* communications; the bird *is* mentioned; the ocean's mystery persists; it's not all solid land (perhaps with housing developments on it). Ashbery's tone also makes me reread Stevens's "ghostlier demarcations" as, suddenly, not all that "ghostly" (in the sense of being figments of the imagination); in comparison with Ashbery, Stevens seems to refer to ghosts in the sense of spiritual presences or apparitions. In short, Stevens's poem seems haunted by something more robust than anything in which Ashbery is able to believe. Yet there is still in Ashbery's poem a dense texture of image and sound that implies he remains haunted (or perhaps seduced) by lyricism.

Of course, many readers and writers these days are even more skeptical about speaking for nature (for birds and oceans) or for other people or about the seductions of sound in poetry than Ashbery's poem suggests he is. While Ashbery rejects some of what he hears in poems like "The Solitary Reaper" or "The Idea of Order at Key West," he is still echoing Wordsworth's and Stevens's poems. I suppose this makes sense: it is difficult to have an argument with others without speaking their language. That is, Ashbery's sea, which "keeps on writing," at least by extension argues with Wordsworth's image comparing a singing reaper to a bird breaking the silence of the seas and, similarly, the "line-drawing / Of a woman" questions Stevens's image of a woman singing by the sea in Key West. At the same time, Ashbery makes us go back to images from earlier poems, especially those by Wordsworth and Stevens. This too makes sense. After all, you do not bother to argue with what you don't feel merits a response.

I am not necessarily suggesting that Ashbery wholly admires Wordsworth and Stevens (although he certainly has praised Stevens's poetry); I am saying that an argument is still a conversation and that Ashbery's images would carry less weight if he and we had not felt moved by earlier lyrical gestures (images of oceans that seem to speak to us, for example).

Wordsworth's "The Solitary Reaper" ends: "That music in my heart I bore / Long after it was heard no more." I've been suggesting that Ashbery still bears Wordsworth's music in *his* heart and certainly is aware of how the sound of poetry continues to move us. I'm also suggesting that later poetry like Ashbery's keeps earlier poems like Wordsworth's alive. As Eliot said, however, when a new poem is added to a (he might say "the") tradition, it changes everything that has come before. Indeed, Ashbery's poem *both* calls attention to *and* changes Wordsworth's poem. That is, after reading "Le Livre Est Sur La Table," it is difficult not to take a stand on whether or not the reaper is taken over by Wordsworth as a figure for his own imagination or whether both Wordsworth and Stevens use images of singing women only to enable their own songs. I have already tipped my hand as to my interpretation: I think when Wordsworth writes "Stop here, or gently pass!" his warning anticipates Ashbery's (and, as I read him, Stevens's) suggestion that images may be merely projections by poets or their speakers. As I said earlier of "The Solitary Reaper," on my reading it already poses the problems Stevens and Ashbery increasingly emphasize, namely how poetry can represent others or how we can give voice to what is outside us. Then, again, it may be that reading Ashbery and Stevens has influenced my reading of Wordsworth's poem.

I want to add one final note about how contemporary critics and poets often prompt us to raise issues that may not have been in the minds of earlier poets. This is probably both inevitable and healthy. As long as you don't misrepresent or assume *a priori* what a poem says, you can move to assess what you have read in light of contemporary problems. My point is that not only are poems in conversation with each other and with history, but our conversations with poems are also perhaps inevitably inflected by the issues most relevant to *our* culture. I would simply advise caution, noting that there is a kind of cultural exchange you miss – even a failure of generosity – if you do not first at least try to hear the way poems speak also to and from other cultures and eras than your own.

Terms used

ballad   end anacrusis

Useful further reading

Jay Clayton and Eric Rothstein, "Figures in the Corpus: Theories of Influence and Intertextuality," *Influence and Intertextuality in Literary History* (Madison, Wisc.: University of Wisconsin Press, 1991): 3–36.

Wai Chee Dimmock, "A Theory of Resonance," *PMLA*, 112 (Oct. 1997): 1060–71.

T. S. Eliot, "Tradition and the Individual Talent," in *The Sacred Wood: Essays on Poetry and Criticism* (London: Methuen, 1976 [first pub. 1920]): 47–59.

Ramon Fernandez, "I Came Near Being a Fascist," *Partisan Review*, 1 (Sept.–Oct. 1934): 19–25.

John Guillory, "Canonical and Uncanonical: The Current Debate," in *Cultural Capital: The Problem of Literary Canon Formation* (Chicago: University of Chicago Press, 1993): 3–82.

James Longenbach, *Wallace Stevens: The Plain Sense of Things* (New York: Oxford University Press, 1991).

William Wordsworth, *Poems, in Two Volumes, and Other Poems, 1800–1807*, ed. Jared Curtis (Ithaca, NY: Cornell University Press, 1983).

Chapter 9

Forests and Trees, or Playing with Poems

This brief last chapter is less of a conclusion than a commencement, a way of encouraging you to go and explore more and new kinds of poems on your own. I want in particular to repeat something I said at the very beginning of this book: there are whole poetic traditions that I have not even mentioned here. What I hope I have provided are tools for reading – and for finding pleasure in reading: tools you can bring to a far wider range of poetry than I have had the space to include.

Indeed, through most of this book I have concentrated, first, on close reading, paying careful attention to the way individual poems variously use formal structures and gestures, modes, sounds, syntax, rhythms, diction, and tone. I have also tried to choose poems that speak to one another, even though this decision limited my choice of poems. Finally, and relatedly, because I think it is an important feature of poetry, in each chapter I focused on how poetic forms and modes, as well as themes and subjects, are changed over time, so that I read (for example) pastoral poems or sonnets across historical and cultural boundaries; as literary critics put it, I read **diachronically**. This has led to some peculiarities that stem partly from my attempt to let you eavesdrop on and participate in conversations and partly from my own taste. To cite just two examples, you may have noticed that all the poems in this book written before 1900 are British; all those written later are American. Moreover, I've not discussed any poems written between 1817 and 1935. This does not mean that the muse departed from Great Britain and sailed across the Atlantic at the turn of the twentieth century. Nor does it mean there was a great silencing of poets through most of the nineteenth century. As you can see by reading through any broad-based poetry anthology, there are earlier American poets and later British poets, not to mention later nineteenth-century poets from both sides of the Atlantic, whose work is well worth reading. Indeed, there are entire libraries of exciting poetry written in English by poets who are neither British nor American. Again, however, I have tried to give you the tools to read all sorts of poems, even those not mentioned here; I hope, too, I have whetted your appetite for reading more broadly. There is one thing I think I can promise you, namely that the more poems you read, the more you will hear in what you read, and the more you hear, the more you will want to read.

I would like also to point out that the poems I *have* discussed can be reread. Although I have spent most time on close readings of poems and on reading diachronically, I have also tried to point out how poets are equally engaged in and with the actual, historical world in which they live. But I have not spent much time reading **synchronically**, which is to say in terms of single periods, without considering historical antecedents. If you read any broad survey of poetry in English, you will notice that most are arranged in terms of periods: early modern poetry (of the sixteenth and seventeenth centuries, sometimes divided into Renaissance and baroque, or metaphysical, poetry) or Romantic poetry (usually dated from 1798 through 1830) or modern or modernist poetry (from the first half of the twentieth century). While I have not talked much about periods, or what some critics have called **period style**, which is to say the kind of poetic language and subjects typical of a given time period, I have actually given you poems that should allow you to think about literary history in this way. What follows is a timeline, listing all the poems discussed in this book, now rearranged historically:

EARLY MODERN POETRY

Wyatt, "The Long Love That in My Thought Doth Harbor" (1557)
Sidney, "Loving in Truth" (1582)
Shakespeare, "Sonnet 18" (*c.*1595)
Marlowe, "The Passionate Shepherd to his Love" (1599)
Raleigh, "The Nymph's Reply to the Shepherd" (1600)

Donne, "Batter my heart . . ." (*c.*1621)
Milton, "Il Penseroso" (1631)
Marvell, "The Mower Against Gardens" (1681)

EIGHTEENTH-CENTURY POETRY
Finch, "A Nocturnal Reverie" (1713)

Collins, "Ode on the Poetical Character" (1746)

Smith, "To Dependence" (1784)

ROMANTIC POETRY
Wordsworth, "A Night Piece" (1798)
Wordsworth, "Ode" (1802–4)
Wordsworth, "The World Is Too Much With Us" and "The Solitary
   Reaper" (1807)
Shelley, "Ozymandias" (1817)

MODERN AND MODERNIST POETRY
Stevens, "The Idea of Order at Key West" (1935)
Frost, "Design" (1936)
Williams, "To Greet a Letter-Carrier" (1938)

Miles, "Purchase of a Blue, Green, or Orange Ode" (1941)

CONTEMPORARY AND POSTMODERN POETRY
Ashbery, "Le Livre Est Sur La Table" (1956)
O'Hara, "The Day Lady Died" (1959)
Wright, "A Blessing" (1963)
Levertov, "O Taste and See" (1964)
Bishop, "Filling Station" (1965)
Nemerov, "Quaerendo Invenietis" ("The Spiral Way") (1973)

Giscombe, "(the future)" and "(1962 at the edge of town)" (1994)

Although you first encountered Shakespeare's Sonnet 18 here in a
chapter on sonnets and Marlowe's "The Passionate Shepherd to his Love"
in a chapter on pastoral, the two were written at roughly the same time.
Thus, Shakespeare's poem, which begins "Shall I compare thee to a summer's day?," may have at least as much in common with Marlowe's poem,
which opens "Come live with me and be my love," as with other sonnets
like Shelley's "Ozymandias" or Frost's "Design." Shakespeare's and Marlowe's distinctive uses of wit or of the commonplaces of courtly love might
become of more interest in a study of Renaissance lyric than they are in
diachronic studies of the sonnet or of pastoral. It is not that you cannot
read literary practices both synchronically and diachronically – indeed,
sometimes you need to do both – but it is difficult to do both equally well

at the same time. Especially since poems make meaning in so many ways – from their use of line breaks or punctuation to their inclusion of contemporary literary and extra-literary speech to the ways they refashion earlier literary gestures – if you try to say everything about a poem at once, you will end up with the verbal equivalent of what my printer does when there is a paper jam and all the lines are printed on top of one another. I would add, too, that these days critics interested in poetry from a certain period often find that there are more kinds of poems to be found than any anthology could reprint; these would include poems by those to whom a given culture paid little attention (working-class writers, for instance) as well as apparently eccentric work (like Emily Dickinson's or Christopher Smart's) – poetry that may have had little influence in its own day – or even what we might find flatly uninteresting. Yet all these kinds of voices would have informed the ears of readers and writers in a particular period. They help define the boundaries of what could be considered "poetry" in a given time and culture. In other words, there are literary and historical concerns that come to light when you read poems in the context of their period, but (typically for poetry) there really is no list of features that you can use to pigeon-hole what all poems from a particular period will sound like or must be about. Certainly, all "Romantic" poetry is not about nature (think of "Ozymandias"), and all early eighteenth-century poetry is not satire in heroic couplets.

Older-fashioned anthologies, of the sort I read when I was a student, used to offer just such lists. For instance, they often called eighteenth-century poetry "Neo-Classical Poetry," and divided the century into two halves, an "Augustan Age" or "The Age of Pope" (including primarily satire, of which I have here included no examples whatsoever), followed by "The Age of Sensibility" or "The Age of Johnson," with poems that did not quite fit that last category sometimes dubbed "pre-Romantic" poetry, as if the second half of the eighteenth century were filled with poets who were merely anticipating Wordsworth, Coleridge, Shelley, Keats, and Byron (listed as the major Romantic poets in such anthologies). It is true that the three poets I have included from the early, middle, and late eighteenth century do not sound like one another. Yet Finch is not an urbane satirist (of the sort often taken to exemplify the early eighteenth-century period style), and both Collins and Smith are interesting each in his or her own right, not just as harbingers of poetry to come (even if "To Dependence" can be read in tandem not only with sonnets but with pastorals or, for that matter, with poems that address political themes, like Shelley's). Indeed, as I noted in the previous chapter, both critical frameworks and later poems can change how we characterize earlier poetry. A look at the table of contents of different editions of, for instance, *The Norton Anthology of Poetry* will show you that the choice of featured poets and poems has changed significantly over time. I assume this is in part because scholars have recovered the work of poets (Finch, for example, or Smith), whose work was not previously reprinted. The inclusion of these poets shifts our sense of what poetry in their day was like. It is also the case that later poets may allow us to hear new resonance in poems we might previously have ignored (as Stevens and Ashbery sent me back to reread Wordsworth's "The Solitary Reaper").

Reading poems as part of a single period poses further challenges, as well. For example, I have labeled the poems by Stevens, Frost, Williams, and Miles "modern and modernist poetry." Miles is set apart because she is of a younger generation, although I gave you one of her very early poems, written only three years after Williams's "To Greet a Letter-Carrier." Many anthologies would call poetry from the early part of the twentieth century "modern" (setting poets who, unlike Frost, clearly experimented with form into a special category, namely "modern*ist* poetry"); similarly, many anthologies would mark the beginning of a new literary period after World War II, calling poems written after 1945 "contemporary poetry" (or, again, if the poets are self-consciously experimental in the way Ashbery's or Giscombe's poems are, "postmodern poetry"). Most would include Miles's work (if they included her poetry at all) as "contemporary poetry," because most of her poetry was written after 1945. You can, I think, see new and interesting features of Miles's work, if you realize she began defining herself as a poet when Stevens and Williams and Frost were the older, well-known poets on the block. Yet it is also useful to read Miles in terms of her contemporaries: she was born the same year as Elizabeth Bishop, for example, and their work first appeared in print at the same time. So when periods start and stop, or whose work belongs to what period, become questions to consider when you are reading poems synchronically. Despite the way in which some current and most older anthologies categorize periods, it does not really make sense to assume that poetic fashions – or period styles – change like clockwork every fifty years, with clear distinctions marking the turn from one period to another.

In short, to think about poets in terms of *standardized* periods has some real drawbacks; however, thinking of poets and poems synchronically is illuminating. You might, for instance, want to consider that the poems you read here by Ashbery, O'Hara, Wright, Levertov, Bishop, and Nemerov were all written within twenty years of one another. When, in the very first chapter, I noted how radical Williams's style appeared to be compared with Nemerov's style, I was fudging a little, certainly overstating my case. That is, the other contemporary American poetry I've given you from the mid-twentieth century suggests that it is Nemerov, not Williams, whose style looks most uncommon for the slightly later period in which Nemerov wrote, even if his diction and rhymed, iambic pentameter couplets are more historically traditional. And, of course, in the first chapter I also suggested that Nemerov's riddle is rebellious in its own way. "The Spiral Way," that is, forces readers (when it first appeared, readers who would have read a good deal of free verse) to think about what expectations they bring to apparently more traditional work. I have entitled this final chapter "Forests and Trees," thinking about the fact that knowing what first looks old-fashioned or traditional about Nemerov's piece – in the larger picture, whether diachronic or synchronic – does not tell you everything you need to know about how "The Spiral Way" works. It looks unusual for its period; it appears to be more traditional if you consider poetry from 1773 to 1973. It is also a poem, you may recall, that on close reading actually plays with and challenges how its untraditional traditional form raises expectations in its readers. Reading the piece only in the context of poems in rhymed couplets or only in the context of early 1970s American poetry, you might, if you did not read with care, miss the tree for the forest. Or, to make my point less metaphorically, we always do read poems in some context, but they are far less interesting if we use them to *illustrate* a form or a period style or even a grand theme, rather than attending first to their singularity.

The above caution does not negate the fact that part of how particular poems make meaning is still by invoking various intertexts (historical or contemporary, literary or not). I offer you the timeline above in hopes that you might go back to reread some of what I have given you here (or go read other works written at the same time) to think about how your view of the poems does or does not change (or deepen) if you read them alongside other writings from the same period. I've also, as I suspect you noticed even before looking at my timeline, given you four pieces written by Wordsworth. This is not because Wordsworth is the center of poetry in English (although he does seem to have haunted a large number of other poets), but because I wanted you to have at least a glimpse of what it might mean to read a poet, rather than a form or mode, as developing over time. Actually, in light of the large amount Wordsworth wrote, four poems is not very many. However, I would encourage you to read several books by the poets who have most interested you, both to think about how individual poets change their styles and subjects over time and to see where what I've contextualized in terms of features of style or form or mode lived first, namely with other poems by the same writer, often – by the seventeenth century, in any case – in carefully crafted books.

I have one final point I want to make. The subtitle of this chapter is "playing with poems." I've suggested above that poems (my metaphorical trees) may look different in different contexts (my forests). At the end of the previous chapter, I mentioned that critical questions – the questions that most interest us – also provide contexts for or inform how we read. That is, although all poems will not yield interestingly to all questions and although poems themselves position their readers, which pieces we read – what we call the poetic **canon** – will to some degree depend on which questions we ask. If, for example, you are interested in women's voices in poetry, then, looking at the poems I've offered here, presumably you will begin to link – to hear intertextual resonances between – the pieces you have read by Finch, Smith, and Bishop (though you would probably not include Raleigh's "The Nymph's Reply to the Shepherd"). Would you also include Miles's poem? Levertov's? Neither clearly depends on being identifiably by a woman or on being heard as spoken by a woman. Yet, of course, Miles and Levertov wrote as women. As critics sometimes say these days, each wrote from the **subject position**, the perspective, of a woman. Whether or not this fact informs the subject position of the speakers in their poems is an open question, but an interesting one, as is the question of whether women's perspectives change in different cultures and different periods. You could, indeed, raise the same questions about gay poets, that is about poets who are not or were not heterosexual. Ashbery's, O'Hara's, Bishop's, and probably Marlowe's poems might all be revisited in this light; they would form another, different canon or set of intertexts.

Of course, you might alternatively be interested in what poems are about or in the images they use. If, for example, you were interested in the poetic *representation* of women, positive or negative, rather than in women's poetic voices or the subject position of women writers, you might construct yet a different line of poetry, one that would include male writers like Wyatt, Sidney, and Shakespeare as well as women writers like Bishop. Whether you would include Finch or Smith or O'Hara would depend on whether you think it is important that Finch's and Smith's speakers are represented as women or that "The Day Lady Died" includes Billie Holiday. Framed by such questions, you would probably not include any of the pieces I've given you by Donne, Frost, or Williams (among others), although had I selected different poems by these same poets, you might have found them of more interest on this score. So, which poems as well as which poets will capture your attention depends on the questions you raise. I might, in fact, set you the challenge of revisiting what you've read here to imagine a tradition of "green poetry," poetry that, either by the perspective it fosters or by what it represents, seems responsive to ecological concerns.

I will here turn you loose to pursue your own questions and to engage in conversation with a variety of poems. You might even wish to be (or to talk with) a practicing poet. I would note that at least a few of the poets whose work I've included are still very much alive, although I have also attempted to introduce you to earlier poets and poems that you might not otherwise encounter either in a classroom or in your normal course of reading. My fondest hope is that you will find on your own more poems that you will love, or that will challenge you, or even with which you will want to argue. Poetry may not be a language spoken by or speaking to huge numbers of people these days. Nor need it be so. I began this book by noting that it is nonetheless no more esoteric than any other practice in which communities of people engage (like cooking or sports) and certainly no more difficult than any other language. If you have read through the poems in this book as an active reader, I trust you can now comfortably approach poems on your own and read them and keep reading them with both understanding and pleasure.

Terms used

canon   subject position
diachronic   synchronic
period style

Index

Numbers in **bold** type indicate pages on which a term or concept is defined or explicated. ***Bold italics*** indicate extended discussion of the specified text.